Immigrant Family

Immigrant Family

THREE CENTURIES
IN AMERICA

Norman Kelker

Inks and Bindings
888-290-5218
www.inksandbindings.com
orders@inksandbindings.com

Dedication

I dedicate this work to my late parents, Aaron Hubbell Kelker and Martha Taylor Kelker, to my wife Hanna, our children and our grandchildren. I also remember my late brother John.

Hanna has been a loyal and loving partner throughout our long marriage, and I owe so much to her. Precious to both of us are our son Adam (born 1974) and our daughter Kristina (born 1978).

Our grandchildren are a source of pride and constant joy. Adam and his wife Michelle Fierro Kelker have two wonderful sons, Aleksander (born 2004), Dominik (born 2008) and a delightful daughter Sophia (born 2013). It has been a delight to see them grow and mature.

Our daughter Kristina and her husband Daniel Gerschel have two lovely daughters, Anabelle (born 2018) and Sasha (born 2021). We love and adore them.

The Swiss Immigrant Kelker family arrived in America in 1743. This book tells their story and their descendant's stories over three centuries to today. Their successes, failures, contributions, problems and challenges are related through biographies of those who led lives that were in some way interesting, from the 1743 arrivals to a 21st century soap opera star. There are some fascinating and entertaining characters along the way. It's American history told through the lives of the Kelker descendants.

Contents

Kelker Quotes

"As long as my name is Kelker, there is not [a call for Sunday rail service], for we will obey the Lord rather than man. It would be cruel to man and the horses, and I for one would not remain in a company that ran their cars on Sunday." (Historical Society of Dauphin County Scrapbook Collection of Harrisburg newspapers, Z-2006)

—Rudolph Frederick Kelker, Harrisburg City
Passenger Railway Company treasurer,
in 1888 expressing his opposition
to streetcar service on Sundays

"The Sioux [Dakota] Indians of Minnesota must be exterminated or driven forever beyond the borders of Minnesota."

—Alexander Ramsey in an address to the
Minnesota legislature, September 9, 1862

"It is due to myself, as well as to all concerned, that I should declare any such statement, whether made by Mr. Jackson or any other person, as absolutely untrue, and my deep regret that Mr. Jackson should either of his own volition or at the instigation of any other person make an assertion so utterly devoid of truth."

—Luther Reily Kelker, in response to being
accused of jury tampering, March 24, 1897

Acknowledgements

S o many to thank:

My wife Hanna has been an immensely helpful critic, and I thank her for her patience and understanding over the years of putting this book together.

Writer and editor Alan Lockwood has been invaluable to the completion of this book. He untiringly read and reread evolving chapters with the critical eye of an experienced and knowledgeable professional. His suggestions on language, structure and organization were critical to this inexperienced writer. I could not have completed the manuscript without his generous assistance.

Ken Frew, the Historical Society of Dauphin County's librarian and archivist, has been invaluable to my research. He untiringly located documents in the society's vast Kelker archives, and his always helpful responses to my many requests provided much of the information about the Kelker family in Harrisburg. Historical Society staff members Rick Hartman, Steve Wydra, Chris Turner and volunteer Larry Geesey provided much needed assistance. Ramsey Davenport supplied extensive genealogical information and photos, and Erik Fasik provided a timely photograph from his collection. Carol Bergman, my writing class teacher, provided a big boost.

Two Harrisburg area independent historians provided interesting and useful information on the area's Black history. Calobe Jackson, a lifelong Harrisburg resident and Barbara Barksdale, a lifelong resident of nearby Steelton, collectively possess a vast knowledge of the area's Black history that they generously shared.

The Historic Harrisburg Association under the able leadership of David Morrison provided useful information and encouragement. My dear friends Ames Sheldon and Andy Currie deserve thanks for their interest, helpful suggestions and for arranging a personal tour of the Alexander Ramsey mansion in St. Paul, Minnesota.

And special thanks to Del Alexis Jupiter for her splendid research that revealed the origin of the Black Kelkers.

A much belated and much deserved thank you goes out to Rudolph Frederick Kelker, a founder of the Historical Society of Dauphin County who in 1883 published the Kelker family record with extensive genealogical and biographical records. Richly deserved belated recognition also goes to RFK's two sons, Luther Reily and William Anthony. LRK served as the state of Pennsylvania's first archivist and in 1907 published a vast three volume history of Dauphin County. William Anthony recorded local history and left many records. Upon his 1908 death he left the family home and its valuable contents to the Historical Society of Dauphin County. His home became the historical society's home. My gratitude to our son Adam, a Geographic Information Systems (GIS) specialist, for preparation of the maps in Chapter 7.

To all, many thanks.

Introduction

This book is a story of the Kelker family in America. It begins in 1743 and ends in the early twenty-first century. It is told from biographies of family members whose lives are in some manner distinguished. It is not an encyclopedic record of births and deaths but glimpses of the history of a family now in its tenth generation in the United States. The story begins with the1743 arrival of Swiss immigrants Heinrich and Regula Kölliker, their ten-year-old son Anthony and four-year-old daughter Susanna, and it ends with NASA space scientists and explorers Andrew Stofan and his daughter Ellen, and soap-opera star Robert Kelker-Kelly.

The book tells the stories of Heinrich and Regula Kölliker and their descendants over nearly three centuries. It begins with the journey and voyage from Switzerland to Pennsylvania, where the new arrivals survived as farmers using that era's primitive agricultural methods. It continues with Anthony and his descendants over the generations with an innkeeper, an iron worker, a saddler, a businessmen, a politician, historians and a traffic engineer, and ends with family members exploring the planets and starring in soap operas. The lone connecting thread is the line of descent from Heinrich and Regula Kölliker to Anthony and Mary Magdalena Kelker and on to the present.

The history presented here is in no way unique. Except for Native Americans every US citizen is an immigrant or a descendant of immigrants, and every one of us has a family history and a story to tell. So, like every family history, mine is not unique. But I did have the unique benefit of rich archival sources that reveal details of the lives and times of my ancestors, and I chose to write about those who lived lives that were interesting in particular ways. Most achieved some success, and many acted charitably, showing concern for their fellow citizens and for their communities and, to their credit, acted upon those concerns. The history also reveals some whose actions were highly questionable, and I have tried to faithfully record those individuals and their indiscretions.

Historians can only report and interpret to the extent that records exist and are accessible. I have been more than fortunate to have access to extensive accounts of the Kelker family history from the beginning of their time in America to the present. In 1883, Rudolph Frederick Kelker (1820–1906), a prominent Harrisburg, Pennsylvania resident, prepared and published an extensive family record that has been extremely useful. The Historical Society of Dauphin County in Harrisburg holds a rich and extensive collection of Kelker family archives from the generations that lived and prospered in Harrisburg throughout the nineteenth and early twentieth centuries. Online genealogical and historical websites offer access to vast archival material. Newspapers.com has been a rich source of information about the Kelker descendants I write about.

This book does not present all of Heinrich and Regula Braetscher Kölliker's descendants. It explores one of the two family lines that descend from the time of their Swiss immigration. The other family line descends of Anthony's brother Rudolph, born in Pennsylvania in 1747, and his wife, Maria Weidman. I have written about the line that descends from Anthony and Mary Magdalena Kelker.

I have added addenda to most of the chapters. While combing through documents, newspaper articles and historical accounts I came across stories that were interesting but didn't necessarily fit into the narrative flow. Some of these addenda are enlightening and some are trivial, but they add a little insight to the lives of the subjects.

The often-recited catchphrase "America is a land of immigrants" is trite but true. And this book reveals only one of the millions of family stories that have been told or are waiting to be told. It has been a fascinating and revealing exercise as well as a source of satisfaction to reveal some of the history of these selected descendants. I hope that this book in some way stirs your curiosity about where you come from and influences you to search out your own family story. I can assure you that it's a worthwhile and engaging exercise.

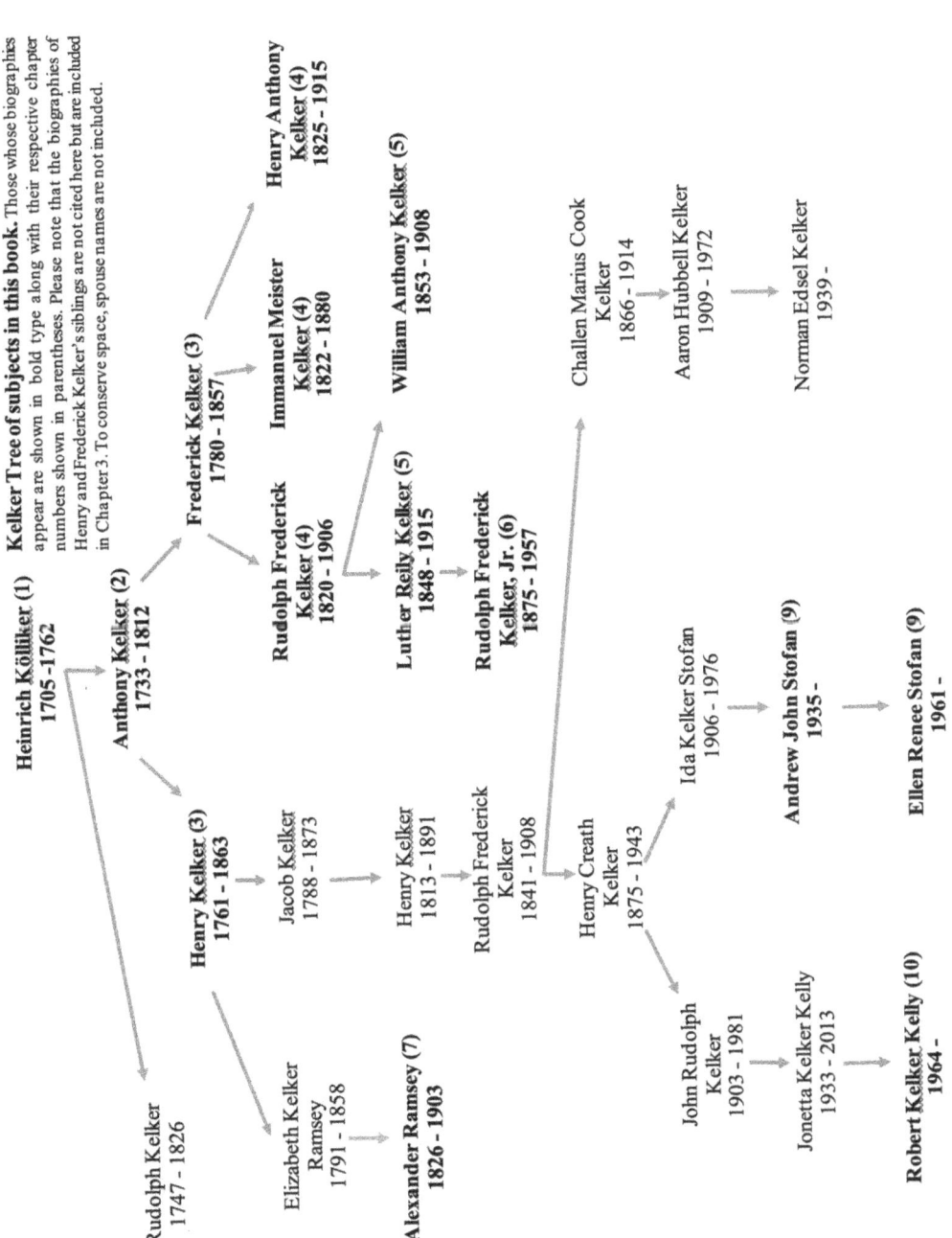

Kelker Tree of subjects in this book. Those whose biographies appear are shown in bold type along with their respective chapter numbers shown in parentheses. Please note that the biographies of Henry and Frederick Kelker's siblings are not cited here but are included in Chapter 3. To conserve space, spouse names are not included.

CHAPTER 1

From Zurich to Pennsylvania:
The Köllikers Arrive in America

Note: Chapter 1 is taken largely from a chapter that appears in an account of the history of the eighteenth-century Swiss migration to the American colonies, by A. B. Faust, in Faust and Brumbaugh (Faust, A. B., and Brumbaugh, G. M., 1920, "Lists of Swiss Immigrants in the Eighteenth Century to the American Colonies," publisher unknown). The article, along with the account's preface, also by Faust, is a valuable account of the Swiss emigration and the social, economic and political conditions under which it took place. The book also contains a list of the Swiss emigrants who left from the canton of Zurich between 1734 and 1744, their birth dates, the villages where they lived and the year they departed. The list was compiled in 1744 by the central authorities in the canton of Zurich as a census of emigrants. Pastors in local communities prepared the emigrant lists.

Departure from Zurich. The Kelker family in America began with Heinrich Kölliker and his wife, Regula, who emigrated in 1743 from Herrliberg in the canton of Zurich, Switzerland, to the American colonies with their five children and Heinrich's sister Verena (Veronica). They were one of many families from Switzerland's French- and German-speaking regions that made the long and dangerous trek to the colonies. The Swiss emigration took place throughout the eighteenth century, with the peak flow occurring between 1734 and 1744. Approximately 25,000 Swiss arrived in the colonies during that century, with about 12,000 arriving during the peak period. (Faust p. 24)

The trip to the colonies was a difficult and dangerous undertaking. It required somehow getting to the harbor in Southampton, England, the point of departure for most of the Swiss, and traveling on a crowded sailing vessel for a transatlantic journey of several months. The voyage was extremely risky.

Passengers faced overcrowding, sickness, the threat of pirates, stark living conditions and limited protection when occasional severe weather struck. Many died en route. The Kölliker's voyage, for example, lasted twenty-eight weeks, and three of their five children died on the way. Their ship landed at Carolina where they were received at a Swiss colony. Then, like most incoming Swiss Germans, they somehow made their way to Pennsylvania.

So why did these people leave their Swiss homes for such a long, dangerous journey to an unknown land? Eighteenth-century Switzerland was indeed a pleasant place to reside, but, alas, only for the nobility. Life was much more difficult for the rest of the population. During the 1730s and 1740s, ruling patrician families in Zurich and other cantons exerted strong control that left little opportunity for any citizens to improve their living conditions. Protest was not tolerated, and any rebellions were immediately put down. Young noblemen enriched themselves by forming armies of young Swiss men to fight in foreign wars. Faust estimates that in 1740, 69,000 Swiss mercenaries were serving in French, Austrian, Spanish, Sardinian and Dutch armies. These mercenaries did not share in profits gained from the ventures, and many did not return from the battlefields.

Miserable living conditions and the inability of citizens to improve their lives were the principal reasons fueling the desire to emigrate. But added stimulus was provided by stories from returning Swiss adventurers proclaiming opportunities in the new land. Adventures in the New World began in 1710 with the establishment of New Bern, a Swiss colony at the meeting of the Trent and Neuse Rivers in what is now North Carolina. It was established by Christoph von Graffenried who brought over a group of Swiss and German settlers. Hostilities with the Tuscarawa Indians and a lack of supplies led to New Bern's quick collapse in 1711. But in 1732 a second Swiss colony was established, surviving for a longer period and serving as point of entry for arriving Swiss settlers. The colony, Purrysburgh, named after Jean-Pierre de Purry, its founder, was established on the banks of the Savannah River in what is now Jasper County, South Carolina. Purrysburgh survived for several decades before it dissolved. This is the presumed landing site for the Köllikers. While we have no record of where they landed, their names do not appear on the list of Swiss immigrants who arrived at Pennsylvania, the only other landing site for them.

The number of Swiss who left for the colonies might have been larger had the Swiss government not reacted to limit the flow, fearing significant loss of population. Like other European countries, maintaining a critical population mass that included farmers, soldiers, tradesman and other workers and taxpayers was critical to a country's strength and survival, especially a small country such as Switzerland. So at various times throughout the 1700s legislation was passed to limit and obstruct emigration. Zurich, for example, issued a decree on November 3, 1734 forbidding its people from traveling to Carolina, preventing prospective emigrants from selling their property, making it illegal to distribute literature promoting emigration and setting out punishment for agents found to be promoting it. A second decree, issued on January 29, 1735, increased punishment for anyone purchasing land sold by emigrants and dictating more severe punishment for enticing anyone to leave. These measures may have slowed emigration, but the Zurich government was not able to shut down the flow, and significant numbers were able to depart.

We do not know what conditions drove the Köllikers to leave in 1743. Did they have to make significant sacrifices to accommodate anti-emigration laws in force at that time? Did they pay any bribes? Did they have a long-held desire to depart, or was it a relatively quick decision triggered by some event? There are many questions, and we can only speculate on the answers from what we know of prevailing conditions. But we do have one bit of history of their departure, a letter (see below, translated from German) from the minister in their Swiss village, Herrliberg, that supports their departure, speaks for the family's good repute and attests to their commitment to the Reformed Christian Church.

> It is shown by these presents, that Heinrich Kölliker, born at Herrliberg, on Lake Zurich, is the son of estimable parents, and has, by holy baptism, been united with the Reformed Christian Church. Likewise, it is also his intention that Barbara, his wedded wife, together with his three sons and two daughters, all of good repute, as far as is known, to leave their fatherland of their own accord and emigrate to Pennsylvania or Carolina, in order there permanently to settle and herewith take with them their church right for themselves and for their descendants. To this journey we wish them success, the divine blessing, health and the attainment of their object. For the sake of greater security I have written the above with my own hand and certified it with my seal.
>
> Hans Conrad Ziegler
> 8th day of June, 1743, Minister at Herrliberg and Wezwyl

On to Pennsylvania. We know that the Kōllikers left in 1743 for a voyage of twenty-eight weeks, and we presume that they landed at the Purrysburgh colony in what is now South Carolina. A record of their leaving (Faust and Brumbaugh includes the list prepared by the Swiss government) contains the names of all Swiss who left for the colonies between 1734 and 1744. The table below shows the Kōlliker names from that list together with other data derived from the Kelker Family Record. Sadly, three of the children, Heinrich, Anna and Jan, did not survive the journey.

Heinrich and Regula Bratscher Kōlliker's Swiss- and American-born Children
(From the Kelker Family Record)

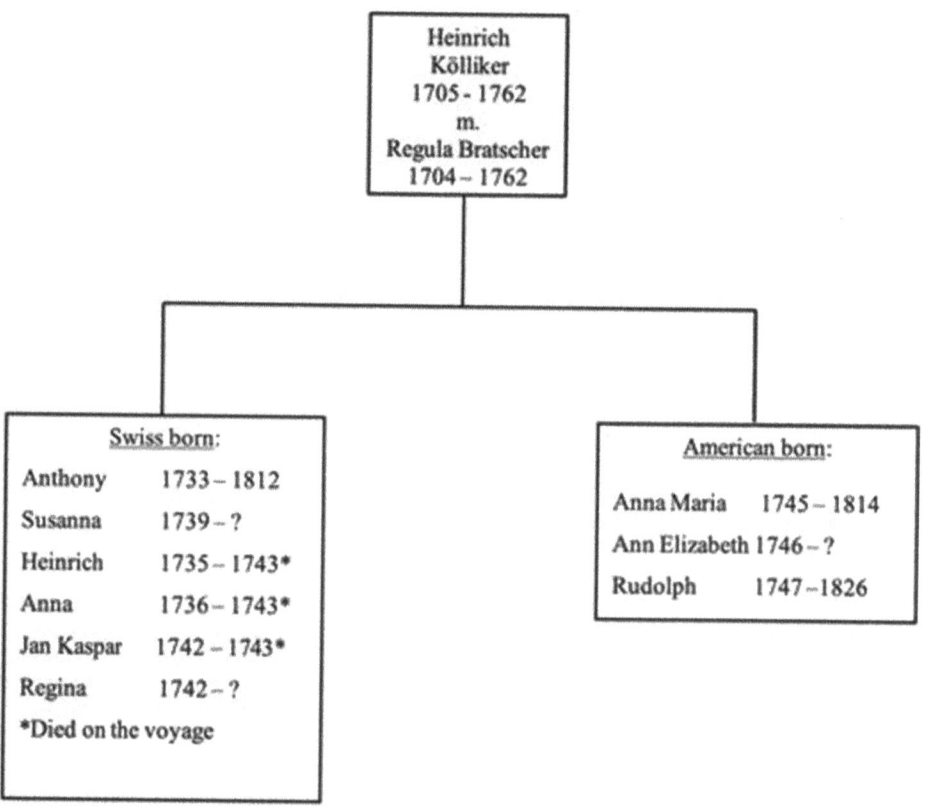

Heinrich Kōlliker 1705-1762 m. Regula Bratscher 1704-1762

Swiss born:

Anthony	1733-1812
Susanna	1739-?
Heinrich	1735-1743*
Anna	1736-1743*
Jan Kaspar	1742-1743*
Regina	1742-?

*Died on the voyage

American born:

Anna Maria	1745-1814
Ann Elizabeth	1746-?
Rudolph	1747-1826

Note: A John Jacob is listed in the Kelker Family record as born in 1740, but he is not listed on the Swiss census of emigrants from Zurich (Faust and Brumbaugh). That he is not recorded leaving Switzerland with the other family members could mean that he died before departure. A Regina is listed in the Kelker Family Record born sometime between 1742 and 1745. She may have been born and died after the family's arrival in Pennsylvania. Heinrich's sister Verena is not listed as having traveled with the rest of the family (page 59, Swiss census), but she is listed on page 66 of the census as "Verena Kölliker, of Herrliberg, having departed in July or August of 1743. She most likely traveled with the family. The Kelker family record does not show a birth year for Ann Elizabeth and Rudolph, but their baptism years are given. Since baptism usually took place shortly after birth, their birth and baptism years are very likely the same.

The new arrivals settled among other Swiss immigrants in Lebanon County, Pennsylvania, on land about four miles from the town of Lebanon. Heinrich became Henry, Kölliker became Kelker and three more children were born (see Table above). They farmed and Henry became an active member and an elder in the Reformed Church (Berg Kirch, or Hill Church) located five miles northwest of Lebanon. Church records show that Henry assisted in the construction of the church in 1744 and that all early entries in the church book are in his handwriting.

Henry's will and an inventory of his estate give us some evidence of how the family lived and prospered at their Lebanon farm. Henry's properties included the farm and the house that he built, along with timber lots he owned in the town of Williamsburg. (Last Will and Testament of Henry Kelker, 1761, in the Kelker Family Record, p. 65) We don't have much information about the family's life in Pennsylvania, but from what we do have we can surmise that they made a successful transition to rural Pennsylvania farm life. Among the few existing bits and pieces is a short description of the original family home that Henry built from logs (Kelker Family Record, p. 65). It is part of a note written circa 1857 that refers to a 1742 land-sale document for the property where Henry had built the family's log house in 1744. The 1742 land-sale document concerns the property's sale by a Matthew Clark to a Jacob Eberly. The note (below) relates that in 1857 the land was divided into two farms by its then owners, a Jacob Lichty and his son-in-law, Joseph Gingrich. The 1857 note reads in part: The part occupied by Gingrich (1857) is where Henry Kelker lived. The house of Henry Kelker stood in the garden in front of the present house, just across the road. Mr. Lichty in 1857, then seventy-four years of age, told R. F. Kelker [Henry's great grandson] that he built the present house in 1808 out of logs of the old house, which was built in 1745 [no doubt by Henry Kelker]. According to the tin weather vane which was erected on the gable end of the house, and which Mr. Lichty remembers distinctly, had the date 1745 cut in it. He says that in rebuilding the house he had to replace only the foundation logs of the old house, the others being in good condition. The farm is situated about four miles north of Lebanon, near the public road leading to Jonestown

The Last Will and Testament of Henry Kelker, 1761
(Kelker Family Record, pp. 65, 66)

In the name of God, Amen! I Henry Kelker of the township of Bethel and County of Lancaster; Yeoman; being weak in body and of sound mind and memory, blessed be God for his mercy, I publish this my last Will & Testament the twenty-eighth day of December in the year of our lord one thousand seven hundred and sixty one, in the following manner: First, I recommend my soul into the hands of God who gave it to me, and then my body to be buried in a Christian and decent manner, at the discretion of my Executors. And what worldly goods the Lord hath been pleased to bless me with, I devise as followeth: that is, I allow all my lawful debts to be paid, and the remaining part of my personal Estate, I give to my loving Wife, the thirds thereof; and the other two thirds I allow to be divided in equal shares between all my Children, Sons and Daughters alike. And I allow my wife to live on the Plantation and assist to raise up my young Children without any interruption during her widowhood, and that none of my Children shall have any demands for any of their shares of the personal estate, until my wife intermarry. And I give also to my Wife, her choice of the Lots I have in Williamsburg and timber of my plantation, to be taken at the cost of my estate, to Build one house of the dimensions of twenty six by twenty eight feet. And my real estate I give and allow to be divided among my Children, all an equal share thereunto, after my Wife is discharged therefrom according to law. And I make and appoint my Wife and my Son Anthony, Executors of my last Will and Testament to manage and order according to the true intent and meaning thereof.

In Witness whereof I have hereunto set my hand and seal.

Signed: Heinrich Kölliker

Inventory of Henry Kelker's Estate. (Kelker Family Record, p. 66) A reading of the February 8, 1762, inventory of Henry's estate that is included in his will gives us some further indication of the family's success. They made productive use of their farmland as shown by the large number of farm implements and farm animals in the inventory. Henry's will lists among numerous other items, four books, three Bibles, a windmill, two sheep, a gun, two spinning wheels, cooper ware, thirty pounds of hemp, six hoggs (sic), five dozen catechism books, a meal chest and thirty bushels of rye.

We can only imagine what life had been like for the Köllikers and other Swiss immigrants of that time. The Köllikers would find a rewarding life in the New World, but it came about after months of hardship, suffering and tragedy. The family had traveled from their Zurich home to England for a perilous sea voyage during which three of their young children died. They landed in a primitive Swiss colony in densely forested Carolina and then had to make it to Lebanon, Pennsylvania, where they faced the challenge of starting a new life. But in spite of all the uncertainty about their new life they must have been immensely relieved to have at last reached their American destination.

But the Heinrich Kölliker / Henry Kelker family made it. They managed a productive farm and handled their affairs well enough to own other properties. Their heirs live on. Their legacy is the large numbers of Kelkers and other heirs who share a remarkable family history.

Chapter 2 continues with the life of Heinrich and Regula's son Anthony and his wife, Mary Magdalena.

Addendum
Henry's Grandchildren Deliver His Headstone

Henry, an active member of Hill Church, was buried in the church's cemetery in 1762. A century later, three of Henry's great grandchildren, the Kelker brothers Rudolph Frederick, Immanuel Meister and Henry Anthony had a headstone prepared and placed at the burial site.

The Kelker Family Record (pp. 67, 68) contains a description of the preparation and delivery of the headstone:

> On the 26th day of October, 1867, R. F. Kelker shipped by Freight car No. 163 on the Philadelphia & Reading Railroad from Harrisburg, Pa., where it had been prepared by Henry Brown, under his direction one large Headstone made of the best quality Hummelstown red sandstone, measuring seven feet long twenty-six inches wide and eight inches thick, together with a heavy footstone of appropriate size. These were conveyed to Annville, Lebanon Co., Pa., by the cars, and from thence, hauled by wagon to the grave yard of the Hill Church ("Berg Kirch") about two miles north-east of Annville, by John Heilman & Brothers and erected by them in the church yard.

> The gravestone inscription reads: "In Memory of Henry Kolliker [Kelker] Born in 1705, Emigrated from Herrliberg, Canton Zurich, Switzerland, and settled in Bethel [now Swatara] Township, Lebanon County, in 1743. One of the Elders of the Reformed Congregation Hill Church in 1745. Died in 1762; also Regula Bratscher, his wife."

Photo courtesy of
Ramsey Davenport.

CHAPTER 2

Anthony Kelker

Swiss Immigrant, Revolutionary War Officer, Dauphin County's First Sheriff, Pennsylvania State Legislator

No one represents the Kelkers in America more significantly than Anthony Kelker (1733–1812), my great-great-great-great-great-grandfather. Anthony with his wife, Mary Magdalena Meister, and his brother Rudolph and his wife Maria Weidman form the bridge between the Swiss Köllikers and the approximately four thousand American Kelkers, black and white, scattered throughout the United States today (United States Census, 2000). Born in the canton of Zurich, Switzerland where he spent his first ten years, ten-year-old Anthony left with his family on their long and difficult voyage that ended in the Dutch country of south-central Pennsylvania. He grew up there on the family farm near Lebanon. He received what little education was offered at that time, but despite his lack of formal training he went on to serve with distinction as an officer in the Revolutionary War, as the first elected sheriff of Dauphin County and as a representative in the Pennsylvania state legislature. According to the Commemorative Biographical Encyclopedia of Dauphin County, Anthony Kelker was remembered as "a man of strict integrity, an unflinching patriot, and highly esteemed by his fellow-citizens." (Commemorative Biographical Encyclopedia of Dauphin County, Pennsylvania: Containing Sketches of Representative Citizens, and Many of the Early Scotch-Irish and German Settlers, 1896, Chambersburg, J. M. Runk & Company, p. 176)

We know little of Anthony's life before he entered military service at age forty-two on August 28, 1775, four months after the Battles of Concord and Lexington (April 19) and fourteen months before the signing of the Declaration of Independence (July 4, 1776). Shown below is a copy of his lieutenant's commission (Kelker Family Record, p. 127) in the Battalion of the Associators of Lancaster County, among the few known records of his military service. Egle's archive (*Pennsylvania in the War of the Revolution, Associated Battalions and Militia, 1775–1783*, vol. 1, 1887, ed. by Egle, W. H. and Meyers, E., State Printer, Harrisburg) mentions only that Anthony was active in the campaign of 1776 but offers no details of those activities or assignments.

SEAL,

LIBERTY, SAFETY

& PEACE

Pennsylvania, ss:

In Assembly

To Anthony Kelcker [sic], Gent., 28 August, 1775.

We reposing special Trust and Confidence in your Patriotism, Valour, Conduct and Fidelity, Do by these Presents, constitute and appoint you to be Lieutenant of a company of foot [soldiers] in the second Battalion of the Associators in the County of Landcaster, for the Protection of this Province against all hostile Enterprises, and for the Defence of American Liberty, You are therefore carefully and diligently to discharge the Duty of a Lieutenant as aforesaid, by doing and performing all Manner of Things thereunto belonging. And we do strictly charge and require all Officers and Soldiers, under your Command to be obedient to your Orders as their Lieutenant. And you are to observe and follow such Orders and Directions, from Time to Time, as you shall receive from the Assembly, during their Sessions; and, in their recess, form the present or any future Committee of Safety appointed by the Assembly of this Province, or from your superior Officer, according to the Rules and Regulations for the better Government of the Military Association in Pennsylvania; and pursuant to the Trust reposed in you. This Commission to continue in Force until revoked by the Assembly, or by the present or any succeeding Committee of Safety.

Signed by Order of the Assembly,

John Morrow, *Speaker*

Anthony fought in 1777 at the Battles of Brandywine (Sept. 11) and Germantown (Oct. 4). We know only that he survived those battles, and that he had been active in the campaign of 1776 (Kelker Family Record, p. 72). Both battles were resounding defeats for the Continental Army. At Brandywine, forces under George Washington were forced to flee the battlefield after the British got around Washington's right flank and into the vulnerable rear areas. That decisive advantage forced the Americans to fight their way out. The success of the escape is credited to Polish General Casimir Pulaski who defended the rear. (Battle of Brandywine—Wikipedia) The loss at Brandywine, in which 1,300 Americans were killed, wounded and captured, left the British commander-in-chief, William Howe, an uncontested path to Philadelphia. General Charles Cornwallis then marched 3,000 British troops unimpeded into the city on September 26.

After the battle Howe stationed 3,000 of his men in Philadelphia but kept the greater part of his force, about 9,000, at nearby Germantown. Seeing the British army divided and sensing a tactical advantage, Washington attacked the Germantown force on October 4. Heavy fog caused considerable chaos and confusion in the morning's fighting. The American columns were unable to overcome any of Howe's formations and were forced to retreat, losing 1,111 men killed, wounded and captured. Howe's forces withdrew to Philadelphia while Washington and his men moved on to Valley Forge where they spent the winter. (Wikipedia, Battle of Brandywine)

Though Anthony's activities following the defeats at Brandywine and Germantown aren't known, on June 2, 1778, he was issued a pass (shown below, from the Kelker Family Record, p. 128) allowing him "to pass unmolested to the states of Maryland and Virginia, to visit his Friends and to transact his "lawful Business" there." What "lawful Business" he was transacting we don't know, but it was very likely of a military nature.

> Lancaster County, ss
>
> In the Common Wealth of Pennsylvania. Permit the bearer hereof Anthony Kelker, to pass unmolested to the states of Maryland and Virginia, to visit his Friends and to transact his lawful Business there, and from thence to return to his place of abode in Lebanon Township. He being a Lieutenant in the Militia, and a Friend to the American Cause. Given under my Hand and Seal at Lebanon, the second day of June Anno Domini 1778.
>
> (Signed) John Thome
>
> To all whom it may concern.

Just seventeen days later Anthony received an appointment as wagon master of Colonel Greenawalt's Battalion (Kelker Family Record, p. 128).

> In the Name and by the Authority of the Supreme Executive Council of the Common Wealth of Pennsylvania
>
> To Anthony Kelker :
>
> I, reposing especial Trust and confidence in your Patriotism, valor, conduct, and Fidelity Do by these Presents constitute and appoint you to be Waggon-Master [sic] of Colonel Greenawalt's Battalion District in the county of Lancaster. You are therefore carefully and Diligently to discharge the duty of Waggon-Master by doing and performing all manner of things thereunto belonging. And I do strictly charge and require all persons under your command to be obedient to your orders, as Waggon-Master of the said district, and you are to observe and follow such orders and directions as you shall from time to time receive from me or from your superior officers, in Pursuance of the acts of Assembly of this State. This Commission to continue in force untill [sic] your term by the Laws of this state shall of course expire. Given under my hand and seal this Nineteenth day of June Anno Domini 1778.
>
> James Bayly
>
> *Waggon–Master General for Lancaster County*

The Revolutionary War ended in 1783 with the British defeated at the Battle of Yorktown. Two years later Anthony was elected as the first sheriff of Dauphin County. The paragraph below is from an article in the *Harrisburg Telegraph* (Dec. 29, 1871, p. 3) that tells us something about his appointment and the sale of his farm, most likely between the end of the war and his election to sheriff in 1785. The R. F. Kelker mentioned in the article is Anthony's grandson, the preparer of the Kelker Family Record.

SHERIFFS OF DAUPHIN COUNTY AND 1ST ELECTIONS

> Our roll of sheriff's [sic] of Dauphin county opens with the name of Anthony Kelker. He had been a farmer, but having sold his farm resided in the town of Lebanon at the time of his election to the office of first sheriff of Dauphin county, in the year 1785. He was a patriotic man. It is said that he sold his farm for a load of hay. The explanation of it seems to be that the Continental money received therefore was

but of little or no value, and as some compensation for losses sustained, his fellow citizens were pleased to confer on him the high honor and profit of the office just named. His descendants, R. F. Kelker and brothers, are well and favorably known in our midst at this day, and deservedly rank amongst our best citizens.

The reference to selling his farm "for a load of hay" indicates that Anthony's finances were in poor shape following the war. This is not surprising since runaway inflation had destroyed the postwar economy. In 1775, at the beginning of the war, the Continental Congress issued paper dollars, referred to as Continentals. As the war progressed the currency steadily depreciated until May 1781 when it became so worthless that its use was halted. The Continentals' fall resulted from too many being released into circulation and from the British dumping large numbers of counterfeit Continentals through purchasing American goods. Anthony was probably in desperate enough straits in the harsh postwar economy that he had little choice but to sell his property.

The statement in the 1871 *Harrisburg Telegraph* that "his fellow citizens were pleased to confer on him the high honor and profit of the office" indicates that the voters of Dauphin County recognized his military service and sympathized with him over his financial losses. Anthony may have even used those factors as a campaign strategy. In any case, the article is from the perspective of a reporter getting information nearly a century later from Anthony's grandson, Rudolph Frederick Kelker.

It should be noted that Anthony's son Henry (1761–1823) and his American-born brother Rudolph (1747–1846) also served in the Revolutionary War. According to Pennsylvania State Archives, Revolutionary War (Militia, 5th S. Vol. VII, p. 127), Rudolph entered service in the Second Battalion of the Lancaster County Militia on October 17, 1780. Henry served in the same battalion and his enlistment commenced on August 20, 1781 (at twenty-one) and ended on October 20 (p. 133). Henry served under Lt. Philip Greenawalt (or Grunenwalt). The Kelker Family Record (p. 77) shows that he married Lieutenant Greenawalt's daughter Elizabeth (1761–1820).

Anthony's move from Lebanon to Harrisburg to begin his appointment as Dauphin County sheriff marks the beginning of the Kelker family's long tenure in the city. He served from 1781 to 1782 as a deputy sheriff of Lancaster County. In 1785 when Dauphin County was split from Lancaster County, he became its first sheriff and served from 1785 to 1788 (Kelker Family Record,

p. 71). Shown below is evidence of Anthony's duties as sheriff, in a writ that he posted in a Philadelphia newspaper.

> **W**HEREAS an alias Supœna has issued, directed to me, the Sheriff of Dauphin county, from the Justices of the Supreme Court of Pennsylvania, in a certain bill presented to the same court by *Joseph Wright*, against *Catharine Wright*, the wife of said Joseph, for a divorce, upon a suggestion of adultery and other misbehaviour; by which said Supœna I was commanded to summon the said Catharine Wright to appear before the Justices of said Supreme Court, at Philadelphia, on the twenty-fourth day of September next, to answer the premises.
>
> These are therefore to notify the said Wright, to be and appear at the return of the said writ, to answer as aforesaid.
>
> August 18, 1788.   ANTHONY KELKER, Sheriff.

Anthony was elected at sixty as a Democratic-Republican to the Pennsylvania House of Representatives where he served from 1793 to 1794. (Kelker Family Record, p. 72)

Anthony's exemplary life is evidenced by his devotion to his family, his community and to his country. His short biography in the *Biographical Encyclopedia of Dauphin County* states that "Mr. Kelker was a man of strict integrity, an unflinching patriot, and highly esteemed by his fellow-citizens." His and Mary Magdalena's seven children represent the first generation born in this country. Anthony's descendants, along with those of his brother Rudolph, make up thousands of US citizens today.

Anthony's siblings. Rudolph Kelker (1747–1826), Anthony's American-born brother, with his wife, Maria Weidman, are the progenitors of the second line of Kelkers. Rudolph was born about four miles from Lebanon. He married Maria on March 22, 1768, and they had six children, with only two, John (dates unknown) and Jacob (1775–?), surviving into adulthood. The Kelker Family Record (p. 123) notes that Rudolph's nephew Frederick and grandnephew Rudolph Frederick Kelker attended his funeral at Lebanon.

Note: Anthony and his sister Susanna (1739–?) were the only Kölliker children who survived the ocean voyage with their family. Four other children—Regina (?–?), Anna Maria (1745–1814), Ann Elizabeth (1746–?) and Rudolph

(1747–1826)—were born after the family's arrival in Pennsylvania. Regina is listed in the Kelker Family Record, but no birth, baptism or death dates are given. We do know that she married a Peter Shally. Anna Maria married a William Dinges, and after his death she married his brother John Jacob Dinges. She and John Jacob are buried in the Lebanon Old Reformed Church cemetery. Ann Elizabeth is listed in the Kelker Family Record but, except for her baptismal date of December 12, 1746, no information is provided. She may have died as an infant. Rudolph married Maria Weidman. He died in Lebanon in 1826. Swiss-born Susanna married a Frederick Bollman. She died at Myerstown (no date of death is recorded in the Kelker Family Record).

Chapter 3 continues with the lives of Anthony and Mary Magdalena's children, the first generation born in America.

Addendum
Anthony and Mary Magdalena Kelker's Furniture

Photo by Steve Wydra

The case of drawers. Anthony left behind two pieces of well-preserved furniture that are now in possession of the Historical Society of Dauphin County and are on display in the Harris-Cameron mansion in Harrisburg. Shown is his case of drawers. According to his grandson, Rudolph Frederick Kelker, (see memorandum below that accompanies the case of drawers) Anthony obtained the case of drawers, or chest on chest, in 1775 from the British loyalist Patton family in Lebanon, Pennsylvania. As described in the legend below, in 1836 it came into the possession of Rudolph Frederick Kelker who had it transported to Harrisburg through the canals that then connected Lebanon and Harrisburg.

The piece was kept in Rudolph Frederick's home at 9 South Front Street. Upon his 1906 death the piece was passed to his son, William Anthony who, upon his 1908 death, left the home and its contents to the historical society. The historical society occupied the Kelker home until 1941 when it was demolished to make way for the Dauphin County Courthouse. The case of drawers and the society's archival collection were then transferred to the Harris-Cameron mansion where they remain today. According to the society's records (accession no. 1941.7) the piece was restored from 1989 to 1994. It is now in splendid condition with brass handles that appear to be original although some locks are missing.

Rudolph F. Kelker's Nov 2, 1899, memorandum on the case of drawers' history that is on display along with the case of drawers:

This case of drawers was the property of Anthony Kelker and his widow Mary Magdalena Kelker, the former of whom died in Lebanon, March 10, 1812 and the latter Dec 30, 1818, after which it was used by their granddaughters Margaret, Catharine, Mary and Susanna Kelker children of Henry Kelker. After that Margaret and Catharine had died and Mary and Susanna had left Lebanon, it was given by Leonard Greenawalt Executor of Anthony and Henry Kelker it was given to Rudolph F. Kelker on the occasion of his visit to Lebanon in 1836. On the 8th of November 1836 Frederick Kelker paid Robert Harris $2.25 freight by Canal boat to Harrisburg Captain Loomis for the Case of drawers—from Lebanon by Union Canal to Middletown & thence by Penn Canal to Harrisburg. Feb 4, 1837 Kelker paid David Greenawalt $3.61 the cost of box? & lumber and which he had advanced to Israel Eubich of Lebanon, for making the same. Anthony Kelker bought the Chest of drawers at a sale of property of the Patton family who removed from Lebanon to Butler. Anthony Kelker bought the Chest of drawers at a sale of property of the Patton family who removed from Lebanon to Philad(elphi)a.

Anthony's walnut desk. The desk remained in the Kelker family from the time Anthony acquired it in 1785 until William Anthony's death, in 1908, when it, along with the case of drawers, were passed on to the historical society. It was used by Rudolph Frederick Kelker as indicated by a "Foreign Missions" label over one of the compartments (RFK was active in foreign mission for his German Reform Church). The desk is identified as Anthony's property by his carved name and the year 1785 on the rear panel. I think we can presume that it was Anthony who carved his name most likely in 1785, or perhaps sometime thereafter, so the desk is more that two-hundred years old.

Anthony's 1785 desk.

Removable panel
with inscriptions.

Anthony's desk on display at the Harris Cameron mansion in Harrisburg. He very likely acquired the desk in 1785, as evidenced by his name and date carved on the back side (see opposite). The arrow shows the removable panel (secret compartment) that when removed reveals the inscriptions on the side panels (Photos opposite)

Above, the carved backside of Anthony's desk, and below, the inscribed panels of the secret compartment.

The inscribed panels of the secret compartment. Rudolph Frederick Kelker wrote on the right panel above:

> This desk was the property of Anthony Kelker, my grandfather in Lebanon and was used by him in 1785 and was bought by me from my Uncle John Kelker about 1854.
>
> Rudolph F. Kelker

It has now (1887) been in our family for more than a century.

The left panel inscribed by William Anthony Kelker reads:

WA

William Anthony Kelker

Born September 20, 1853

CHAPTER 3

Anthony and Mary Magdalena's Children:
The First American-Born Generation

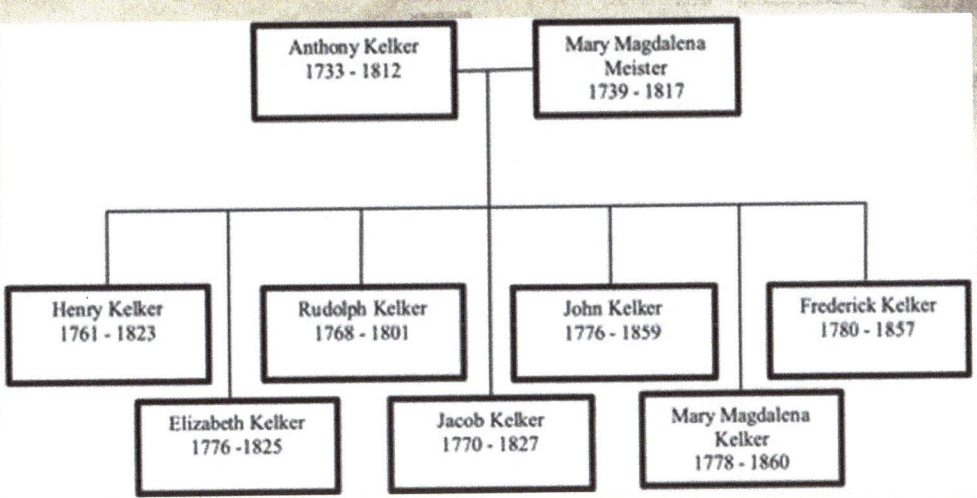

Anthony Kelker
1733 - 1812

Mary Magdalena
Meister
1739 - 1817

Henry Kelker
1761 - 1823

Rudolph Kelker
1768 - 1801

John Kelker
1776 - 1859

Frederick Kelker
1780 - 1857

Elizabeth Kelker
1776 -1825

Jacob Kelker
1770 - 1827

Mary Magdalena
Kelker
1778 - 1860

Anthony and Mary Magdalena's five sons and two daughters were born over a period of nineteen years. The sons distinguished themselves as soldiers, businessmen, officeholders, churchmen and active leaders of charitable causes. Thanks to their recorded successes and failures, that we can now find in recorded in newspapers and historical collections, information that can be pieced together that gives us an idea of how they lived their lives and the roles they played in their community. Not so with the daughters who, according to the laws and society's standards of the time, spent their lives confined to the home caring for their children and maintaining the household (see Chapter 8 for a discussion of Kelker women). Women had no opportunity to pursue career paths outside the home. Men ran the world and women were not allowed into the more public levels of participation. The unfortunate consequence of this repression is that women, denied opportunities to succeed in any profession, do not figure prominently in the history of that time. Through no fault of their own we have, with some exceptions, few records of their time. And without historical information there is not much we can say about daughters Elizabeth and Mary Magdalena.

Elizabeth Kelker Grunenwalt Gillum (1766–1825) and Mary Magdalena Kelker Wolf (1778–1860). What little we know about Anthony and Mary Magdalena's two daughters is recorded in the Kelker Family Record. (pp. 73–75), Elizabeth was born near Lebanon. She married Christian Grunenwalt (1758–1796) of Lebanon and bore three children. When Grunenwalt died in 1796 she was left a thirty-year-old widow with three children. But in 1799 she married a John Gillum, and when he died (date unknown) she was again left a widow. She then resided in Harrisburg with her brother Frederick and his family at 9 South Front Street until her death, on July 30, 1825.

Mary Magdalena was born in Lebanon twelve years after Elizabeth. She married Henry Wolf of Jonestown, and when he became Dauphin County Sheriff in 1809, the couple moved to Harrisburg. The Wolfs home on the northeast side of Market Square was destroyed by fire in 1818, but Henry rebuilt the property. When he died in 1831, Mary Magdalena, like her sister, moved in with her brother Frederick and his family. She then moved to a dwelling on South Second Street where she lived until she died on August 23, 1860. She is buried in the Harrisburg Cemetery where her grave is marked by a marble headstone placed there by her nephews Rudolph Frederick, Immanuel Meister and Henry Anthony.

Her obituary notice published by her pastor and shown in part below gives us an example of how earnest and active women of that time made the most of their restricted lives. For Mary Magdalena it was devotion to church.

> Nearly thirty years of her life were spent in widowhood. Having devoted herself to the service of God at an early age, she maintained her profession strictly to the last. Her attachment to the Church was strong and unwavering […] Christianity was for her the attainment of full christian womanhood […] Her visits among her friends and acquaintances were frequent; and into whatever family she entered, she had always something to say for Christ and his church. Spiritual Carelessness on the part of any would pain her deeply […] She had lived to follow nearly all the friends of her youth to the grave. The sickness that ended her days was of short duration. In it she felt that she would die. She had nothing to fear. She told me that, though, she had dear friends who cared for her, still "to be with Christ was

far better." Several hours before her death she fell asleep, in which her spirit fled away. Rest in Peace.

Henry Kelker (1761–1823). Henry Kelker, Anthony and Mary Magdalena's first child, was born about four miles from Lebanon on June 20, 1761. From what little information is available about his life, we know that he was the registrar and recorder of Lebanon County, Pennsylvania from 1821 until his death in 1823. He served in the Revolutionary War in the Second Battalion of the Lancaster County Militia and that his duty commenced on August 20, 1781 (at twenty) and ended on October 20 1781 (PA Archives, Revolutionary War, Militia, 5th S. Volume VII, p. 133), Henry served under Lt. Philip Greenawalt (or Grunenwalt) (PA Archives, p. 127). The Kelker Family Record (p. 77) states that he married Lieutenant Greenawalt's daughter Elizabeth (1761–1820) and that they had eight children.

Aside from Henry's military service his greatest distinction seems to be that he was the grandfather of Alexander Ramsey, who would become first governor of the Minnesota Territory, second governor of Minnesota, mayor of St. Paul, US senator from Minnesota and secretary of war in the Rutherford B. Hayes administration. Ramsey was the son of Henry and Elizabeth's daughter, also named Elizabeth, and Thomas Ramsey (1784–1826), a blacksmith and a veteran of the 1814 battle in defense of Baltimore. (See Chapter 7, Alexander Ramsey.)

Rudolph Kelker (1768–1801): Iron, Slaves, Cannonballs and Fatherhood. Rudolph, Anthony and Mary Magdalena's third born, was apparently a bright and ambitious young man who displayed his talents early. At twenty-three he was promoted to manager of the charcoal furnace at the sprawling works of the Cornwall Iron Furnace in Lebanon, then one of the largest iron producers in the country. However, his life was cut short by an illness of unknown origin, and he died at thirty-three, leaving behind a son.

Although Rudolph received only what little early education was then available, he displayed early signs of his abilities. In 1785, at seventeen, he began work in the Dauphin County Sheriff's office where his father, Anthony, was serving as the county's first sheriff. According to the Kelker Family Record (pp. 73, 74) he "rendered much assistance in that office" during his three-year tenure. He then worked as a clerk in a Lancaster County office, but his career took a significant upward move on April 1, 1791 when he entered the employ of the Cornwall Iron Furnace.

Iron. The Cornwall furnace was among the largest iron producers in the late 1700s when iron was a driving force in the new nation's economy. Farmers used tools and farm implements; the military used cannonballs, guns, wagons and other items; and industry required tools, machines and other iron-containing products. To meet market demand Cornwall and other ironworks maximized output by operating blast furnaces 24 hours a day, 365 days a year. Full-time operation required an ever-ready supply of iron ore, charcoal and other materials that had to be maintained to satisfy the furnace's voracious appetite. The Cornwall ironworks was ideally situated on a site supplied with all the materials required for producing iron.

Iron ore: The blast furnace was ideally situated close to a huge lode of iron ore located near the surface. This was of great benefit since the ore was readily available and could be easily mined.

Limestone: The ironworks' property contained a plentiful supply of limestone, a key ingredient for smelting, i.e., the removal of impurities during production.

Wood for charcoal: The ironworks was situated in a large dense forest supplying timber that was processed into charcoal. Charcoal burns at the high temperature required for extracting iron from iron ore.

Air blast: A rapidly flowing stream on the property was engineered using a paddle wheel and bellows to generate the air blast for the iron furnace.

The benefits of having supply and production needs readily available at the site allowed Cornwall to operate as a fully integrated facility with all the advantages of cost saving and efficiency. (Cornwall Iron Works, Wikipedia)

Slaves. Rudolph Kelker joined the ironworks in 1791as a clerk. He must have impressed his boss, Robert Coleman, with his capabilities because only a few months after beginning his employment he was made manager of the charcoal furnace. Rudolph's appointment at age twenty-three to a position so essential to company operations indicates that Coleman must have seen considerable promise in the recent hire. His job was to maintain a steady supply of charcoal to feed the constantly roaring blast furnace. To accomplish this he had to procure his production materials, maintain a production schedule and supervise his workers. His labor staff, like many at other facilities in the company, consisted of paid workers, indentured servants, free blacks and black slaves.

Slaveholding was still legal but fading in Pennsylvania in the 1790s. The company's slave workforce began to decline after 1780 when the Pennsylvania legislature passed legislation for the gradual elimination of slavery in the state. The legislation did not immediately free all slaves, only those who were born in Pennsylvania after 1780. However, the newly "freed" slaves were not free until they reached twenty-eight. Those born before 1780 remained slaves for life. The act also banned the importation of slaves from other states. Company records list eleven slaves working at Cornwall in 1776, but only one in 1792, the year after Rudolph began his employment. (Miller, F. K, 1951, *The Rise of the Iron Community: An Economic History of Lebanon County, Pennsylvania from 1740 to 1865*, Volume XII) Records of the USDT, Lebanon Township, Dauphin County, state that "by 1798 Robert Coleman still owned 5 slaves who worked under Kelker's supervision at Cornwall." (Wenger, D. E., 2008, *A Country Storekeeper in Pennsylvania*, Pennsylvania State University Press, University Park, Pennsylvania, p. 89) The discrepancy is likely a result of the company's methods for accounting for its slaves. Cornwall may not have listed them since they were the personal property of Robert Coleman.

In any case we have little information of Rudolph's dealing with slaves, although we do have an interesting record of his actions regarding a runaway slave known as Governor Dick. According to Bill Knapp, a historian of Lititz, Pennsylvania, Dick was the last slave purchased by Coleman. He produced charcoal for the Cornwall Furnace at a heavily forested mountaintop site near Mount Gretna, six miles from Lebanon. The site exists today as Clarence Schock Memorial Park although some refer to it as Governor Dick Park.

Governor Dick is a man of legend. So many stories are told about him that it is often difficult to determine fact from fantasy. But we do know a few things; he is listed aged fifty in a 1780 Lebanon County slave registry, and he lived and worked at the Mount Gretna site where he was a skilled axe man and a very competent collier, that is, a maker of charcoal. He left little evidence of his time at the mountain. Considerable efforts to locate his living quarters have not been successful. Only a few areas of blackened earth where he produced charcoal are still present. He fled the site in April 1796, at sixty-six. Dick must have been a skilled asset to the Cornwall Furnace because the company made efforts to retrieve him. Rudolph Kelker posted a reward notice for the runaway slave in the *Lancaster Journal* (see below) offering $20 for his return. The notice describes Dick as bald with large feet and "a remarkable scar on the great toe of his right foot occasioned by its being split with an axe." Governor Dick was never found, and no one knows what happened to him, although some have speculated that he went to Hartford, Maryland, where he had previously lived.

Twenty Dollars Reward.

RAN away from Cornwall Furnace, Dauphin County, on Sunday the 17th of April last, a Negro Man, called *Dick*, (alias) *Governor Dick* : he is an elderly man, bald headed, about five feet ten inches high, stout made, has a down look, is flightly marked on each of his temples with the small scores usual to some of the natives of Africa, has large feet, and a remarkable scar on the great toe of his right foot, occasioned by its being split with an axe. He is by trade a rough carpenter, and values himself greatly on his dexterity in that occupation. Had on when he went away, a new drab-coloured coatee, with metal buttons, jacket and overalls of the same, a new wool hat, and took with him some old clothes. As he lived in the early part of his life in Hartford county, State of Maryland, it is probable he has shaped his course to that quarter. Whoever secures the said Negro so that the owners may get him again, shall receive the above reward, and reasonable charges, if brought home.

      RUDOLPH KELKER, jun.

July 8th, 1796.

Another reference to Rudolph and a slave is found in the "Index of owners." (Ainsworth, John., Dauphin Co., Pennsylvania, Slave Records [1782–1825]) He is listed as a slaveholder along with Curtis Grubb, a part owner of the Cornwall Furnace. The listing reads: "Kelker, Rudolph Jr. [Curtis Grubb estate executor]." The slave or slaves in question are not mentioned. This may have been in reference to Governor Dick, but no other information is given. There is no evidence that Rudolph ever owned a slave.

Cannonballs. Although Rudolph is credited with management of the charcoal furnace his role in the following transaction indicates that he was involved with company affairs beyond the production of charcoal. A supply of 280 12-pound cannonballs manufactured for the Revolutionary War remained in storage at the Cornwall facility from 1776 until 1798. (Papers of the War Department: 1784–1800 Collection: Library of Congress: Samuel Hodgdon Letterbook, 1798–1799) On June 14, 1798, a Samuel Hodgdon of the War Department in Philadelphia, then the nation's capital, wrote to Robert Coleman requesting delivery of the supply of shot to Philadelphia "with all convenient dispatch." On June 20, Coleman replied that he was having difficulty delivering the load because he could not procure transport since wagons were being used by farmers for the ongoing harvest. But he assures Mr. Hodgdon that he had given the manager of the Cornwall Furnace "directions to exert every diligence to procure teams." On July 3, Rudolph Kelker sent a handwritten receipt to the War Department (see below) that went along with delivery of the shot. A John Smith wrote an acknowledgement of receipt of the balls that was signed upon delivery and an inventory statement signed by Sam Hodgdon that appears at the bottom stating that 274 balls, and not 280, had been delivered. (Papers of the War Department: 1784–1800, RG4)

Sirs   Cornwall Furnace 3rd July 98

By the bearer Jacob Fisher you

will receive Two hundred eighty can

non balls weighing 12lb each, part of

the shot belonging to the United States

remaining at this place since the

revolution ~ for carriage you'll please

to pay him Twenty two Dollars ~

I am with respect
Your Able Serv.
for Robt. Coleman Esq.
Rudolph Kelker

July 6, 1798 Two hundred & seventy four twelve
Pound Round Shot   signed John Smith

Total Number Rec'd at Cornwall Furnace ~280
                    Rec'd at Philad   ~274
                                             6 Deficient
Sam Hodgdon, Esq.   William ???

Rudolph Kelker's July 3, 1798, letter confirming delivery of 280
12-pound Cannonballs to the Department of War

Twelve Pound Cannon Balls on Display at the Cornwall Iron Works Museum.

Twelve-pound Cannonballs from the Revolutionary War at the Cornwall Ironworks Museum,
Lebanon, Pennsylvania. These are the same kind of shot delivered from the Cornwall Iron Works
to Philadelphia. Photo by Hanna Kelker.

Fatherhood. In addition to his duties as manager of the Cornwall furnace Rudolph had the responsibility of caring for his son. His fatherhood is revealed in Diane Wenger's remarkable book, *A Country Storekeeper in Pennsylvania: Creating Networks in Early America, 1790–1807* (cited above). The country storekeeper of its title was Samuel Rex of Schaefferstown, and he supplied goods to the people and industries in and around Lebanon County. By combing through Rex's well-preserved and extensive business records, Wenger was able to create a picture of the commercial activities and the life of Lebanon County at that time. The historian's thorough research reveals that Rudolph held accounts at Rex's store to pay for his son's living expenses.

Rudolph apparently had close relations with Rex, and he frequently visited Schaefferstown to purchase goods for his son at Rex's store and to see his son who lived and went to school there. It appears that Rex played a significant role in taking care of the boy's needs. His records show that he paid for school supplies and paid a tailor to make clothes for the boy. He kept a running account of the boy's expenses for which he was reimbursed by Rudolph. When Rudolph fell ill before his death, in 1801, Rex was named as one of his executors. Rudolph's will (on file at the Dauphin County Courthouse, Harrisburg) provided £200 to be managed by Rex for the boy's care until he reached maturity. The identities of the boy and the boy's mother are not known, with no identifying records yet found.

Rudolph fell ill of an undiagnosed disease in early 1801, and as his condition worsened he resigned his position at Cornwall. He died on May 30, 1801, (Pennsylvania Vital Records, Volume II, pp. 551, 552) Funeral rites were performed by Rev. John Anders Shultze, who later served as the sixth governor of the state (1823–1829). Rudolph was buried in the cemetery of the First Reformed Church in Lebanon. According to his glowing obituary in the *Lancaster Intelligencer* (June 3, 1801, p. 3, see Addendum): "Mr. Kelker might have been expected to reside much longer among us: But, Alas! Heaven thought otherwise; and relieved him from a tedious and lingering disorder, which, from its commencement, he bore with the fortitude of a Man and a Christian."

Addendum

Rudolph Kelker's Obituary (1801). We know little of Rudolph Kelker except for the few records that remain. His *Lancaster Intelligencer* obituary, although by no means objective, gives us reason to appreciate his life.

Note: Reading may present a slight difficulty given that printed English then used the German *s* that looks like an English *f*.

Mount Vernon Furnace, June 1, 1801.

DIED, on Saturday morning laſt, at Lebanon, Dauphin County, *Rudolph Kelker*, Jun. Eſq. in the prime of Life. His death is one of the many inſtances to remind us of the incertitude of our ſituation in this World, and its ſublunary enjoyments. In the general courſe of human Nature, Mr. Kelker might have been expected to reſide much longer amongſt us: But, alaſs! Heaven thought otherwiſe; and relieved him from a tedious and lingering diſorder, which, from its commencement, he bore with the fortitude of a Man and a Chriſtian.

Few young Men have died more regretted. His numerous Friends and Acquaintances will long bear teſtimony of his worth. The amiableneſs of his character made him generally eſteemed. No one could know him intimately, without having the higheſt reſpect for him. To a diſpoſition naturally cheerful and benevolent, was added manners the moſt engaging and prepoſſeſſing; which never failed to intereſt all who knew him in his favor.

As a Man of Buſineſs, he was active, induſtrious, and perſevering. His judgment, of itſelf correct and acute, was much improved by the application and aſſidious attention which he paid, in the line of life* in which he had for ſome years been engaged: And, as he had already proved himſelf a valuable Member of Society, no doubt, had he come to be farther advanced in years, his talents and Abilities would have ſhown more conſpicuouſly; but Death cut ſhort his blooming proſpects; and, as it cannot efface the memory of what he has been, it leaves us to imagine what he might have been, had he been ſpared a little longer.

Since Fate, however, decreed otherwiſe, we muſt bow, with ſubmiſſion, to that Divine Will which called him hence: But the impreſſion of his many eſtimable qualities will be indelibly ſtamped on the Affections, on the Hearts, of thoſe who were intimately acquainted with him. This ſtrong Record will remain, never to be effaced; and Friendſhip will drop a ſympathizing Tear, when Recollection brings to mind the Virtues of the amiable, and ever to be regretted, *Kelker*.

* *Iron Works.*

Jacob Kelker and the origin of the Black Kelkers in America. Many black Kelkers exist in the United States today. Their family origin has been carefully traced by genealogist Mrs. Del Alexa Egan Jupiter in her scholarly and extensively researched family history. (Jupiter, D.A.E., 1994, *Agustina of Spanish West Florida and Her Descendants*, Genealogy Publishing Service, Franklin, North Carolina) In this magnificent effort tracing the origins of her family (including the Kelkers) Mrs. Jupiter exhaustively studied large numbers of court and census records and historical documents. Through these she has precisely traced the origin of the black Kelkers to Jacob Kelker (1770–1827), Anthony and Mary Magdalena's fourth child, and Elizabeth Lewis, "a free woman of color" as she was described in territorial Florida's first census, in 1830 (Jupiter, p. 34). Jacob and Elizabeth apparently never married, but they had two sons.

Jacob left Lebanon at twenty-three in 1794 on what turned out to be a long, meandering journey through the South, making many stops along the way before arriving in the far-western end of the Florida panhandle, at Escambia Bay. (Kelker Family Record, p. 74) Mrs. Jupiter's research reveals that sometime after 1822, the year Florida became an organized US territory, Jacob acquired 640 acres of third-rate land on the east side of Escambia Bay as a donation grant approved by US commissioners and Congress. He resided there until his death, in 1827 (see map below). The property is still referred to locally as Kelker Fields and is currently owned by the American Cyanamid Company. (Jupiter, pp. 28–31) The map below shows the location of Jacob's property at Escambia Bay near Pensacola.

Two children are known to have been born to Jacob Kelker and Elizabeth Lewis: John (~1812–1893) and Frederick (~1812–~1878). Jacob named his boys after two of his brothers, John and Frederick, continuing the recurring naming pattern in the Kelker family. John married a Cecilia Gomez (1830–1903) and they had nine children. Frederick married circa 1865 a Nancy (last name unknown) and they had one son. (Jupiter, pp. 35–39) Mrs. Jupiter's research reveals that the many black Kelkers today descend from Jacob and Elizabeth.

Escambia Bay in orange, site of Jacob Kelker's Florida land. Map prepared by Adam Kelker.

Frank "Doc" Kelker and Dr. Henry Creath Kelker of Cleveland. It seems that as the black and the white Kelker families grew in number over the generations neither was aware of the family connection. But some recognition appeared in 1941 when Mrs. Susan Kelker of Pensacola, Florida, whose husband was Jacob and Elizabeth's grandson, raised the question in a letter to Dr. Henry Creath Kelker of Cleveland, Ohio (my father's uncle). Dr. Kelker replied by recalling some of his lineage and noting that his "great grandfather was a son of Henry Kelker brother of this Jacob who went South." Dr. Kelker then asks Mrs. Kelker: "Do you believe him to be the same man that was your husband's grandfather?" His letter clearly suggests that he had been unaware of the connection until she had informed him. His letter goes on to mention Frank Kelker of Cleveland. "There is a Frank Kelker, who is a teacher at Central High School here, who came from Dover, Ohio & he said his people came from Florida. He is a colored man and a very fine man & and greatly respected here in Cleveland." Doc Kelker, as he was known, was an outstanding athlete, a career high school teacher and a prominent civic leader in Cleveland.

As a high school student at Dover High School he earned eleven varsity-sport letters as an elite athlete competing in football, basketball, track and baseball. He was the first high school athlete to achieve All-Ohio honors in both football and basketball in the same year (http://www.timesreporter.com/sports/x123454799/Dover-names-first-HOF-class?zc_p=1#axzz2XBkwZHRe). Frank Kelker went on to an outstanding college football career at Western Reserve University. He was selected for *Sports Illustrated*'s 1962 Silver Anniversary All-American Football Team. (http://clevelandsportshall.com/kelker-frank-1-doc/)

KELKER (Class of 1934)—Frank "Doc" Kelker was the first Ohio high school athlete to be named All-Ohio in both football and basketball in the same calendar year, and is regarded by many as Dover's greatest athlete ever. Kelker led the Tornadoes to the state basketball title in 1933 and the football team to a 30-1 record during the 1931, 1932, and 1933 seasons, including two victories over Massillon. Kelker was equally gifted in track and baseball. As a 9th grader he was the first Dover High athlete to run the 100-yard dash in 9.9 seconds, which is still the school record. As a member of the baseball squad in 1932 and 1933, Kelker's unofficial stats included a .521 batting average with 12 doubles, seven triples, five home runs and 22 stolen bases. During those two years, the Dover diamond teams posted a record of 23-4, including a victory over state champion Warren. In total, Kelker earned 11 varsity letters at DHS. (from the TimesReporter.com) http://www.timesreporter.com/article/20101010/NEWS/310109976

My father and Frank Kelker. My father, Aaron Kelker (1909–1972), knew Frank Kelker, at least well enough to greet him on Western Reserve's campus. In the late 1930s my father was studying for his masters degree in biology at Western Reserve University in Cleveland, Ohio while Frank Kelker was a student there. When they met on campus, they would greet each other with a mutual "Hi Kelker." I am certain that neither one had any idea that they shared a common ancestry, and just assumed they somehow coincidentally had the same last name.

The Kelkers, black and white, living in the United States now number about four thousand, according to the 2000 US Census. They inhabit cities, towns, suburbs and rural areas all over the nation. Members of each branch, as with my father and Doc Kelker, are with a few exceptions unaware that the other exists and of their shared lineage. This story of the two Kelker families revealed to us by Mrs. Jupiter informs us and is a remarkable bit of history, a lesson to us all about where we come from and who we really are.

Addendum
Jacob Kelker's Long, Meandering Journey from Lebanon to Florida's Panhandle. Jacob Kelker, the fourth born of his parents Anthony and Mary Magdalena, was by trade a saddler. He was also a hatter, and he and his partner Jacob Friedley operated a hatting business in Harrisburg at Market Street and River Alley. In 1794, Rudolph entered a partnership with a Frederick Farnsler, and they moved to Lynchburg, Virginia and started a saddlery business. But Farnsler's father called his son back to Lebanon, and the partnership was dissolved. Jacob then moved deeper into the South and after many starts and stops ended up in Florida's Panhandle. The Kelker Family Record (p. 74) describes his circuitous route to Escambia Bay where he remained until his 1827 death.

> From some of Jacob's letters subsequently received, it appears that he remained a while in Virginia, thence removed to Nashville and to Knoxville, thence to Natchez and to New Orleans. Returned again to Natchez, and from thence to Mobile and thence to Pensacola. From Pensacola he went to his lands at the head of Escambia Bay, where he resided for some time, but being much afflicted, he removed to the town of Florida, where he died September 4, 1827. As Florida then belonged to Spain, there was but little intercourse with the United States and but little was known of his family here. He was unmarried.

The next to last sentence indicates that Jacob's family in Lebanon knew nothing of his relationship with Elizabeth Lewis and the birth of their two sons. And the last sentence further indicates that they also knew nothing of Jacob's Florida life. The 1883 Kelker Family Record makes no mention of Jacob and Elizabeth's children. Only from the remarkable work of Mrs. Del

Jupiter do we know of Jacob and his role in the origin of the black Kelkers that she uncovered research for her family history. (Jupiter, pp. 35–39)

John Kelker: Sheriff, Innkeeper, Politician. The fifth of Anthony and Mary Magdalena's seven children, John Kelker (1776–1859), was born in Annville in Lebanon County and he grew up there on the family farm. He received only the little available education, but it had little if any ill effect on his career. He went on to serve as Dauphin County Sheriff, Dauphin County Treasurer, an active member of the Democratic Party and a successful innkeeper. And, like the rest of his family, he was devoted to the German Reform Church. (*Commemorative Encyclopedia of Dauphin County, Pennsylvania*, 1896, J. M. Runk and Company, Chambersburg, Penn.) John married Sabina Schantz in 1798, and they had seven children, one of whom died in infancy. The family resided in Lebanon then moved to Harrisburg in 1813 after John was elected sheriff of Dauphin County. (Kelker Family Record, p. 82)

Photo from the Historical Society of Dauphin County

Note: The position of sheriff in Dauphin County seems to have been something of a Kelker family affair. Anthony served as the county's first sheriff, from 1775 to 1788. His son-in-law Henry Wolf, husband of daughter Mary Magdalena, became sheriff in 1809. Mary Magdalena's brother John was elected sheriff in 1812. John was the county's first sheriff to serve after its eastern portion became part of Lebanon County (Kelker Family Record, p. 72).

John's Inn. What bits of history we have indicate that the inn John Kelker owned and operated must have been a successful enterprise. Newspaper accounts from that time indicate that the success of the inn (or public house or tavern, as it has been variously described) came about from John's warm and welcoming personality. Evidence of this comes from a Harrisburg Telegraph article (Dec. 30, 1871, p. 3) on the history of Dauphin County's sheriffs by a writer (no byline) recounting his memories of the inn and effusively praising its innkeeper:

> Someone has said, rather ironically, that the heartiest welcome he ever met with was at the inn. However this may be in general, a good tavern is a good thing, and the visitor at Mr. Kelker's, if deserving, was sure to meet with a kind reception, and received good entertainment, as the writer can personally certify […]

The inn, located on North Second Street near Walnut Street (*Harrisburg Telegraph*, April 30, 1881, p. 6), provided a living for John and his family. But, more than a place of business, it was a frequent site for meetings of the local Democratic Party of which John was an officer and a fully committed party man. Meeting notices published in local newspapers give us records of the local party's use of the inn. But John did not limit the use of his public house to Democrats. The notice shown below announces a meeting to be held at the inn of the stockholders of the Downingtown, Ephrata and Harrisburg Turnpike Road Company. We can presume that John was a stockholder.

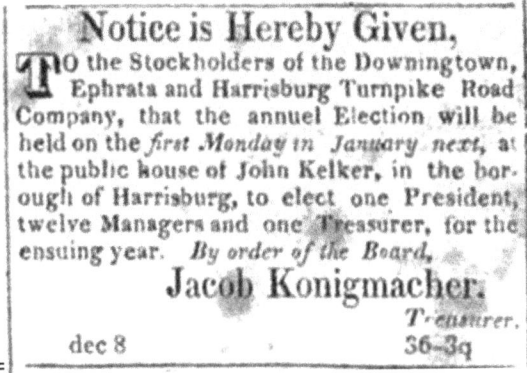

Lancaster Intelligencer, Dec. 8, 1826, p. 3.

We know little else of John's life. But it appears that he was an honest man, solid citizen, reliable public servant, good family man and a welcoming innkeeper.

Frederick Kelker: Anthony and Mary Magdalena's Youngest Child, Hardware Merchant, Landowner, Community Activist, Good Citizen.

Image of Frederick Kelker from a photo pentaptych showing five Kelker generations.

Photo by Norman Kelker who is in possession of the pentaptych.

A Brief Biography. Frederick Kelker (1780–1856) entered the world in Lebanon, Pennsylvania, on October 29, 1780. He was the last of Anthony and Mary Magdalena's seven children born over nineteen years. Frederick is most remembered for his active role in the life of early Harrisburg and for his business success.

He spent his early life in Lebanon and moved to Harrisburg in 1805 at twenty-five. He arrived just fourteen years after incorporation of the borough, then with a population fewer than one thousand (Harrisburg, Pennsylvania, Wikipedia) and the death of John Harris Jr. (john harris jr. harrisburg pa, Yahoo Search Results) Seven years after Frederick's arrival, Harrisburg, then with a population of about 2,500, became the state capital. Frederick was not the first of his family to settle in Harrisburg. His father, Anthony, had moved there to serve as first sheriff of Dauphin County (1785–1788) and as member of the Pennsylvania House of Representatives. (1793–1794) (Kelker Family Record, p. 91) Frederick's life set a pattern that was followed in Harrisburg by his children, grand-children and some great-grandchildren who spent their lives there involved in business, church, charitable work and community service.

Frederick became a prominent and respected citizen thanks to his success in business. His path to success in matrimony, however, was fraught with difficulty and disappointment. On August 31, 1806, he married Lydia Gemberling (1786–1812). (Records of Salem Reformed Church, Harrisburg, Dauphin County, Pennsylvania, 1790–1808) One child was born to the couple, Mary Magdalena in 1806, but she died in 1810. Then Lydia contracted consumption (tuberculosis) in February 1812. On April 27, after several weeks of confinement to her bed, she died at twenty-six leaving Frederick a thirty-two-year-old widower with no children. (Kelker Family Record, p. 88)

In 1817, Frederick became engaged to Anna Maria Forney of Hanover, Pennsylvania. But his second attempt at marriage ended sadly just before the ceremony when Anna Maria died suddenly at twenty-five. The Kelker Family Record (p. 89) contains an interesting 1869 letter from a Henry Wirt to Frederick's son, Rudolph Frederick Kelker, describing Wirt's visit to Miss Forney's grave.

> Dear Bro. Kelker:
>
> At your request, as made of me when I was in Harrisburg last, I have examined the tombstone of the Miss Forney who it seems was engaged to be married to your father, but who died about the time the matter was to be consummated.
>
> My mother, who well recollects the circumstances, says that the tombstone was put there by your father, though of this there is no evidence on the stone itself. It is a large marble slab on brick foundation, and has the following inscription:
>
> Sacred to the memory of
>
> Anna Maria Forney, Daughter of Adam and Rachael Forney, born June 23, 1792, departed this life October 5, 1817, in the 25th year of her age.

Few were her pangs, nor long with woe opprest [sic];

Short was her passage to the port of rest;

Life and its joys she thought not worth her stay;

Just viewed our troubled globe and soared away.

With my respects to Mrs. Kelker and your family,

I remain, truly yours,
Henry Wirt

Frederick's third attempt at marriage was, at last, successful. On May 7, 1820, he married Catherine Fager (1798–1846). (Ancestry.com, Pennsylvania and New Jersey, Church and Town Records, 1708–1985). Three sons, Rudolf Frederick, Immanuel Meister and Henry Anthony were born to the couple (see Chapter 4). The marriage lasted twenty-six years until Catherine's death, in 1846. Records indicate that she was an exemplary wife and naturally committed to helping others.

Catherine lived in a time when the laws of government and social restrictions kept women confined to the home with essentially no opportunity to enter any profession beyond domestic duties. But church and charity provided a chance for women like Catherine to participate in rewarding activity, and she took full advantage. A few words from her short biography (below) written by her son Rudolph Frederick (Kelker Family Record, pp. 89, 90) give us an idea of how she worked outside the home for the benefit of others.

> Catherine (Fager), second wife of Frederick Kelker was the daughter of John Fager, a hatter by trade, and Sarah (Cleckner) his wife, who settled in Harrisburg about the year 1785. Catharine was born at Harrisburg on the 24th of October, 1798, baptized December 2, 1798… She took a very active interest in the first organization of the Sunday school of the Lutheran Church, and labored diligently for its success as a manager and teacher. After her marriage, she withdrew from the Lutheran, and united with the Reformed congregation, of which her husband was a prominent member. She was a woman of exemplary piety, humble, devoted, unostentatious, and remarkable for her meek and gentle spirit. In the Church, and in the sewing circle, Sunday school mission society, and benevolent society, her labors were unremitting. She was deeply interested in the education and maintenance of poor young men studying for the Gospel ministry, and heartily engaged in every good work. She was the light of the family circle, given to hospitality, and was a most

affectionate wife and mother. She enjoyed through excellent health until her last illness, which continued for three weeks, when in the triumphs of faith she fell peacefully asleep in Jesus, on Saturday morning, August 15, 1846.

Devotion to family was highly regarded and practiced by Frederick and Catherine. In 1826, in an exemplary act of kindness, they took in and raised Alexander Ramsey, the son of Frederick's niece Elizabeth Kelker Ramsey, who was suddenly widowed when her husband, Thomas Ramsey, committed suicide. His death left Elizabeth in a state of poverty with five young children.

Eleven-year-old Alex joined the Kelker sons Rudolph Frederick, Immanuel Meister and Henry Anthony and grew up with them essentially as a fourth brother. Alex Ramsey had a distinguished career in politics. Among other high positions he served as the first governor of the Minnesota Territory and a two-term US senator from Minnesota (See Chapter 7, Alexander Ramsey).

Business. Frederick spent a successful and profitable career in business, first in mercantile trade operating a hardware firm and then profiting from the buying and selling of land and homes in and around Harrisburg. He began his business career in 1801 at twenty-one when he joined the Oves & Moore hardware firm in Lebanon. In 1805, when the firm moved to 5 South Front Street (later re-designated 9 South Front Street) in Harrisburg, Frederick moved there along with the business. In 1811, at thirty-one he purchased the interests of Oves & Moore and became the sole owner, and in 1813, he purchased the Front Street house and ran the business under the name F. Kelker & Company.

9 South Front Street, Harrisburg, Frederick Kelker's home and the site of his hardware business. This photo is one of the oldest in the Historical Society of Dauphin County archives that is not of a person. Previously #5 South Front Street in Harrisburg (note the "5" on the right door), it was 9 South Front Street when the photo was taken on February 5, 1858 by A. C. Smith. The home was built in 1798 by Henry Islett. Frederick Kelker moved from Lebanon to Harrisburg in 1805 and started a hardware business here. Frederick died in 1857 and the business was moved by Kelker and Brothers to Market Square. Rudolph F. Kelker had A. C. Smith take the photo before demolishing the house to make room for a new house, which was later given to the Historical Society of Dauphin County and served as our home from 1908 to 1941. Photo ID: C02799. (Caption and photo from the Historical Society of Dauphin County, http://www. dauphincountyhistory.org/)

Frederick ran the business successfully until 1823 when he became ill and sold the business to George Oglesby and Samuel Pool, who changed the name to Oglesby & Pool. When he recovered sufficiently, he turned his attention to buying and selling homes and land in and around Harrisburg, a practice that made him a wealthy man.

The town of Steelton and the building of the first steel mill in America are part of Frederick's real estate legacy. Two of his most notable land acquisitions, large parcels in Baldwin (now Steelton), led to the development of the local steel industry and the development of the town of Steelton. Upon his death, in 1857, he left the two land parcels, nearly one-hundred acres, to his sons Rudolph Frederick and Henry Anthony. In 1866, the sons sold their land to the newly formed Pennsylvania Steel Company for the construction of the first US steel mill. They then used their gains to purchase land in Baldwin where they laid out and sold housing lots. Their actions gave rise to the village of Steelton (see Chapter 4).

The Harrisburg National Bank. Among Frederick's many business, civic and charitable activities was his long service as a director to the Harrisburg National Bank. He bought a hundred shares of the original stock issued in 1814 and was a member of the first board of directors. (Wallace, H. B. 1914, *A Century of Banking*; Harrisburg National Bank, Harrisburg, PA)

Frederick was the first of three generations of his family to serve as a director. His sons Henry Anthony, Rudolph Frederick and Immanuel Meister, and Henry Anthony's son Henry Anthony Jr. also served as directors. Through the years they served with many prominent Pennsylvanians. A few are listed below:

—Robert Harris, son of Harrisburg's founder, John Harris, Jr.

—Jacob Haldeman, a successful iron manufacturer, wealthy land owner responsible for laying out New Cumberland in 1816

—James Buchanan, in 1831, twenty-six years before becoming the nineteenth US President was a stockholder and was elected a director

—William Wallace, son-in-law of William Maclay, one of Pennsylvania's first US senators, headed the Presque Isle Land Company, developer of Erie, Pennsylvania

—Alexander Ramsey, Minnesota Governor, US Senator and Secretary of War in the Rutherford B. Hayes administration, was a stockholder

—Francis R. Shunk, Pennsylvania governor from 1844 to 1848, became a stockholder in 1818

—Simon Cameron, US Senator, Ambassador to Russia and Secretary of War in the Lincoln administration, was a stockholder

The bank was founded in 1814 and served the Harrisburg community for many years under the able oversight of many prominent Harrisburg citizens. The bank opened two years after Harrisburg became the state capital, at a time when the young, growing village town was feeling the need for a financial institution to serve its farmers, businessmen and builders. The bank's building committee of Robert Harris, son of Harrisburg's founder, and two other directors bought a house at 21 South Second Street that the bank occupied until it bought and took over a South Market Square building then occupied by a Philadelphia Bank branch. The Harrisburg National Bank moved to the new site and opened for business in 1817.

Religion. Like the rest of his family, Frederick was devoted to the German Reform Church. He was faithfully involved in many aspects of the church and was highly regarded for his service. He presided at a meeting on November 17, 1820 that was called to establish the church's first Sunday school, and he was prominent in "measures adopted for erecting the church building." (*Commemorative Biographical Encyclopedia of Dauphin County*, p. 205) Strong religious belief was not unique to Frederick. His Swiss ancestors and generations of Harrisburg Kelkers that would follow him were strongly adherent to their religious beliefs and were active supporters of their church.

Community Service. As with almost all the Kelker men of Harrisburg, Frederick was inevitably drawn to serving in government and in community service. He served the small but growing Harrisburg community as town-council president in the early nineteenth century. (*Harrisburg Telegraph*, June 2, 1897, p. 1) When public schools were first established in Pennsylvania he served as a director of the common schools. (*Commemorative Biographical Encyclopedia of Dauphin County*, 1896, J. M. Runk and Company, p. 205)

A Slavery Friendly Ordinance. An interesting account of Frederick's actions as town-council president appeared in the *Harrisburg Telegraph*. (June 2, 1897, p. 1) The report is disturbing because it reveals his role in passing an ordinance that essentially turned the Harrisburg constabulary, in the words of the *Telegraph* article, into "a body of slave-snatchers and slave hunters." The three-part ordinance's first section laid out a requirement that, beginning on May 10, 1821, "every free person of color" living in the town was required to appear before the chief burgess and provide his or her home address, names of all family members and any others residing in a home, the trades of all residents, and any changes of address. Every black person was required to pay twelve and a half cents to receive a certificate with a penalty of a dollar for every twenty-four-hour delay in registering.

The second section required all innkeepers and residents who accommodated any black person as a guest for twenty-four hours or longer to report to the burgess or any borough constable the names of such individuals, who were then required to register with the burgess and pay the registration fee.

The third section reveals the slave-catching intent of the ordinance: "that it shall be the duty of the high constable or any of the constables of said borough, in case any strange person of color [in the language of the time] shall be found therein, not having complied with this ordinance, to take him or her forthwith before any justice of the peace within said borough to be dealt with according to law in such manner as is directed with respect to vagrants and idle or disorderly persons." The ordinance was passed to monitor closely every black person in Harrisburg in a search for runaways who when identified would be taken before a magistrate and returned to bondage under his or her owner in a slave state. The ordinance placed a heavy and unjust burden on local free-black residents, who were forced to pay to participate in the scheme, and the constabulary that was mandated to serve slave states' interests.

We ask why Frederick Kelker, a man dedicated to charitable causes and a devout Christian, was party to this scheme to identify and capture slaves fleeing to their freedom. Pennsylvania began the gradual elimination of slavery in 1780, and by 1821 few slaves were held in the state. But large numbers of runaways passed through Pennsylvania on their way north, and US laws provided for their capture and return. The constitution when written included procedures for the return of runaway slaves, and the law was reinforced and clarified by Congress in 1793 (Fugitive Slave Clause, Article IV, Section 2, Clause 3 of the Constitution). Free Blacks in Pennsylvania and other free states lived imperiled by slave hunters who roamed those states looking for runaways. Placing Harrisburg blacks under surveillance added to their peril and was a clear imposition on their lives. We can only speculate about what drove Frederick to enact such legislation. He did live in a time when large numbers of whites, even in free states, believed that blacks were inferior and therefore were more sympathetic to the institution of slavery. We can also speculate that the ordinance might have been passed against his objections. It is possible that he was not favorable to the ordinance, but he did, in fact, sign it into law. Without knowing what drove him to enact such a law it can appear that he was but going along with the tenor of his times, i.e., that racism and slavery were accepted practices. We should note here that Frederick's older brother Rudolph, as part of his employment at the Cornwall ironworks in Lebanon, supervised black slaves and acted to retrieve a runaway who fled the ironworks (see this chapter's section on Rudolph Kelker). However, Frederick's son Rudolph Frederick would later hide runaways in his Harrisburg stable and help them to move along the underground railroad on to freedom in Canada (see Chapter 4, RFK section).

Frederick's life. On balance we must acknowledge that Frederick's life was one of goodness and devotion to his fellow man. A section of his biography from the Kelker Family Record (pp. 87, 88) describes his good character, warmth, generosity and concern for his fellow man. But read it with the caveat that it was written by his son, Rudolph Frederick, whose objectivity is, understandably, lacking:

> From the time of his retirement from business until his decease he manifested great interest in the welfare of his successors in business, and there was perhaps no year in which a portion of his capital was to a greater or less extent used by them whenever they desired it. He was remarkable for punctuality and integrity. A close observer of human nature and safe counselor, being often appealed to by his fellow-citizens; calm and modest in his demeanor, he was not to be swerved from his purposes, when he felt that he was in the line of duty. His habits of industry and economy led to the acquisition of competency, and the latter half, especially, of his long life was devoted in his own quiet and unobtrusive way to the amelioration of the condition of the poor sick, and friendless. In the vigor of manhood he filled many minor positions in the community in which he lived, always rejecting political preferment [...]

Grandson and biographer Luther Reily Kelker gives us some further insight into Frederick's life and character from a brief biography in Volume I of his weighty three-volume history. (Kelker, L. R., 1907, *History of Dauphin County*, Pennsylvania, Lewis Publishing Co., Chicago, New York)

He was averse to political distinction but occupied various responsible positions; for several years he was a member and president of the borough council: a director of the Harrisburg Branch of the Philadelphia Bank, and was a director of the common schools at their first establishment. He was remarkable for punctuality and rectitude of conduct, was held in deep respect for his knowledge of human nature, wise judgment and conservative character, and his advice was frequently asked by his fellow citizens in important affairs. He acquired a comfortable estate, and while he was always charitable, the latter half of his life, was especially devoted to aiding the poor, the sick and the friendless, quietly and unobtrusively, but effectually. He was prominent in the affairs of the Reformed church, of which he was a member; he presided at the meeting on November 17, 1820, to establish the first Sunday school, and was active in the erection of the church edifice which yet stands as a monument to his effort.

Frederick died on July 9, 1857. His final moments were recorded by his son, Rudolph Frederick, who was with his father at his death. (Kelker Family Record, pp. 87, 88)

His last moments commenced on the evening of the 21st of June, 1857, and it became apparent that he would not recover. He was visited by his pastor, Rev. D. Gans, and also by Rev. George Marquart, pastor of the Evangelical Church of Harrisburg. He particularly enjoyed the visits of the latter, who faithfully administered the consolations of religion. He had patiently waited for many years for the great change, and was therefore prepared for it. About twelve hours before his departure he sank into a deep sleep, in which he breathed heavily. Believing that he might thus pass away, his oldest son [i.e., Rudolph Frederick] felt anxious to have one more assurance from him of his resignation to the divine will. He accordingly aroused him from his slumber saying, Father, you seem to be about to leave us, can you still trust in Jesus? To this he replied in a very emphatic manner, raising and clasping his hands together, "Oh my, yes." These were his last words on earth, and at one o'clock on Sunday morning, July 12, 1857, he entered upon the enjoyment of the eternal Sabbath above.

He was buried on July 14 in the family plot at the Harrisburg cemetery. Funeral services were performed in English and German.

Frederick's business pursuits and his devotion to his church and his community set the pattern for the next two generations of Harrisburg Kelkers. His and Catherine's three sons, Rudolph Frederick, who would prepare the Kelker Family Record, Immanuel Meister and Henry Anthony, were all successful in the hardware business and other business ventures in Harrisburg.

They also followed their father's example as prominent citizens who served Harrisburg with distinction.

But amidst the fulsome praise for his life and his many admirable accomplishments, we cannot fail to acknowledge Frederick's actions regarding the 1821 ordinance supporting the practice of capturing and returning people purported to be runaway slaves. Indeed, the ordinance was fully in accord with the constitution, which sanctioned the practice. And he lived in a time when many in both slave and free states felt that blacks were somehow destined to be slaves. So should we excuse him for following national law and public opinion? Or should we hold him up to those who acted against the prevailing law and ignored public opinion by aiding runaways escaping to freedom? Let me suggest that we look at the whole of his life and recognize his many contributions, service to his community, his charitable acts and his devotion to his family. But let us keep in mind the ordinance and how we should judge that action against his many good works.

Chapter 4 continues with the lives of Frederick and Katherine Fager Kelker's sons, Rudolph Frederick, Immanuel Meister and Henry Anthony.

Addendum

Frederick Kelker and Fire Safety. As town-council president in early Harrisburg, Frederick, like others in that position, dealt with the many concerns of the community, some significant and some trivial. Below is an example of his performing his duties by addressing the threat of fires, a major concern among Harrisburg's early citizens. In 1822, he issued and signed a fire-safety ordinance laying out laws governing the use of fire. In a time before electricity the dependence on fire for heat, light and cooking presented an ongoing hazard, and in the event of a fire little help could be expected from a primitively equipped, poorly trained fire department.

AN ORDINANCE

To prevent fires in the Borough of Harrisburg.

Section 1. *Be it ordained by the Town Council of the borough of Harrisburg*, That from and after the due promulgation hereof, it shall be unlawful for any person or persons, their servant or servants, to carry fire from one house to another in the borough of Harrisburg, except the same be secured in a close vessel.

Sect. 2. *Be it further ordained by the authority aforesaid*, That the practice of burning shavings, straw or other inflamable matter in the streets and alleys; the projecting of stove-pipes through roofs, sides and ends of buildings, the smoking of lighted pipes and segars in and near barns or stables, and carrying lighted candles into the same are hereby severally declared unlawful, &c. be, and

Sect. 3. *Be it further ordained by the authority aforesaid*, That if any person or persons shall be found disregarding the provisions contained in this Ordinance, and being thereof convicted before the Chief-Burgess, or in his absence or inability to act, before the Assistant Burgess, he, she, or they, shall forfeit and pay for every such offence, the sum of FIVE DOLLARS, to be recovered as other fines are made recoverable by the ordinances of the borough.

Enacted into a law, July 13, 1822.

F. KELKER,
Pres't of the Town Council.

Attest—J. Downey, Town Clerk.

A notice posted by Frederick Kelker acting in his duty as President of the Harrisburg Town Council. (Harrisburg Chronicle, 12 Aug 1822, p.1)

CHAPTER 4

The Second Generation Born in America
Rudolph Frederick, Immanuel Meister and Henry Anthony Kelker

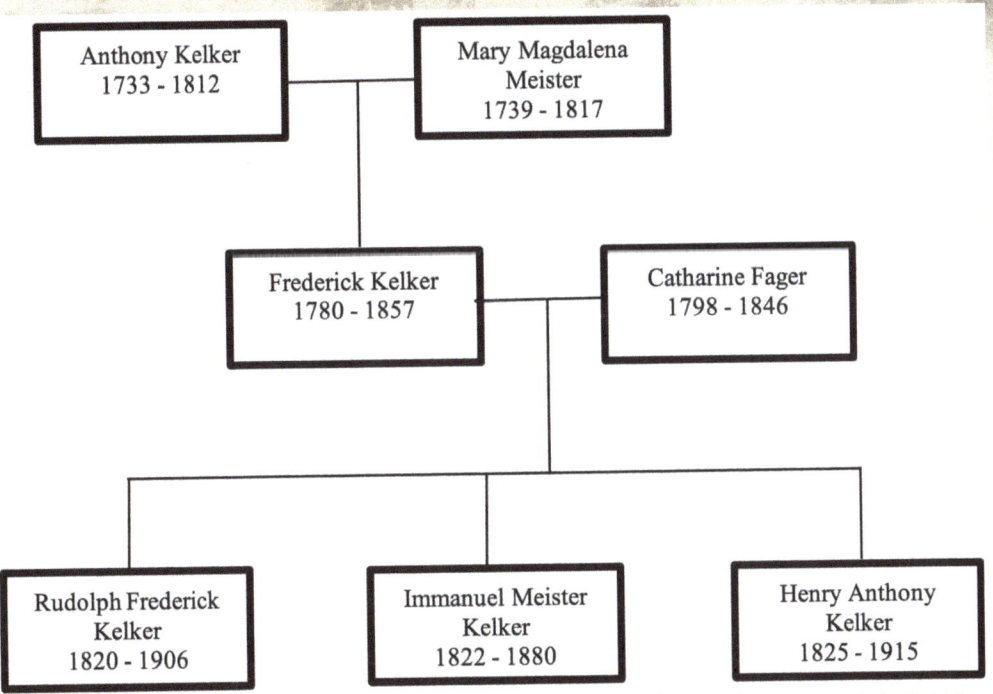

Frederick and Catherine's three sons lived lives that seemingly replicated that of their father. We could almost write each one's story by copying Frederick's biography. All three began in the hardware business and, except for Immanuel Meister, ended up in real estate. And, except for Immanuel Meister again, they were active in Harrisburg politics. Following tradition, each was deeply religious, devoted to and active in the Reformed Salem Church. And all three spent their entire lives from birth to death in Harrisburg where they enriched themselves and worked to make life better for the local citizens.

Photo: courtesy of Ramsey Davenport

Rudolph Frederick Kelker: Hardware, Religion, Temperance, Real Estate, Good Citizen.

Rudolph Frederick Kelker (1820–1906), the oldest brother, left a big footprint in Harrisburg. His life was occupied with business, church, Bible study, the Harrisburg community, temperance, the Historical Society of Dauphin County, the YMCA, the Almshouse, the German Society, establishing the town of Steelton and just about everything else that was happening in and around Harrisburg. With but little formal education he was successful in almost everything he touched. He left his name in perpetuity with the naming of Harrisburg's Kelker Street.

RFK lived his entire eighty-six years as a citizen of Harrisburg devoted to his community. He was endowed with a keen business sense that he used to grow his inherited money. While wealthy from his business dealings, he untiringly devoted his time and effort to helping his fellow citizens through leadership roles in charitable and civic activity. His motivating presence seems to have been everywhere in Harrisburg where he was active in countless organizations, committees and activities.

Rudolph Frederick Kelker was born February 17, 1820, in Harrisburg. At eleven he entered the Harrisburg Academy where he studied for three years. In May 1834, he began studies at the Classical School of the German Reformed Church in York, Pennsylvania. But in August he was forced to leave because of a serious illness, and on his doctor's advice he abandoned all efforts to seek further schooling (Kelker Family Record, p. 99), and he received no further formal education.

Born to a wealthy family, he could have lived a comfortable life without the burdens and challenges of a business career and community activism. But the story of his life, from inherited wealth to acquired wealth and a lifelong commitment to aiding his fellow citizens, gives us a picture of a man concerned for the welfare of others. Deeply religious, he put his church's teachings—"love thy neighbor," for example—into practice.

He was fifteen when he entered the world of commerce by joining the hardware firm owned by Messrs. Oglesby and Hinckley. That the business had been previously owned by his father, Frederick, might have had something to do with his being hired for his first job. He spent three years with the firm, gaining valuable business experience, but in May 1838 a period of ill health forced him to resign. During his recovery he spent his time tending his father's many properties in and around Harrisburg.

At twenty-two, in November 1842, RFK returned to the hardware business. He purchased Mr. Hinckley's share of the hardware firm, most likely with his father's money, and shared management with Mr. Oglesby until March 1846 when Oglesby died. It was during this period that he married Mary Anne Reily, on June 17, 1844 (See Addendum for a short biography of her life). Their first child, Frederick, was born in September 1845 but died when he was four. Following Oglesby's death, RFK operated the business by himself for a year before forming a partnership with his brothers Immanuel Meister and Henry Anthony under the name Kelker & Brother. He remained in the partnership until 1851 when for a third time he became ill and was forced to leave the firm. Two sons were born during this period, Luther Reily in 1848 and Rudolph Frederick who, unfortunately, died at three in 1850. A fourth son, William Anthony, was born in 1853. Mr. Kelker did not return to the hardware business or to any other mercantile pursuit (Kelker Family Record, p. 96). At thirty-three, he walked away from the hardware business and went on to a life of church, business and community service.

RFK and the German Reformed Church. Like his parents, grandparents, great-grandparents and Swiss ancestors, Rudolph Frederick Kelker led his life as a devout Christian fully committed to the beliefs and practices of the German Reformed Church. From his first days of Sunday school to his last day he devoted his time, energy and service to his church. He served as a deacon, an elder, a Sunday-school teacher, bible class teacher and superintendent. His religious activities extended beyond his Harrisburg church to participation in the Pennsylvania State Sabbath School Association, the American Sunday School Union and the American Tract Society (a publisher of Christian literature). He also served as trustee of Marshall College, a religious institution, and he continued as a trustee of Franklin & Marshall College after the two schools merged. His active participation in a long internal controversy over the

Reformed Church's form of worship led to the founding of Ursinus College. Deeply involved in the rites, rituals and activities of his church, RFK put his Christian beliefs to practice through generous acts of charity. He served as Harrisburg's director of the poor, as a principal figure in the founding of the Harrisburg City Hospital and actively supported and participated in numerous other charitable efforts. (Rudolph F. Kelker 1820–1906, from the Kelker archives at the Historical Society of Dauphin County, Harrisburg, Pennsylvania)

The Salem Bible Class. Perhaps RFK's greatest contribution to his church was as a Sunday school teacher and a leader of Bible-study groups. His Sunday-school participation began when he was three and continued throughout much of his long life. From 1836 at sixteen until 1850 he served as teacher, and from 1850 to 1870 as superintendent of the Sunday school. He then, at the request of the consistory, took charge of the adult Bible class of twelve students. Whether through his persuasion, personality, effort or all three, class enrollment grew at a rapid rate. In his first year the class size reached ninety members, and in 1874 reached a hundred and sixty-one. But that year, amid an internal controversy over the German Reformed Church's form of worship (see below for a history of the controversy), the consistory relieved him of his teaching duties, and another pastor was assigned to replace him. His dismissal was done without regard to his teaching success but because his anti-ritualistic views were not in agreement with those of the consistory.

Soon after his dismissal Mr. Kelker received an invitation to organize and take charge of a new adult Bible-study group, and he then organized the Salem Bible Class. It was open to men and women of all denominations, even those with no church affiliation. His initial class consisted of twelve individuals, but the numbers began to swell almost immediately. (*Harrisburg Telegraph*, June 12, 1902, p. 11) At the end of the first year, he was teaching seventy-six students, and with the growing numbers the class needed to move twice to larger quarters. Finally, in 1885, the class found sufficient space at the YMCA. (*Evening News*, Harrisburg, Dec. 17, 1937, p. 18) By 1902, near the class's final days, 959 people had studied with Mr. Kelker. (*Harrisburg Telegraph*, June 12, 1902, p. 11)

He nurtured, supported and devoted himself to the Salem Bible Class. According to a 1903 newspaper account (*Harrisburg Telegraph*, Oct. 6, 1903, p.

4), "In all those years, .(i.e., the thirty-three years that the Bible class existed) except when prevented by sickness, Mr. Kelker has never missed a session, and his watchful eye over his class has been that of a shepherd." Newspaper accounts of Bible-class meetings describe a joyous atmosphere and a loving respect for Mr. Kelker. An account of an 1879 meeting (*Harrisburg Telegraph*, Dec. 24, 1879, p. 1) gives us an idea of the high esteem in which he was held. During the meeting he was addressed by a Reverend Gause who presented him with a surprise gift, "a large silver fruit basket, a cut-glass dish, mounted on a silver base and stone, and two large bouquet holders, of silver and painted ware. The basket was filled with bananas, pears and grapes, the salver with cut flowers, and the bouquet holders each with a bouquet." Reverend Gause then addressed Mr. Kelker:

> In your position, sir, as teacher in this class, as teacher of adults, always a work of labor and responsibility, we are here to testify how well you discharge them: to assure you, if you have any doubt on the subject, that you do your duty faithfully, lovingly, and ably. On that point you need not have any doubt, and slightly to testify their regard and appreciation for your unselfish labor in their behalf, the class has authorized us to present these [sic] article of silver, filled with rich fruits and flowers. Take them sir, and with them our deep and sincere love and appreciation for you and yours.

Mr. Kelker, surprised by the gift and kind words, replied:

> I do not know what to say [...] You have overwhelmed me [...] Ten years ago, when I took charge of this class, it was a little thing, a small beginning, which has widened and lengthened until it now presents proportions for which we may all feel grateful, as being the result of our individual exertions and the blessings of God [...] as your cooperation and zeal in our work rendered it an easy and a delightful task to act as your teacher. The class has grown wonderfully. Its members in ten years have gone to all parts of the country and even to the Canadas, while as teachers they have been accepted in almost all the Sunday schools in the city. Are not these gratifying facts?

The newspaper article further reported: "With much more that was fervent and eloquent, Mr. Kelker warmly thanked the members of the class for the gift and asked them 'to pray for him for strength still further to discharge his duty until the time comes when the Master calls him home!"

The Salem Bible Class spread its influence beyond Harrisburg, even to far-away Asia. A *Harrisburg Telegraph* article (Dec. 21, 1889, p. 1) tells us that the Bible class, working with the church's Board of Foreign Missions, was educating a young seminary student at the Seminary of the Reformed Church in Sendai, Japan. The Bible class at its meeting in December 1889 heard an address in English by a Rev. Masayoshi Oshikawa, president of the Theological Seminary of the Reformed Church in Sendai, who informed the group of that young student's progress.

The Bible class sent money for several years to the American Tract Society to organize Sunday schools in mountain areas of the South. Many class members, educated and strongly influenced by the Salem Bible Class, moved on to other parts of the country where they in turn taught Bible classes.

Mr. Kelker diligently led the Salem Bible Class for over three decades, but as age and ill health overcame him, he was forced to cede his leadership in 1901, five years before his passing. He was succeeded by Charles Gumpert, a longtime member of the class. The Salem Bible Class ended its thirty-three-year existence on Sunday, October 4, 1903. According to the *Harrisburg Telegraph* (Oct. 6, 1903, p. 4) the final meeting was led by Mr. Gumpert, who:

> [...] addressed the class on Paul's charge to Timothy. His words were strong and earnest. He then spoke a few words of farewell. The reverend Mr. Stein, of St. John's Reformed Church, also addressed the class. When the aged teacher [Mr. Kelker] with feeble steps, took his seat at the desk where he had sat so many years, and said, "This is the last time," they felt the full significance of the words. The closing hymn, "Blest be the tie that binds," was sung, followed by prayer by Mr. Kelker and benediction by the Rev. Mr. Stein, and the bible class was no more.

Rudolph Frederick Kelker and the merger of Franklin and Marshall Colleges. Devotion to his church and his recognition of the need for formal education (including religious education) are reflected in Mr. Kelker's service to Marshall College, a German Reformed Church institution. He joined the college's board at a time when the school was experiencing financial problems and then continued his service through difficult times that led up to and beyond the school's merger with Franklin College, in 1853.

Twenty-five-year-old RFK was invited to join Marshall's Board of Trustees in 1845. The opportunity undoubtedly came about from his father's wealth, public service and devotion to the German Reformed Church, and from his own devotion and service to the church. After the merger with Franklin College, he served on Franklin & Marshall's board, whose chairman, James Buchanan, would become America's fifteenth president. Historical records indicate that RFK served with devotion, professionalism and confidence, and that his service benefitted both institutions.

Considering RFK's religious devotion and dedication to the German Reformed Church, it seems only appropriate that he should have served on the board of a college united with that church. The fact that he never attended college and had only a brief early education seemed not to matter to him or to Marshall College. It was, apparently, his religious credentials and his early success in business that were recognized by the college.

Marshall College was established in 1836 in Mercersburg. It arose from the Theological Seminary of the Reformed Church, established in 1825 in association with Dickinson College, a Presbyterian institution in Carlisle, Pennsylvania. Despite high hopes for the seminary's success its early years were plagued with problems. The difficulties arose from financial issues and the inability to realize the expected benefits of being part of Dickinson College. So, in 1829 the church synod approved a move to York, Pennsylvania. The move saved the institution from collapse and to a period of prosperity. At the urging of Dr. Lewis Mayer, the head of the seminary, the synod approved elevating the seminary to a high school, and it began as the Classical School when it opened in 1832. As enrollment grew and educational offerings increased the institution was renamed the High School of the Reformed Church in 1835. But despite its success the institution was losing money.

At a meeting of the Board of Visitors in June 1834 it was agreed to establish a "literary institution" in a place where money could be raised to erect buildings. The institution moved to Mercersburg in 1836 where Dr. Mayer convinced the local community to subscribe to a donation of $10,000. The Pennsylvania legislature approved the charter, and the school, now offering both theology and literary programs, was moved to Mercersburg where it opened that year as Marshall College. The name was chosen in honor of the recently deceased US Chief Justice John Marshall who, as stated in the school's charter, was selected for his "exalted character, great worth, and high mental attainments." Marshall College continued in Mercersburg until 1853 when, faced with financial difficulties, it moved to Lancaster after merging with Franklin College. (Dubbs, J. H., 1903, *History of Franklin and Marshall College: Franklin College, 1787–1853*, Franklin and Marshall Alumni Association, Lancaster)

Franklin College, like the United States of America, was founded in 1787. Unlike Marshall College, which was strictly German Reform, Franklin College began as multi-denominational. Two ministers from the German Reformed Church and two ministers from the Lutheran Church established the institution. Its charter, printed in both English and German, incorporated the institution as "a College and Charity School." The new school was named for Benjamin Franklin "from a profound respect for the talents, virtues and services to mankind in general, but more especially to this country, of His Excellency Benjamin Franklin, Esquire, President of the Supreme Executive Council." Trustees of the college named in the charter included three who had signed the Declaration of Independence and at least seven who had served as officers in the Revolutionary War. The ministers who served as the first trustees were equally represented, as prescribed in the charter, with seven from the German Reformed Church, seven from the Lutheran Church, one Roman Catholic priest and one Moravian minister.

The college opened as a co-educational institution in Lancaster with seventy-eight young men and thirty-six young women enrolled. However, shortly thereafter women were excluded, and the school remained all male for 182 years. Despite its early promise Franklin College did not grow as expected due to continuing financial struggles. In the late 1840s, those problems caused departments to be consolidated and plans for expansion to be canceled. Faced with these continuing struggles plans were put forth to seek a merger with another college. (Dubbs, 1903)

The process of merging the two struggling colleges began in response to a proposition sent on December 6, 1849 from Franklin College to the chairman of Marshall's board of trustees. After considerable discussion Marshall's board voted for the merger with sixteen yeas and ten nays with RFK voting with the majority. Immediately following passage of the resolution he served on a committee of seven whose charge was "to inform the Board of Trustees of Franklin College of the determination of this board [...] and to do other acts or things required to carry forward and accomplish the objects in view." In 1853, after four years dealing with all the necessary tasks and details and after approval by the state legislature, Franklin & Marshall College opened in Lancaster with a formal ceremony on June 7. (Klein, H.M.J., 1936, *A Century of Education at Mercersburg, 1836–1936*, Lancaster Press, Inc., Lancaster, p. 333)

James Buchanan, six years before becoming the US president, played an important part in the merger. He had gained prominence as a lawyer active in community affairs in Lancaster. He was chairman of Franklin College's board of trustees and after the merger he continued as chairman of the Franklin & Marshall board.

Today, Franklin & Marshall College is a 2,300-student liberal-arts institution of high academic standing open to all faiths and races. The institution continues to strive to meet the goals set out by its first president, Frederick Rauch: "The fortune of our lives and our government depends not exclusively on useful knowledge but on our character as citizens, and to form this character by cultivating the whole [person] is the aim of education in the proper sense." The school's mission statement affirms that "the College expects students to see connections, to discover community, and to understand the centrality of service to the human endeavor." [Franklin & Marshall—Mission and History (fandm.edu)]

A Controversy over Liturgy: RFK and the founding of Ursinus College. Nowhere is Mr. Kelker's devotion to the German Reformed Church on display more than in his involvement in the church's controversy over its liturgy and the consequent founding of Ursinus College. The church spent thirty-three years, from 1845 to 1878, embroiled in the controversy. On one side were those who felt compelled to adhere to a form of the traditional liturgy in which the service was conducted from the pulpit with no responses or prayers spoken by the congregation. This was referred to as the "pulpit liturgy," in reference to the minister in his pulpit as the centerpiece of the service, with the congregation doing little beyond sitting and receiving the word. It centered on a human interpretation of God's word and emphasized moral living according to His word. Its adherents were referred to as the Ursinus Movement in recognition of Zacharias Ursinus, the sixteenth-century theologian and leader of the Reformed Protestant movement in the Palatinate (a region in western Germany bordered on Belgium, Luxembourg and France). On the other side were those including RFK who favored services conducted with greater congregation involvement in prayer responses and singing of hymns. Obedience to God's word was to be expressed in offerings of praise and thanksgiving for what God through Christ had done for them. This "altar liturgy" sprang from an 1844 address, "The Principle of Protestantism," delivered by Phillip Schaff, a young theologian. Schaff was attacked for his views and tried for heresy, although he was later acquitted. This liturgical practice came to be referred to as the Mercersburg Theology or the low-church movement. (*The Ursinus School*, Ch. 3, John C. Shetler, http://d3n8a8pro7vhmx. cloudfront.net/ unitedchurchofchrist/legacy_url/1225/HH1chap03Ursinus.pdf?1418424671)

In 1847, the church's Eastern Synod appointed a committee to prepare a new liturgy. What resulted was something closely aligned with the pulpit liturgy of the Ursinus Movement. It was met with controversy, but the committee continued its work and in 1857 produced a provisional liturgy, but that version did not come into general practice. Mr. Kelker stepped into the controversy in 1859 when he was named one of five trustees of the newly organized Eastern Synod where he became a major force in support of the Mercerburg altar liturgy. In 1866, the Eastern Synod published what was termed the New Order of Worship. (Good, J. I., 1902, *Developments in the Nineteenth Century, The Historical Handbook of the Reformed Church*, electronic version 2004, the Synod of the Reformed Church in the U.S.) Here, Mr. Kelker came forth as a leading voice in the liturgical controversy when he railed against the 1866 New Order of Worship, feeling that the changes in the English translation were not warranted. In 1877, he called for a convention of ministers and elders of the Eastern Synod to meet in Meyerstown to protest that the doctrines and cultus of the New Order of Worship were not representative of and were contrary to the Reformed Church. An outgrowth of the convention was the establishment of Ursinus College, as an institution representing the Mercersburg Theology. The new college was established in 1869 in Freeland (now Collegeville) with a charter that authorized the teaching of the classics and theology. J.H.A. Bomberger was named the first president.

But the liturgical controversy continued. In 1879, a Peace Commission was established to attempt to settle the differences in doctrine, cultus and government. Mr. Kelker served as one of twelve elders and twelve ministers chosen by the General Synod of the German Reformed Church. The body met in Harrisburg for what turned out to be eight days of discussion. But an agreement was reached that finally ended the long liturgical battle. Harmony was restored. A final "perfected" version was made in 1884 and was adopted as "The Directory of Worship of the Reformed Church in the United States." (from Rudolph F. Kelker 1820–1906, p. 3, from the Historical Society of Dauphin County)

Today, Ursinus College exists as a private undergraduate liberal-arts college of about 1,650 students. Although founded on the tenets and practices of the Reformed Church it is now a nonsectarian institution and welcomes students of all religious backgrounds. It does however continue to observe the vision of its first president, the theologian Bomberger, to enrich students in preparation for contributing to society.

Mr. Kelker also served his church during several years in high office as the first president of the board and later as treasurer. He then served on the board of foreign missions of the general synod from 1863 to 1890 (except for three of those years). He was a member of the synod's committee that prepared the "Triglott Tercentenary Heidelberg Catechism," published in 1863 in recognition of the 1563 Heidelberg Catechism written by the early Protestant reformers Zacharias Ursinus and Caspar Olevianus. He voiced strong disagreement with the final version, feeling that many of the changes in the English translation were not warranted. (Rudolph F. Kelker 1820–1906, from the Kelker archives at the Historical Society of Dauphin County, Harrisburg, p. 3)

Mr. Kelker saw life through a religious lens, and as such he acted in accordance with the moral teachings of the German Reformed Church. His almost every action seems guided by a strong sense of Christian charity. This is seen in his overriding sense of concern for others and in his devotion to charitable works. Even his business affairs seem to have an element of fairness and concern. He did enrich himself through his business dealings, but gaining more wealth was not his highest priority. Following his very profitable sale of lands in what is now Steelton (see below) he devoted himself intensely to charitable and community concerns.

We can wonder what Mr. Kelker's life would have been without his strong religious faith. Would he have been as devoted to the welfare of his fellow man and as enriched by caring, thoughtfulness and charity? Probably so, as those traits were probably in his genes. But his religious beliefs reinforced those fine qualities and intensified his concern for those less fortunate. He did so to the benefit of many.

RFK, the Pennsylvania Steel Company and the town of Steelton. Mr. Kelker's father, Frederick, had been a successful businessman who acquired wealth through ownership of many properties in and around Harrisburg. The son, whether by nature or nurture, was also possessed with business acumen that he used to succeed. His early hardware store tenure provided valuable experience, as did his experience tending his father's properties. At twenty-two he ran the hardware business with his partner Mr. Ogleby and then ran it alone after Ogleby's death. The firm continued its success when his brothers Henry Anthony and Immanuel Meister joined the Kelker & Brothers partnership. So, whether by heredity or by learning, with little formal education but with intelligence and a good sense for business, RFK succeeded.

His great business coup was the sale of his Baldwin land for the construction of America's first steel mill and, with his brother Henry Anthony, the establishment of the town of Steelton. The story begins in 1738, when the property on which the steel mill now stands had been warranted to a Thomas Renick. In 1747, it was granted by patent to a Richard Peters, secretary to the Penn family, "as a tract of land in Paxtang Township, Lancaster County." Frederick Kelker acquired the property with purchases in 1830 and 1843 for which he paid $37 per acre. Upon his death in 1856, the land (in two parcels) was left to Rudolph Frederick and to his brother Henry Anthony. At that time, the site was undeveloped with only six families living in the area.

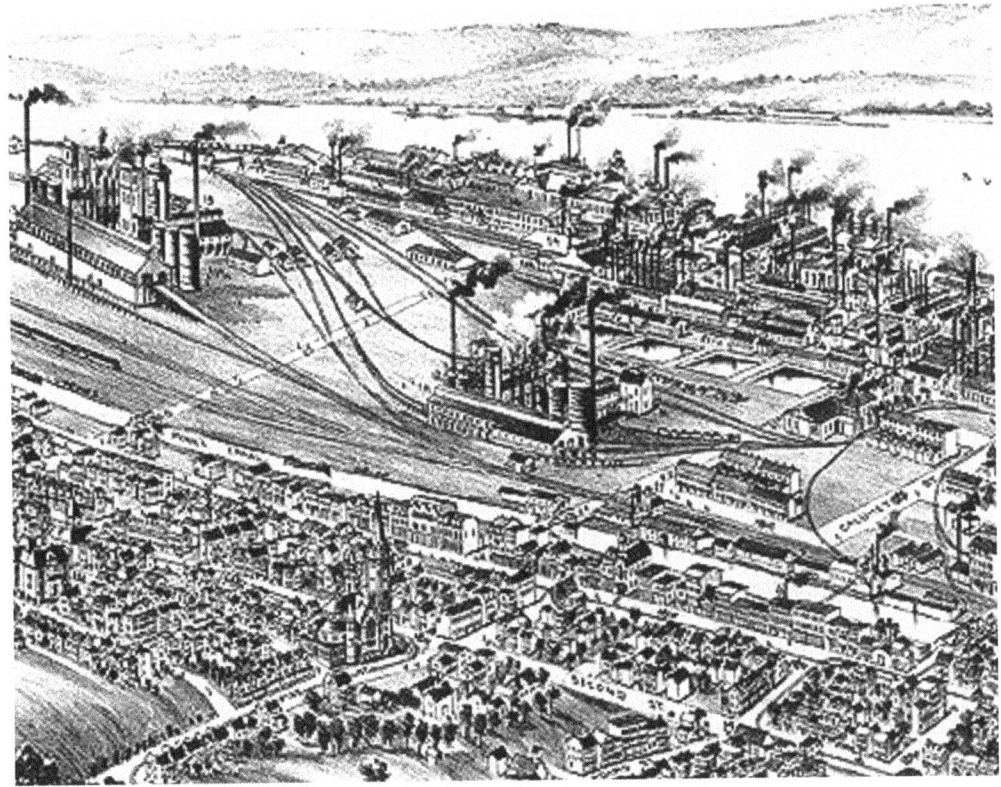

Early undated drawing of the Pennsylvania Steel Company site in Steelton. [sketchsteelton.jpg (432×254) (dickinson.edu)]

A period of rapid change got underway with the brother's 1866 sale of the "Kelker Lands," a total of ninety-seven acres, to the newly formed Pennsylvania Steel Company. The company paid $300 per acre netting the sellers a total of $29,175, a very considerable sum at that time. The site was attractive to the company for its location near the Cornwall iron-ore deposits in Lebanon, from which ore could be readily transported to the mill by the Philadelphia & Reading Railroad (P&R). The site was also attractive because its location on the bank of the Susquehanna River provided for convenient shipping.

The first products, railroad-track rails, rolled out of the plant in 1867. Steel production at the site continued over the years, through good times and bad times, through plant expansions, strikes, economic depressions, bankruptcies and ownership changes. Bethlehem Steel Corporation bought the plant in 1916, and when Bethlehem went bankrupt in 2001 it was taken over by ISG and then by Mittal Steel. The plant is operated today by Luxembourg-based ArcelorMittal, the world's largest steelmaker. ("Rails, Baldwin, Our Place," by Paul van Meter, posted on the viaductgreene blog, April 1, 2012). It employs about 436 workers and occupies 251 acres of land (ArcelorMittal, Steelton, ArcelorMittal USA)

After the sale, RFK bought land adjacent to the mill and developed that property into residential lots. He purchased forty-five acres from an Abraham Wolf, twenty-two acres from a Jacob Bender and forty-five acres from his brother Henry Anthony, then proceeded to lay out streets, roads and home lots. Henry Anthony also used his sale earnings to buy land and lay out home lots. Lots were sold at prices ranging from $100 to $250 each. Today's map of Steelton is essentially as Rudolph Frederick and Henry Anthony designed the area. Their financial gain made them among the wealthiest men in Dauphin County.

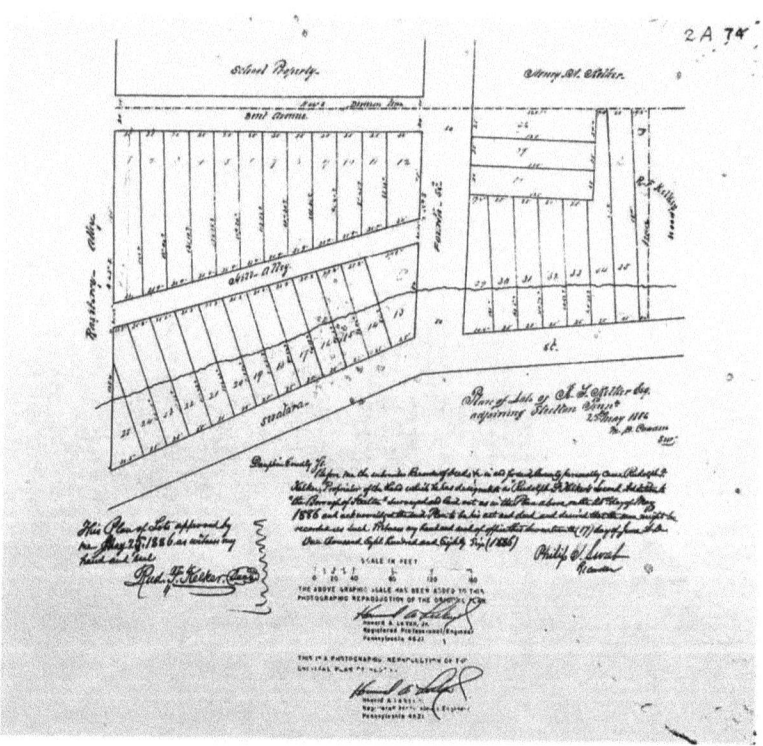

R. F. Kelker's 1886 deed for thirty-six Steelton home lots, one of several developments that he and Henry Anthony laid out in Steelton. (From the registry of Dauphin County Deeds, www. dauphinc. org/deeds)

The Harrisburg City Passenger Railway Company. RFK, his brother Henry Anthony and three partners formed the Harrisburg City Passenger Railway Company in 1874. The history of that venture is presented in the Henry Anthony Kelker section of this chapter.

Civil War Orpans. Rudolph Frederick Kelker, with benevolence rooted deeply in his character, never seemed to pass up an opportunity to serve the less fortunate. The list of his good works is long and testifies to his empathy and caring for his community, a consequence of his deeply felt religious faith and his devotion to the teachings of the German Reformed Church. We see this when at seventeen he and a friend showed concern for those neglected and left indigent by an alcoholic father or husband by organizing the first total temperance society in Harrisburg. His life was marked by that most Christian-inspired call to charitable action. Examples of RFK's charitable service illustrate these efforts.

The Soldiers' Orphan Schools were a statewide network of homes for the care and education of children whose fathers lost their lives in the Civil War (1861–1865). The war resulted in an estimated 750,000 deaths on both sides. (Hacker, J. D., McPherson, J. M., 2011, "A Census-Based Count of the Civil War Dead," pp. 307–348, in *Civil War History*, Vol. 57, Iss. 4, Kent State University Press, Kent) The effect on the widows and children of the fallen soldiers and sailors was devastating. Left with no means of support and nowhere to turn, many children were left to life on the streets where they begged and committed petty crimes. In response to this tragedy many states established schools where war-orphaned children could be housed and educated. Pennsylvania's response to the problem was to establish a statewide system of Soldiers' Orphan Schools.

Credit for establishing the Orphan Schools is given to Andrew Gregg Curtin, Pennsylvania's wartime governor, and to the Pennsylvania Railroad for donating $50,000 to start the project. Curtin claimed that his inspiration for the schools came from an encounter with two shivering, rag-clad street urchins who came to his door on Thanksgiving Day in 1863. He recounted that he was stunned by the contrast of hungry children begging for food on a feast day. Curtin told this story on many occasions, and it is often cited when the history of the Soldiers' Orphan Schools is discussed. However, according to Dr. O. David Gold in his excellent history of the Pennsylvania system (Gold, O. D., 2016, *The Civil War Soldiers' Orphan Schools of Pennsylvania, 1864–1889*, Pendragon Press, pp. 6–13), the story is most likely not true. Gold's meticulous research reveals that the governor mentioned the story a full three years after the purported encounter with the children. In fact, the much more likely story is that he acted as a political strategy.

Pennsylvania, to protect the state's canal system, was collecting a tonnage tax of about $400,000 a year on the railroads. In 1862, in what was probably a thinly veiled payoff to get the tonnage tax reduced or eliminated, the Pennsylvania Railroad offered to donate $50,000 to help recruit soldiers for the protection of the state. Republican Curtin, however, was concerned that the Democrats would accuse him of accepting a political payoff. To avoid any smell of graft the governor proposed using the money to establish a soldiers' home for the care of war veterans. Thomas Scott, the head of Pennsylvania Railroad, agreed to the proposal and in 1864 it went before the state legislature. The Democrat-controlled legislature rejected the measure, but on May 6, 1864, with the Republicans in the majority, funding was approved for a system of Soldiers' Orphan Schools to be established throughout the state. We can give Governor Curtin some credit for the Soldiers' Orphan Schools, but the orphans benefitted mostly from politics and the generosity of Pennsylvania Railroad, albeit with the motive of reducing their tonnage tax. (Gold, p. 11)

> "The Governor of the Commonwealth of Pennsylvania is hereby authorized to accept the sum of $50,000, donated by the Pennsylvania railroad company for the education and maintenance of destitute orphan children of deceased soldiers and sailors, and appropriate the same in such manner as he may deem best calculated to accomplish the object designed by said donation. The accounts of said disbursements to be settled in the usual manner by the Auditor General and the Governor, and make report of the same to the next Legislature.
>
> This act was approved May 6, 1864.

From the Kelker Archives at the Historical Society of Dauphin County, MG 405, box 2

Nearly fifty homes for housing, feeding, education and professional training of the orphans were established throughout the state. (Harford Historical Society | SAH ARCHIPEDIA (sah-archipedia.org); (Paul, J. L., 1876, *Pennsylvania's Soldiers' Orphan Schools*, pp. xiv–xv, Claxton, Remsen & Haffelfinger, Philadelphia) The homes accepted boys and girls, but their mothers were not provided for. They lived apart from their children and were allowed visiting privileges. No home was established in Dauphin County, but two orphan schools were located nearby, the Mount Joy School at Strasburg in Lancaster County and the White Hall School at Camp Hill in Cumberland County. But the Orphan Schools' charter provided that each county set up a committee of superintendents to review applications for admission. (Paul, J. L., 1876, *Pennsylvania's Soldiers' Orphan Schools*, p. 45, Claxton, Remsen & Haffelfinger, Philadelphia) Rudolph Frederick Kelker served as chairman for Dauphin County's superintendents committee. An example of what he was dealing with is this war-widowed mother's letter asking for her children's acceptance to an Orphan school:

> Highspire Dauphin Co. Pa
>
> September 29, 1864
>
> Mr. Bailey,
>
> I am the widow of Samuel Light who was a soldier of the United States and had enlisted for three years, but died by disease contracted by the performance of his duty as such—leaving me and four small children unprovided. The oldest child is a girl & was ten years last July—the next in age is a boy a few months over seven. Being unable to feed and clothe them and educate them without assistance I would respectfully ask if the two oldest mentioned might be admitted into the Institute provided for soldiers orphans. Please write me & let me know where the school is located etc.
>
> Yours Especially
>
> Elizabeth Light

Unlike RFK's many other involvements in management affairs, his duties with the orphan schools were limited to chairmanship of the superintendence committee that reviewed orphan applications and submitted recommendations for acceptance or rejection to the state's Superintendent of Soldiers' Orphans, a Thomas H. Burrowes.

Acceptance notification for Wm. H. and Mary Ann Cleckner to a Soldiers' Orphan School. From Thomas H. Burrowes, superintendent of Pennsylvania's Orphan Schools, to RFK, chairman of the Committee of Superintendence for Dauphin County. (Kelker Archives, Historical Society of Dauphin County)

The Soldiers' Orphan Schools continued until 1889, twenty-four years after the war ended. By then the system had deteriorated to the point that individual homes had become profit-making enterprises. Care was neglected to enhance profits. This corruption was exposed in 1886 in the *Philadelphia Record*'s February 22 issue. The headline screamed "The Soldiers' Orphans, A Syndicate's Traffic Upon Humanity; Official Corruption, Neglect, Discrimination; Bathing Orphans in Pickle Barrels; A Furnace Cellar for A Playroom; Crowded Three and Four Children Into One Bed; Forcing Them To Wear the Same Clothing In Winter and in Summer." An immediate explosion of outrage followed throughout the state. Almost all four hundred posts of the Grand Army of the Republic passed resolutions condemning the alleged mistreatment of the children.

Gov. Robert E. Pattison and his attorney general inspected ten schools and interviewed more than a hundred witnesses. Seven hundred pages of testimony were taken. The inspection tour was widely covered in the press, and on April 15 the findings were released to the public:

> The facts proved by the testimony unhappily establishes the substantial truth of the Philadelphia Record's charges. The testimony shows a most pitiful, cruel and inhuman neglect of the children as well as suggestions of depravity and immoral practices that are too vile for enumeration. The entire system shows human greed, speculation and heartless bargaining.

Amid the outrage, Governor Pattison fired two state inspectors and asked for the resignation of the state's Superintendent of the Soldiers' Orphan Schools but claimed to be powerless to enforce change as the organization had been created by the legislature. The end of the orphan schools finally came in March 1889. The remaining homes in the system were brought under the control of an eleven-man commission that oversaw the closing of some schools and, in 1893, the integration of others into a single public institution, the Industrial School for Soldiers' Orphans, located in Scotland. Governor Curtin's politically driven vision, executed with care and compassion and benefitting so many struggling children, was eventually ended by graft and corruption. (Gold, pp. 100–107)

Temperance. Apart from Mr. Kelker's concern for the plight of war-orphaned children was his concern for those left destitute by alcohol abuse. Throughout his long life he fought for that cause through active participation and by efforts to establish legislation restricting the sale of alcohol.

The fight over temperance and the consumption of ardent spirits has a long history in Pennsylvania and throughout the country. The widespread use of alcohol in Pennsylvania, as elsewhere in the colonies, had begun soon after as the first European settlers arrived. One of William Penn's earliest actions upon his 1682 arrival to what would become Pennsylvania was to build a brew house. Penn announced his construction plans in a 1684 letter to a James Harrison, stating that "I would have a kitchen, two larders, a wash house, a room to iron in, a brew house and Milan oven for baking, and stabling for twelve horses." The brew house was built in 1685.

Penn was not alone in his love for beer. George Washington was a lover of porter, which in his time was imported from England. His passion for his beloved beverage was strong enough that he prepared and kept a small-beer recipe on a sheet of paper during his time as a colonel in the Virginia militia. Benjamin Franklin, James Madison and many of their peers were joyful consumers of beer. (Chalfant, H. M., 1920, *Father Penn and John Barleycorn*, Evangelical Press, Harrisburg, p. 17)

Hard liquor as well as beer was eagerly consumed by the population, at least in part because it was not always easy to find safe drinking water. Most drinkers in colonial times drank in moderation though liquor was widely available. According to "A Brief History of U.S. Drinking" (Gershorn, L., 2016, "A Brief History of U.S. Drinking" | JSTOR Daily), "many Americans opened the day with a drink and consumed rum or hard cider with every meal. People of all ages drank, even toddlers who enjoyed the sugary dregs of their parents' rum toddies." Liquor was an integral part of social interaction. Ardent spirits were commonly served at a variety of social events including funerals, weddings, ministerial ordinations and others. Wages were often paid with liquor. With alcohol use so much a part of social interaction and the economy, the attendant destructive effects of its overuse began to emerge. Many drank in moderation, but many slipped into alcohol dependence, and the havoc wrought by excessive drinking had far-reaching consequences for the social fabric. It was this climate of freely flowing liquor and the miseries it brought to individuals, families and society that gave rise to stirrings of organized resistance to alcohol.

A very significant boost to the early temperance movement was a 1784 tract, "An Inquiry into the Effects of Ardent Spirits Upon the Human Body and Mind," by Dr. Benjamin Rush (1746–1813). Rush, a renowned Revolutionary War surgeon and the founder of Dickinson College, quaintly put forth his unscientific ideas about the ill effects of alcohol on the body as well as its presumed good effects on various organs.

Following on Rush's warnings the prominent Congregational minister Lyman Beecher (1775–1863) produced another influential work, "Six Sermons on Intemperance," in 1828. In it, the father of Henry Ward Beecher, the well-known nineteenth-century preacher, and of Harriet Beecher Stowe, author of *Uncle Tom's Cabin*, railed against intemperance and beseeched his fellow citizens to cease their inaction and to start fighting the evils of strong drink. A paragraph from Beecher's sermon reads:

> Such is the influence of interest, ambition, fear, and indolence, that one violent partisan, with a handful of disciplined troops, may overrule the influence of five hundred temperate men, who act without concert. Already is the disposition to temporize, to tolerate, and even to court the intemperate, too apparent, on account of the apprehended retribution of their perverted suffrage. The whole power of law, through the nation, sleeps in the statute book, and until public sentiment is roused and concentrated, it maybe doubted whether its execution is possible.

A greater awareness of the need to combat the damage that alcohol abuse was having on society emerged in part due to Beecher's widely disseminated sermon. As the temperance movement gained momentum organizations began to appear all over Pennsylvania and the rest of the country. The Pennsylvania Society for Discouraging the Use of Ardent Spirits (later renamed the Pennsylvania Temperance Society) was formed in Philadelphia in 1827. It advocated total abstinence. Soon after, in 1833, the Society for United States Temperate Union began in Philadelphia. Both were active in recruiting members and in promoting the cause (Chalfant, p. 70). Pittsburgh's first anti-liquor organization was started in 1830. (Chalfant, p. 67) All over the state organizations promoting temperance were formed, and as interest in the cause grew the movement began statewide political efforts to eliminate drink.

It was against this backdrop that Rudolph Frederick Kelker entered the temperance movement. In 1837, at the at the tender age of seventeen, he and his friend James Cowden formed Harrisburg's first total temperance society, the Young Men's and Young Ladies' Total Temperance Society of Harrisburg. (Kelker Family Record, p. 98) Total temperance called for the elimination of all beverages containing alcohol; partial temperance, advocated by many, called for the elimination of all hard liquors but allowed for the sale and consumption of beer and wine. In 1841, young RFK served as secretary of the organization (see below, from *The Keystone*, July 28, 1841, p. 1).

TEMPERANCE DEPARTMENT.

Officers of the Young Men's and Young Ladies' Total Abstinence Society, of Harrisburg.

PRESIDENT—David Fleming.
VICE PRESIDENT—Valentine Egle.
SECRETARY—Rud. F. Kelker.
TREASURER—Joseph Allison.
Ex-officio members of the Board of Managers.

BOARD OF MANAGERS.

Hon. John C. Bucher,	Henry C. Hickok, Esq.
John Zollinger,	Samuel D. Ingram,
Henry Hise,	Daniel Eppley,
Robert McElwee,	Stephen Miller,

PUBLISHING COMMITTEE.

Peter C. Keller.	Daniel W. Gross.

At a meeting of the Board of Managers of the Young Men's and Young Ladies' Total Abstinence Society of Harrisburg, held April 6, 1841, the following preamble and resolution, were unanimously adopted and ordered to be published:

WHEREAS, This Board have noticed that several members of this Society have signed applications for Licenses *which course we believe contrary to the spirit of our pledge, and a bad example to the public at large.* Therefore,

Resolved, That we earnestly recommend to members of this association, that they withhold their signatures from all such applications.

In 1840, Mr. Kelker played a significant role in the formation of the Harrisburg chapter of the Washington Temperance Society and represented the society at state conventions. Also referred to as the Washingtonian Movement, it was something of a forerunner of today's Alcoholics Anonymous. The society was founded that year in Baltimore by six heavy drinkers who, after attending a temperance lecture, decided to go sober, and after doing so they started what would become a national society devoted to converting heavy drinkers to abstinence. Recovered alcoholics traveled the country giving public talks and helping alcoholics break their addictions, with membership growing rapidly and spreading nationwide. (Maxwell, M. A., 1950, "The Washingtonian Movement," *Quarterly Journal of Studies of Alcohol*, vol. II, 195, pp. 410–452) I have not come across any descriptions of RFK's participation, but his role in founding the Harrisburg chapter is mentioned in the Kelker Family Record (p. 98) and in "Rudolph F Kelker, 1820–1906" (on file at the Historical Society of Dauphin County).

As the temperance movement in Pennsylvania grew in numbers and in activity throughout the first half of the nineteenth century, it did so in constant struggle with the liquor industry. At a state constitutional convention in 1838, the state temperance society tried unsuccessfully to achieve a complete prohibition of alcohol. At the 1841 convention the movement pushed for a local option law subject to a yearly vote in which towns and communities could elect to be wet or dry. (Chalfant, p. 33) These and other issues were knocked around between the temperance movement, commercial liquor interests and the courts for the rest of the century. However, with the liquor industry successfully influencing key legislators, the consumption of strong drink and its consequent societal damage continued. The Civil War brought a pause to temperance activities, but the momentum resumed in the years following (Chalfant, p. 83), and it was during this period that Mr. Kelker assumed a leadership role in the fight against issuing liquor licenses in Dauphin County. As a member of the Prohibition Executive Committee, an organization of Christian citizens in Harrisburg, he gave voice to the cause by seeking support from state and county newspaper editors, arranging public-speaking platforms and urging ministers to "preach at least twice on the subject before the third Friday of March next, and to give public notice thereof" in a short article about a Prohibition Executive Committee meeting at his Front Street residence. (*Harrisburg Telegraph*, Feb. 11, 1873, p. 3)

RFK's greatest impact on the temperance cause came about from his position as foreman of the Dauphin County Grand Jury in 1871, 1873 and 1879. He used his office to reduce liquor sales by recommending that courts impose stringent standards for obtaining a liquor license to prevent undesirable and dishonest individuals from dispensing alcohol. He considered the existing law "a public nuisance." (Rudolph F Kelker, 1820–1906) In 1873, the presiding judge, John J. Pearson, presented RFK's body of twenty-one jurors with a charge relating to the sale of intoxicating drinks. The judge expressed his belief that there were "too many licensed in the county" and "If the Grand Jury look around through the townships of the county, and the wards of the city and discover and present mere tippling shops or unnecessary houses *they will not be licensed.*" The grand jury's response addressed the judge's charge by characterizing the problems with the existing license system and with recommendations for more strict procedures. The jury's response appears to have been prepared by Mr. Kelker, as it is written in the first person. Among the many points put forth in the response is a condemnation of lawyers and other individuals who assisted and endorsed license applications for disreputable applicants. The response, shown below, and the judge's charge were published in the *Tunkhannock Republican.* (Feb. 26, 1873, p. 4)

It is therefore amazing that many good men (it must be thoughtlessly) are persuaded to sign applications for license, thus lending the influence of their reputation and standing to a business which they would scorn to engage in themselves. And we would appeal to the members of the Dauphin county bar to ponder well the responsibility they assume for the sake of an attorney's fee, be it large or small, which they may receive for obtaining licenses for individuals they personally know to be pests of society, and whose houses if licensed will prove avenues to hell for their citizens. In fine we would appeal to the honorable court, our attorneys, and all good men, without exception, to unite together, and with a relentless grasp of the Moloch[*] of intemperance determined to rid our land of a traffic, which, if successful, will destroy; but the prohibition of which by law will serve to perpetuate our civil and religious liberties.

[*Moloch refers to a Canaanite God associated with child sacrifice; in literature it refers to someone or something demanding a costly sacrifice.]

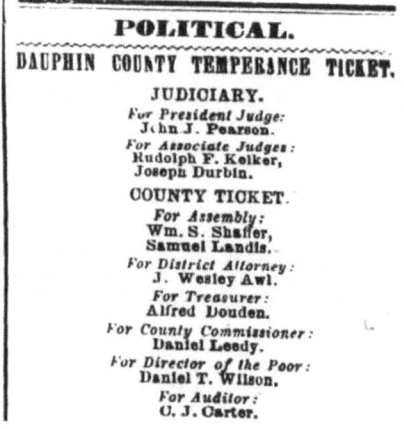

POLITICAL.

DAUPHIN COUNTY TEMPERANCE TICKET.

JUDICIARY.

For President Judge:
John J. Pearson.

For Associate Judges:
Rudolph F. Kelker,
Joseph Durbin.

COUNTY TICKET.

For Assembly:
Wm. S. Shaffer,
Samuel Landis.

For District Attorney:
J. Wesley Awl.

For Treasurer:
Alfred Douden.

For County Commissioner:
Daniel Leedy.

For Director of the Poor:
Daniel T. Wilson.

For Auditor:
O. J. Carter.

In 1871, Mr. Kelker ran unsuccessfully for Associate Judge on the Dauphin County Temperance Ticket along with Judge Pearson.

In addition to his three years as foreman of the Dauphin County grand jury, RFK was appointed by the Prohibition Executive Committee to monitor liquor-license applications in Dauphin County for the purpose of keeping undesirables out of the business of selling alcohol and to monitor those who received licenses to ensure that proper procedures were followed and that legal requirements were met. (Rudolph F Kelker, 1820–1906)

As a dedicated advocate of temperance, he saw the abuse of ardent spirits as a monstrous evil that if left unchecked would destroy society. The collateral damage that hard drink wrought on communities did indeed impose a serious threat to the social fabric. We can understand that the temperance movement saw the elimination of intoxicating liquor as a noble goal and the answer to problems brought on by excessive alcohol use. Harrisburg was overrun with dram houses, families suffered and were being destroyed, and community life was degraded. To many, total temperance was the answer.

We know the history. The Eighteenth Amendment (the Prohibition Amendment, ratified in 1919) would prove a failure that brought about a national crime wave. It did not alleviate the alcohol problem, it made it worse, and the only answer was to repeal it by passage of the Twenty-first Amendment (on December 5, 1933). But let's give the temperance movement its due for fighting for what it perceived to be the betterment of society; with the advantage of hindsight, we can extend some considered praise to the movement. Rudolph Frederick Kelker and so many others put forth effort to improve their communities. Were they wrong, misguided? History may assess they were, but they were acting out of compassion to improve the many lives so tragically impacted by rampant abuse of alcohol. We can credit them for that.

A Hospital for Harrisburg. RFK's devotion to his fellow man and to his community are on full display with his efforts to establish the first hospital in Harrisburg. His position in the community and his ability to get things done played a major role in bringing about the new facility.

On December 3, 1872 thirty-nine men met in the boardroom of Harrisburg National Bank to discuss and plan for a dispensary and hospital to serve the Harrisburg community "for the reception, cure and medical or surgical treatment of the sick and injured." (Crist, R. G., 1973, *Harrisburg Hospital: The First 100 Years*, Harrisburg, p. 1) The need for a hospital had become urgent. Harrisburg's population had reached twenty-three thousand by 1870 (Harrisburg, Pennsylvania Population History, https://www.biggestuscities. com/city/harrisburg-pennsylvania), and the two existing hospitals at the

Almshouse and the Lunatic Asylum had become inadequate for meeting the needs of the community.

The meeting's organizers, realizing that expertise and experience would be needed to meet the challenges they faced chose from their group five prominent and influential individuals with experience in business and community affairs to begin the planning process. They were James McCormick Jr., son of James McCormick Sr., a prominent Harrisburg businessman and head of a business empire of farms and flour mills (James McCormick [1801–1870], The McCormick Family of Dauphin County, psu.edu); Donald Cameron, son of Simon Cameron, political power broker and head of the Republican Party's statewide political machine; William Calder, a wealthy heir and director of several corporations; Rudolph Frederick Kelker, businessman and community activist; and A. Boyd Hamilton, a board member of several Harrisburg organizations and societies.

On February 25, at their second meeting, McCormick Jr. assumed leadership of the project and appointed committees to raise funds and to draft regulations for the hospital's management. He was looking for relevant experience and influence, and for the management committee he found those qualifications in Kelker, Daniel W. Gross and Dr. John Curwen. Mr. Kelker was chairman of the Almshouse Directors of the Poor, a trustee of the Lunatic Asylum and an officer of the Harrisburg City Passenger Railway Company, with extensive involvement in the community, church affairs and in business. Gross was a businessman, a trustee of the Lunatic Asylum, a member of the city council and the school board. Dr. Curwen was the long-time superintendent of the Lunatic Asylum.

Over the next three weeks, the fundraising committee did its job by collecting $5,050 from the organizers and others, with the largest donations coming from the McCormick family. From there things began to move quickly. On March 24, Simon Cameron's handpicked state attorney general quickly certified the legality of the new organization's articles of association. After the state supreme court issued a charter for the enterprise, Cameron's chief lieutenant, Matthew Quay, promptly delivered it to Cameron's hand-picked governor, John F. Hartranft, who signed it. The hospital received its official charter and was incorporated on May 9, 1873. (Crist, p. 4)

With the certification process ongoing, the committee charged with finding a building purchased a brick schoolhouse on Mulberry Street.

(*Harrisburg Telegraph*, May 21, 1873, p. 3) Their action was approved at a May 20 meeting of the organizers presided over by Mr. Kelker. Shortly after the vote of approval, Donald Cameron was elected chairman and took over the chair. A twelve-man committee was then elected to manage the hospital project. Members included Mr. Kelker, both McCormicks, Donald Cameron, Hamilton, Gross, Curwen and Mr. Kelker's brother-in-law, George Reily. (Crist, pp. 1–4)

With state certification and approval, the acquisition of the building and with the governing body in place, the task of putting together a functioning hospital commenced. Here, it may be useful to understand what hospital care in the mid- to late-nineteenth century really was. It was in no way comparable to that provided by today's scrubbed and sanitized medical centers. Most hospitals and doctors were either unaware of or did not follow antiseptic practices. The first demonstration of the benefit of antiseptic practice had been made by Ignaz Semmelweis (1818–1865) in Vienna in the 1840s. Semmelweis showed that the incidence of childbed fever, a common infection in newborns of that period, could be significantly reduced when doctors simply washed their hands. His observation was largely ignored or dismissed for contradicting medical dogma of that time (Ignaz Semmelweis, Wikipedia). In the 1860s, Louis Pasteur introduced the germ theory of disease, showing that microorganisms (germs) were the cause of many diseases (Louis Pasteur, Wikipedia). Following Pasteur's observations, Joseph Lister introduced antiseptic procedures to surgical practice in 1867. Lister showed that when surgeons sterilized their instruments and gloves, there was a marked reduction in post-surgical deaths from infection (Joseph Lister, Wikipedia). Unfortunately, many surgeons again did not accept his proven antiseptic practices.

Medicine of that time was based, in many cases, on wrongheaded assumptions. For example, many doctors then believed in "laudable pus," that is, that the accumulation of pus during an infection was a positive sign of healing. (Varhola, M. J., 1999, *Everyday Life During the Civil War*, Writer's Digest Books, Cincinnati, p. 183) We now know that pus, the accumulation of infection-fighting immune cells that appear at the site of a bacterial infection, is indicative of a disease's progression brought about by invasive proliferating bacteria. Effective treatment, as with antibiotics, limits bacterial proliferation, with a subsequent disappearance of pus, thus leading to faster recovery. Unfortunately, the "laudable pus" theory was subscribed to by too many physicians and surgeons with predictable results.

Nineteenth-century medicine also suffered from controversies over methods of treatment. Many doctors subscribed to the practice of homeopathic medicine, popular in that period but since shown to be ineffective. Practitioners of homeopathy believed that agents that produce symptoms that mimic those of the disease to be treated were effective when administered in low doses. Treatment formulations, or "homeopathics," were chosen from reference books and prepared by dilution or serial dilution in water or alcohol. Sometimes the homeopathic was serially diluted to the extent that no homeopathic molecules remained in the final preparation. (Homeopathy, Wikipedia)

Allotropic medicine, unlike homeopathy, used conventional treatments of that time, many of which are now known to be ineffective or harmful (Allopathic Medicine, Wikipedia). Neither homeopathy nor allopathy was based on scientific evidence. Surgery was most frequently performed without the benefit of antiseptic procedures, with a resulting high post-operation death rate. In the nineteenth century, medical-school education, whether homeopathic or allopathic, was brief, inadequate and little influenced by science. Six months of medical-school education were enough qualification to begin a practice. Until 1875, there was no requirement for physicians to be licensed. Until 1844, Pennsylvania was licensing doctors without any assessment of the applicant's knowledge of medicine. A physician with no understanding of the germ theory could be licensed to treat infectious disease. (Crist, p. 6) Compounding this slapdash system of medical care was the lack of formal training for nurses anywhere in the United States. Nursing care was performed by untrained volunteers or by untrained employees. (Crist, p. 5) Medical practice then was far from acceptable by today's standards, but it was all there was.

Harrisburg's new hospital was dedicated in a ceremony on the hospital grounds at 3:00 pm on Monday, August 4, 1873. Rev. R. J. Keeling of the St. Stephens Episcopal Church opened the ceremony with a prayer. Board president McCormick announced receipt of donations to the hospital totaling almost $10,000 and Mr. Kelker discussed the activities of the board. Robert A. Lambert then addressed the crowd, and after the meeting was closed with a prayer by Rev. William Calder, those assembled were invited to inspect the new facilities. (Crist, pp. 10, 11)

The new hospital hit rough waters before it even opened for business over the issue of allopathic care versus homeopathic care. Allopathic practitioners had little regard for homeopathy, and homeopathic physicians in turn disdained allopathic medicine. Some cities, to deal with the existing incompatibility and be able provide medical care to the community, established both allopathic and homeopathic hospitals. (Crist, p. 13) Harrisburg did not have a homeopathic hospital at that time.

Although both homeopathic and allopathic doctors practiced in Harrisburg, the hospital board, following the lead of the Dauphin County Medical Society, hired a staff of eight allopathic doctors and no homeopathic doctors. An outcry from some homeopathic practitioners and community members brought about enough pressure for the board to make some accommodation. At a hastily arranged meeting held just an hour before the opening ceremony, the board passed a resolution allotting $100 for the purchase of homeopathic medicines.

The eight newly hired allopathic doctors then resigned to protest the board's accommodation to homeopathy and for not being consulted about the decision. The community's homeopathic doctors, meanwhile, merely saw the board's action to purchase homeopathic medicines as a feeble conciliatory gesture. Nor were they impressed by the resignations of the allopathic physicians. So, just days after its grand opening, the hospital had three patients, no doctors and a controversy over allopathy versus homeopathy.

The staff vacancies were quickly filled when Mr. Kelker and Henry McCormick were designated to find replacement doctors. In another mild compromise to the homeopaths, they hired as "Visiting Physicians" two allopathic physicians with tolerant views of homeopathy. Two surgeons were subsequently hired. In the evening of the day of the mass resignation, the Dauphin County Medical Society met and pronounced their rejection of homoeopathic medicine and endorsed the actions of the physicians, stating that "each and every member of the late staff be re-elected by the Managers of said Hospital, and all other practice but that of the regular school of medicine be ignored."

The homeopathic physicians' protests and those of their supporters did not sway the hospital management, although the latter remained willing to accommodate patients seeking homeopathic treatment. The Dauphin County Medical Society remained strongly opposed to any accommodation to homeopathy, and their position was endorsed by the Medical Society of the State of Pennsylvania. The state society, at its annual meeting in 1876, issued a statement that it "unanimously endorsed" the Dauphin County Society for declining "to have anything to do with an Institution that recognizes any system of practice based upon exclusive dogma," (Crist, p. 17)

The controversy continued, as did Harrisburg Hospital's growth as an allopathic institution. An apothecary was hired in 1877 (Crist, p. 20). The first department, Eye, Ear and Throat, was formed in 1885 (Crist, p. 23). An operating room, named for its provider, Sara L. Haldeman-Haly, was established in 1899 (from the Haldeman-Haly Operating Room's opening day program, on file at the Historical Society of Dauphin County, MG 378). As the hospital grew, Mr. Kelker continued to serve and to exert influence (Crist, p. 20). In March 1878, he accepted the position of treasurer and served in that capacity until 1888. (Kelker Family Record, p. 97)

HARRISBURG HOSPITAL
Mulberry Street, Near Front,

APPLICATION FOR ADMISSION TO BE made to the attending managers at the Hospital Wednesday and Saturday afternoons at 2:30.

Persons injured by accident received at all hours, provided they are brought to the hospital within twenty-four hours after its occurrence.

Poor persons receive medical attention and

MEDICINE FREE OF CHARGE

Open every day, except Sunday.
Visiting Surgeon — THOMAS J. DUNOTT M. D., DR. J. P. SEILER.
Visiting Physicians—FRED. W. COOVEE, D., and GEORGE R. HURSH, M. D.
Resident Physician — CHRISTIAN J. FABER, M. D.

FREE DISPENSARY

For all diseases at the hospital from 12 A. M. to 2 P. M. The Resident Physician can be found at all hours at the hospital, unless professionally engaged. Poor persons attended at their homes by the Resident Physician.

JAMES PORTER, Steward.

Notice of Harrisburg Hospital's services.

Harrisburg Telegraph, May 20, 1880, p. 3

At the age of seventy-nine and no longer affiliated with the hospital, Mr. Kelker spoke at the 1899 dedication of the Haldeman-Haly Operating Room. (HSDC, MG 378) His rather lengthy presentation covered the hospital's history from that first organizers' meeting at the Harrisburg National Bank up to the dedication of the operating room. His remarks, filled with references to his religious beliefs, reflected pride in his contributions and hope for the hospital's future. He ended his talk with these words:

> I am sure we all are glad today, that what we have lived to see so much good accomplished by the institution, beginning with but very little means, fostered by kindness and benevolence, and looked after by the Board of Managers from year to year, and now, thanks to our Heavenly Father, we have lived at last to see the culminating point—an operating room with everything that is required for the proper treatment of the sick and injured who may be brought within its walls.

Today, Harrisburg's hospital is a major medical center. It operates as a unit of the University of Pittsburgh Medical Center. It provides contemporary facilities and a full range of diagnostic and treatment services to the residents of central Pennsylvania.

The Sick and Indigent, a Controversy. Helping war orphans, working to reduce the ravages of alcoholism and establishing medical care for his community are all part of Mr. Kelker's legacy. But also recognize his devotion to caring for the sick and indigent as president of the Directors of the Poor for Harrisburg's Almshouse from 1866 to 1872. During his tenure he directed upgrades of the facilities that brought an improved quality of care for its patients. But his tenure was also marked by a raging controversy involving the mayor, county commissioners and the Almshouse over the care of smallpox patients and the institution's ability to provide for their care.

Almshouses, or poorhouses, originated in England during the Middle Ages with the mission of providing housing and basic needs for the poor, elderly and indigent. Most were founded in the Christian tradition of "love thy neighbor" although a few were secular. The first American almshouse was established in Boston in 1622. The tradition of almshouses was brought to the Commonwealth of Pennsylvania with William Penn in the seventeenth century, and by 1896 more than fifty Pennsylvania counties had at least one almshouse, orphanage or charitable organization for the poor and underprivileged. (According to the 1896 report of the twenty-second Annual Session of the Association of Directors of the Poor and Charities of the State of Pennsylvania, Pittsburgh, Oct. 20, 21 and 22, pp. 19–22…)

The Dauphin County Almshouse was authorized by an 1804 act, and in 1806 it began accepting patients in its facility located two miles east of Harrisburg. (Annual Session of the Directors of the Poor, p. 184; Kelker, L. R., 1907, *History of Dauphin County, Pennsylvania*, Lewis Publishing, New York, Chicago, p. 109) The original campus consisted of small buildings that grew inadequate as the patient population increased. By 1866, when RFK was presiding over the Directors of the Poor, the campus was in desperate need of expanded and modernized facilities. He used his influence as a director and as a prominent member of the community to get legislation passed for the construction of new buildings and to get needed improvements in the management of the facility. (Kelker, L. R., p. 109)

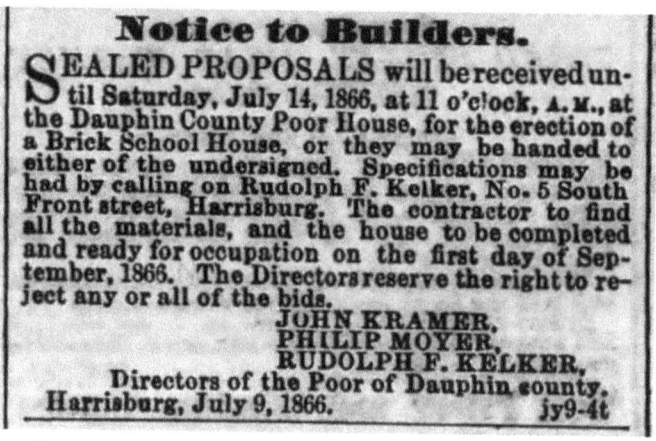

Notice to Builders.

SEALED PROPOSALS will be received until Saturday, July 14, 1866, at 11 o'clock, A. M., at the Dauphin County Poor House, for the erection of a Brick School House, or they may be handed to either of the undersigned. Specifications may be had by calling on Rudolph F. Kelker, No. 5 South Front street, Harrisburg. The contractor to find all the materials, and the house to be completed and ready for occupation on the first day of September, 1866. The Directors reserve the right to reject any or all of the bids.
JOHN KRAMER,
PHILIP MOYER,
RUDOLPH F. KELKER,
Directors of the Poor of Dauphin county.
Harrisburg, July 9, 1866.   jy9-4t

From the *Harrisburg Daily Independent*, July 3, 1883, p. 1.

The upgraded facilities opened in 1868, but a hospital planned for the care and treatment of patients with smallpox and other infectious diseases was not built. The responsibility for this became a contentious issue and a blame game in which RFK, as president of the Almshouse's Directors of the Poor, was a central figure.

This issue of a hospital for the treatment of infectious-disease patients was critical because contagious diseases were prevalent during 1800s. Pennsylvania suffered a smallpox epidemic from 1860 to 1861, and Philadelphia endured another from 1865 to 1873. Typhus, cholera and even yellow fever were also afflicting many. (History of Smallpox—Epidemics in the Americas, http://www.liquisearch.com/history_of_smallpox/epidemics_in_the_americas)

The Almshouse had only a small ill-equipped building where no more than one or two infectious disease patients could be isolated and cared for. In the fall of 1871, with winter approaching and the expectation of increasing numbers of infected patients, the need became pressing. This was made clear in a *Harrisburg Telegraph* report (Nov. 25, 1871, p. 3) on Harrisburg Grand Jury proceedings that put the blame for the delay in construction on the county commissioners:

> The County Commissioners appear to have also unnecessarily delayed obeying the recommendation of the Grand Jury at the August Court, for the erection of an [sic] hospital for contagious diseases. In the words of the court, the appearance of small pox [sic] in Harrisburg and vicinity, and the almost certain appearance of the cholera the coming season, should be sufficient incentives to proceed without delay and provide for those who may be afflicted.

The report went on to note that the grand jury had recommended that a thirty-by-forty-foot frame structure with appropriate facilities under the direction of three physicians would be sufficient.

Shortly thereafter the Directors of the Poor issued a public notice signed by RFK and two other directors (*Harrisburg Telegraph*, Dec. 1, 1871, p. 2) stating that the Almshouse would not accept smallpox patients because there were insufficient facilities on the property. And they put the responsibility for this lack of a hospital directly on the county commissioners:

> THE DIRECTORS OF THE POOR of Dauphin County regret that owing to there being no hospital for contagious diseases on the poor house farm, they are compelled to decline any more persons with small pox [...]

Then came the statement that riled the commissioners:

> Magistrates, constables and all other persons are therefore warned not to send or bring any such persons to the Dauphin County Poor House **until the Commissioners of Dauphin County carry out the recommendations of the Grand Juries of both**

the August and November Courts, 1871, and cause to be erected some suitable buildings wherein such afflicted persons may be properly provided for [...] (emphasis added).

The notice brought a strong response from the *Harrisburg Telegraph* editors and the county commissioners. The *Telegraph* attacked the Directors of the Poor in an opinion piece (Dec. 2, 1871, p. 3) asking how the directors could reject admission of an infected individual when they were the very ones who had failed to get the hospital built:

> Was our involuntary expression as we read the "notice" from the Directors of the Poor, forbidding the bringing of persons infected with small pox to the almshouse. It is both right and proper that the inmates of that institution be protected, but we must earnestly protest against the neglect of the authorities thereof to provide some place for the reception of persons infected with contagious diseases [...] It is true that an infirmary or hospital is sadly needed, and we live in hope that measures will be speedily taken by our public-spirited citizens to found such a charity. But at present, when we are threatened with a spread of small pox contagion, it is the duty of the Directors of the Poor to make proper provision for all who cannot otherwise be taken care of, instead of giving "notice" "*warning Magistrates, Constables and all others not to attempt to send or bring any such persons to the Dauphin County poor house.*" Why have the directors been so derelict? They have acted very strangely throughout this whole affair, and they are highly culpable, in our opinion in delaying until the winter has set in to make arrangements therefor. They may throw the responsibility to the county commissioners, but the community will hold them responsible in the premises. If they desire to show their philanthropy, let them at once go to work and act promptly.
>
> [...] One month more and Rudolph F. Kelker, Esq., retires from the board [...] Mr. Kelker has been the life of the board, and we can hardly believe for his well-known Christian benevolence, that he willingly allowed himself to be overslaughed [sic] by the other directors. We know that several months ago, when the almshouse physician refused to attend smallpox patients, Mr. K protested against this neglect, but was overruled by the others [...]

The county commissioners then followed with a blistering defense of their actions and, like the *Telegraph*, put the blame for there being no hospital on the Directors of the Poor. (*Harrisburg Telegraph*, Dec. 22, 1871, p. 2) The piece, "To the Public," began by referring to the director's December 1 public notice banning infected patients from the Almshouse:

.THE ATTENTION OF THE UNdersigned [sic], the County Commissioners, has been directed by an official notice, published by the Directors of the Poor, to the effect that "until the Commissioners of Dauphin County carry out the recommendations of the grand jury of August and November, 1871," and erect suitable buildings for the accommodation of persons having contagious diseases, no more persons afflicted with the small pox or varioloid [or variola, a milder form of small pox] would be received at the alms house for medical treatment thus reflecting upon the County Commissioners in an unjust and uncalled-for manner, and placing upon them a willful neglect, which belongs elsewhere. The Commissioners, in justice to themselves, deem it proper to also publish an *official* notice, in order that the public may understand and properly appreciate their position upon this important question.

The commissioners then cited an 1866 act of the Assembly:

Surely someone is to blame here, certainly not the Commissioners of Dauphin County; and that the position of the Commissioners may be further understood, they refer to an act of Assembly passed 17th April 1866, and from it they quote for the benefit of the Directors of the Poor and the public generally, viz: "Sec. 1. In all cases where a poor house or houses have been or hereafter shall be erected in any county or counties under any law of the Commonwealth, and the said buildings are found insufficient for the purpose of comfortably sheltering the poor, sick or insane of the proper county, it shall be lawful for the County Commissioners to erect new or additional buildings for such purposes, or for hospitals to prevent the spread of infectious diseases among those sent to such institutions: *Provided that before erecting any such new or additional buildings, the construction thereof shall be recommended by the directors of the poor, an* [sic] *grand jury and the court of quarter sessions of the proper county.*

They then put forth that they had no discretion to initiate the building of a hospital because they received no communication from the Directors of the Poor or the court of quarter sessions:

Aside from the recommendations of the Grand Juries of August and November last, no memorial [i.e., notification] *from the Directors of the Poor, or any communication from the court of quarter sessions of the county, were ever received by the Board of County Commissioners upon the subject,* hence they could take no steps towards the erection of buildings, as the law is plain and explicit that there must first be a recommendation to them by the authorities referred to. It can now be seen that the Poor Directors, in their published notice, have endeavored to place the censure of the delay of building a hospital upon the Commissioners of the county, when in truth and reality it rests in great measure upon them. This a plain statement of fact based upon law, and to every thinking person cannot but at once place us before the public in a proper light.

Four days later, RFK as president of the Directors of the Poor responded in the *Telegraph* (Dec. 26, 1871, p. 2) with another piece titled "To the Public." He began by claiming that the commissioners misunderstood the directors' public notice about smallpox, stating that "No reflection upon the non-action of the Commissioners was intended" and that the director's statement in the December 1 public notice that "no small pox patients would be received at the Poor House until the Commissioners carry out the recommendations of the Grand Juries of August and November Courts" was only to inform the public that the Almshouse with its limited facilities could not accept new patients, for they would then take up the limited space for such treatment that had to be available should any Almshouse residents become infected. He then listed an eleven-item account of events from September regarding the hospital issue: The grand jury in September did not recommend erecting a hospital; in an October 3 meeting the directors unanimously recommended the erection of a hospital and did so again in a November 7 meeting in which they authorized Kelker to memorialize the court; he did notify the court on November 20; the grand jury on November 25 reported that "the county commissioners appear to have unnecessarily delayed obeying the recommendations of the Grand Jury at the August court, for the erection of an hospital for contagious diseases"; on December 7 the grand-jury report endorsing the building of the hospital was approved by the judges. RFK ended "To the Public" by reaching out with some words of conciliation:

> Whatever injustice has been done to our brethren in office we do most sincerely regret. A friendly call on either of the directors at the date of their advertisement would have made this communication unnecessary, and we trust that there will be no further occasion for appearing in public on this matter.

The next volley in the ongoing public debate came from another opinion piece in the *Harrisburg Telegraph*, "The Directors of the Poor and Contagious

Diseases." (Jan. 8, 1872, p. 2) The unsigned article asks why there is no hospital when it was part of the 1867 plans for the new Almshouse buildings.

> [...] a general surprise is expressed that the directors of the poor, expending an immense amount of money in enlarging the building, should have neglected to provide for the sick and infirm, when it will be remembered that the great plea for the necessity of extending the poor house building was for the purpose of erecting a hospital.

The piece then cites as evidence an 1867 notice from the Directors of the Poor addressed to the county commissioners requesting an appropriation for buildings that included a hospital:

> To the Commissioners of Dauphin County.
>
> The undersigned directors of the poor of the county aforesaid, respectfully request that you would make an appropriation of a certain amount of money sufficient for the purpose of erecting the necessary additions to the poor house building, and such alterations as may be deemed expedient and proper in the present poor house, and also a hospital for the keeping of patients who may have contagious diseases, and such other improvements as were designated in the memorial to the directors of the poor of April 25, 1866 and which was approved by the grand jury and the court of quarter sessions of April term, 1866, herewith presented to your honorable body.
>
> We will only add that a due regard to the pressing wants of the poor and the insane committed to our charge call for immediate action.
>
> Rud. F. Kelker
>
> A.H. Boyer

> August 6, 1867, Dauphin county poor house.

The *Telegraph* article then inquires:

> Here is an especial request for a building for the accommodation of persons who are afflicted with CONTAGIOUS DISEASES [sic], and now the whole country is afflicted with this malady, we are told that the directors of the poor have no room whatever for such patients.

Another wrinkle in the ongoing debate appeared in the same January 8 issue of the *Telegraph* with a report on page 3 of a statement from Harrisburg's Mayor Verbeke concerning the admission of a smallpox-infected jail prisoner to the Almshouse. The *Telegraph* pointed out that the statement was being published with the mayor's permission. The mayor wrote that he was notified of the prisoner's condition by Dr. Egle, the prison physician, and that arrangements were then made to send the infected individual to the Almshouse. An application made to the Almshouse for the patient's admission was rejected by the directors because the last two patients that were sent died "out of neglect," apparently because the Almshouse could not care for them. It is not clear from the article but apparently RFK and another director, a Mr. Herr, sent word to the mayor that if the man was sent to the poorhouse he would do it against their protest. The mayor sent the man to the poorhouse anyway.

The article ends with:

> A correspondence on the subject took place between the mayor and R.F. Kelker, Esq., which we desired for publication, but as it was of a partly private nature, the mayor felt a delicacy about allowing its publication.
>
> We learn, however, that subsequently the directors of the poor informed the mayor that they would do what they could to have all cases sent from the city properly attended to.

RFK, in the next day's *Telegraph* (Jan. 9, 1872, p. 2), replied saying that the reason for no hospital was because in 1867 the commissioners never allocated the money for it to be built. He used the same heading that the *Telegraph* used the previous day in attacking him. In the opening paragraph he condemns the *Telegraph* writer(s) for apparent ignorance of the hospital situation:

"THE DIRECTORS OF THE POOR AND CONTAGIOUS DISEASES"

> Mr. Editor—Such is the caption of an editorial in the DAILY TELEGRAPH of last evening. It is impossible to conceive that the writer of the same was ignorant of the fact that the *Commissioners of Dauphin County* and not the directors of the poor built the new alms house. If he did not know this, he should have refrained from writing at all; and if he did know he has grossly assaulted unoffending parties. To say

that the directors of the poor "obtained a very large amount of money, some say over one hundred thousand dollars, to make these improvements and erect a hospital" is totally untrue. They never received one dollar from the commissioners for the purpose, and consequently never expended any. The whole work from beginning to end, was contracted for, carried on, finished and paid for, by the commissioners of Dauphin County at an expense of about $77,000, as has appeared in their own published annual statements [...]

RFK then recounts that in March 1866, after discussion with Judge Pearson, he delivered the proposed legislation for the construction of new buildings to the speaker of the Senate where it was enacted into law. The law made provision that for any county where its poorhouse buildings were not adequate:

> [...] it shall be lawful *for the county commissioners to erect new or additional buildings* for such purposes, or for *hospitals, to prevent the spread of infectious diseases among those sent to such institutions*, provided that before erecting any such new or additional buildings, the construction thereof shall be recommended by the directors of the poor, a grand jury and the court of quarter sessions of the proper county.

Mr. Kelker then recounts that in August 1867 a memorial—that is, a memorandum or letter—was sent from the Directors of the Poor to the commissioners recommending "adequate additions" that included "*a hospital for contagious diseases.*" The buildings were completed in March 1868. The poorhouse was remodeled, with buildings for the steam boiler, laundry and bakery built. However:

> "When these labors were finished they [i.e., the commissioners] ceased from their labors." *The hospital for contagious diseases*, although urgently requested by the Directors of the Poor, was not erected.

He then mentions that the commissioners visited the poorhouse farm on December 5, 1871, and surveyed for a hospital site, and that the directors were asked to submit to the commissioners a request for the hospital, and the directors did so. He closes his piece with a swipe at the *Telegraph* article, a defense of the directors and a reference to the inadequate conditions for caring for patients at the Almshouse:

The editorial in the TELEGRAPH would have been passed by unnoticed, had it not contained serious but false charges against men whose only desire is to serve the public faithfully, and at the same time to stand by the poor and prevent their being immolated in case of sickness, in such a pest house as the present "Dauphin county small pox hospital."

The *Lykens Register* (Jan. 12, 1872, p. 2) published a response to RFK's piece three days later with the same caption: "THE DIRECTORS OF THE POOR AND CONTAGIOUS DISEASES." While not responding to any of Kelker's points, the writer(s) persisted in laying the blame for the lack of a hospital on the Directors of the Poor:

> The correspondence between the directors of the poor and county commissioners has elicited considerable comment in private circles, and a general surprise is expressed that the directors of the poor, expending an immense amount of money in enlarging the building, should have neglected to provide for the sick and infirm, when it will be remembered that the great plea for the necessity of extending the poor house building was for the purpose of erecting a hospital.

The article then quotes the directors' letter of August 6, 1867, in which they call for immediate action to build a hospital:

> Such was the plea of the directors of the poor with the court and grand jury. They obtained a very large amount of money, some say over one hundred thousand dollars, to make these improvements and erect a hospital, and now by the present directors, one of whom, Mr. Kelker, is still in office, and was so whilst the improvements were made, that there is no hospital.

As further fodder for their blame-the-directors position, the article then cites and attaches the directors' August 1867 *Telegraph* editorial in which the Directors of the Poor urge the construction of the hospital. The *Lykens Register* article concludes by condemning the directors:

> Since the above was in type we have seen an article from Rud. F. Kelker, Esq., President of the Board of Directors of the Poor, in which the statements of the Telegraph reflecting on the Poor Directors are pronounced incorrect in essential particulars, and the responsibility for the existing inadequate hospital building

at the almshouse for infectious and contagious diseases is charged upon the Commissioners, under whose authority the present building was erected. Be this as it may, the Board of Commissioners has changed since that time, and the Poor Directors have been compelled to virtually admit that they publicly censured the present Commissioners for neglect of duty at the outset in this controversy, for not performing an act which they [the Poor Directors] had failed to lay before the Commissioners in accordance with the plain requirements of law.

Four days later, the *Telegraph*, while reporting on grand-jury proceedings, proudly noted that Judge Pearson in presiding stated that although the grand jury had recommended the building of hospital on previous occasions "it had been neglected." The article (Jan. 16, 1872, p. 2) did not mention the Directors of the Poor or RFK as the negligent party, although it is clear that the *Telegraph*'s charge was directed at them:

> The want of a proper hospital for contagious diseases was also brought to the notice of the jury, and we were gratified to hear that the TELEGRAPH was cordially endorsed in denouncing those who had neglected to provide this much needed building. His Honor remarked that the grand jury had recommended the erection of such a hospital, and yet it had been neglected. We hope the present will investigate this matter thoroughly, and make the proper recommendation; and we feel gratified to state that the court will do its utmost to have the poor and sick cared for in a humane and proper manner. If any reliance at all can be placed on the rumors regarding the manner in which small pox patients are treated at the poor house, it is really horrible and criminal.

In the same edition, a one-sentence piece reported that the county commissioners:

> have decided to erect a hospital building for the accommodation of parties suffering from contagious diseases on the poor house grounds immediately.

The hospital was at last built, and, as reported in the *Telegraph*. (May 8, 1872, p. 3)

> The building erected for the accommodation of those afflicted with infectious diseases, known as the small pox hospital, adjacent to the almshouse, and under the control of the steward, is commodious and in every way adapted to the purpose for which it

was intended, and the care given by the county physician, Dr. Raysor, as well as the nurses, to the class of unfortunates who have been placed in this building has been unremitting and more than ordinarily successful. The disease (small pox) has been of a malignant type and yet but a very small percentage has proved fatal [...]

So, after all the charges and countercharges, endless discussion and the attendant commotion the hospital was built. RFK, who finished his tenure as a Director of the Poor in February 1872, had little if anything to do with the hospital's construction, but he left a grand legacy. His promotion of the 1867–1868 construction of new buildings and the upgrading of the old Almshouse buildings brought much needed comfort and relief to the residents. Throughout his six years as chairman of the Directors of the Poor, he and his fellow directors devoted themselves to providing for the patients and working to assure that they were safe, comfortable, well taken care of and protected from contagion. The residents were far better off after Mr. Kelker left than before he arrived. Throughout the controversy he never lost sight of his mission, and he showed himself willing to speak out when he felt that he was in the right and when what he felt was best for the unfortunate.

The Almshouse burns. Tragedy struck the Almshouse on July 2, 1883, fifteen years after completion of the new buildings. A fire destroyed almost the entire complex; only the schoolroom and the laundry survived.

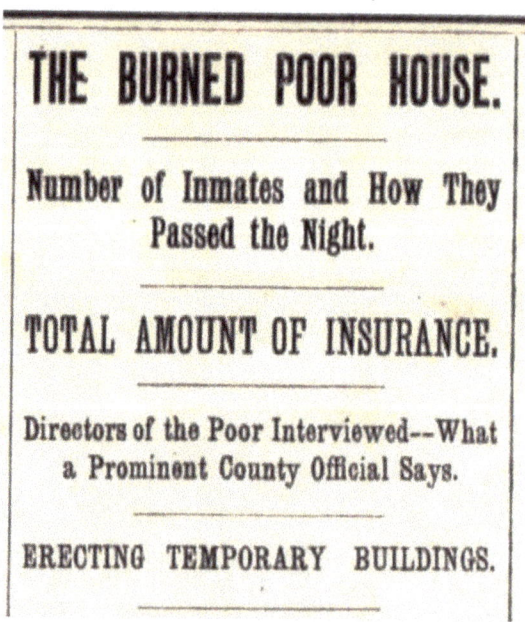

From the *Harrisburg Daily Independent*, July 3, 1883, p. 1.

The fire began in the barn that was within fifty feet of the main building. It then spread to a nearby building as the staff began removing the residents. Those who couldn't walk were removed to a safe distance from the flames. The new main building soon caught sparks from the burning buildings, and it caught fire before all residents were out. But all 185 people were removed, and only one was injured, a woman resident who was severely burned. Harrisburg firemen rushed to the scene, but they were unable to save the buildings due to the intensity of the blazes and a lack of water. (*Harrisburg Telegraph,* July 2, 1883, p. 4) The commissioners immediately proceeded to rebuild; construction began after acceptance of plans by county inspectors.

The rebuilt Almshouse opened in 1884. An inscription, written at the suggestion of RFK, was placed on the base stone of the institution. It read: "In the name of Christ the Gift of Dauphin County to Her Poor and Destitute—Built 1868—Rebuilt 1883." (Kelker, L. R., 1907, *History of Dauphin County, Pennsylvania*, Vol. 1, Lewis Publishing, New York, Chicago, p. 109)

RFK, a stationmaster on Harrisburg's Underground Railroad. Probably nothing speaks to Rudolph Frederick Kelker's benevolence and concern for his fellow man more forcefully than his active participation in helping runaway slaves escape north and to Canada. He did this in violation of the US Constitution and national laws. He was not alone. Many black and white Harrisburg citizens, like so many others throughout the Northern states, braved danger and imprisonment to hide, feed and transport runaways along the vast network of the Underground Railroad. The efforts of these facilitators were brave and noble. They risked their welfare for a just cause.

Mr. Kelker's efforts and those of so many others were a reaction to the inherent immorality of slavery, a practice that began with the 1619 arrival of the first black Africans in the Virginia colony and continued until the 1865 passage and ratification of the Thirteenth Amendment. This seemingly endless period of slavery, an ever-rising crescendo of conflicts leading up to and through the Civil War, was continually inflamed by confrontations between pro- and antislavery advocates, conflicts over the right to recover escaped slaves and disputes over allowing slavery in newly formed states and territories.

Although slavery was practiced throughout the thirteen colonies, the preparers of the US Constitution did not include a provision for slavery, but they did include a provision for the return of escaped slaves. The Fugitive Slave Clause (Article IV, Section 2, Clause 3) required states to return fugitive slaves to the states from which they had fled. Congress subsequently strengthened the provision with passage of the 1793 Fugitive Slave Act that provided procedures for capture and return. Congress further strengthened the earlier act through passage of the Fugitive Slave Act of 1850 when Southern congressman and senators moved to stem the flow of escaping slaves.

The new act was intended to reduce tensions and bring order to controversy over slavery questions, but it did neither. It inflamed those controversies and pushed the country further along the path toward war. The legislation placed an unfair burden on the free states by requiring that local law enforcement and other officials who failed to arrest and hold suspected runaways be subject to a $1,000 fine, a huge sum at that time, and that citizens who hid or housed runaways or failed to report them to authorities were subject to a $1,000 fine and/or imprisonment. The law gave slave hunters full freedom to roam throughout free states and identify, arrest, capture and return alleged escapees, while reducing the legal requirements for ownership claims to a simple sworn affidavit from a slaveholder. The act provided a quick, simple and unjust process for capture and return. Those identified as escaped slaves and their defenders had only limited rights to challenge deportation. They were placed before slave commissioners who had a financial incentive to decide for return; they received $10 for every individual sent back and only $5 for ruling against return.

The law had a devastating effect on Harrisburg and the nation. According to Gerald Eggert (Eggert, Gerald G., "The Impact of the Fugitive Slave Law on Harrisburg: A Case Study," *Pennsylvania Magazine of History and Biography* 109/4, 1985, pp. 559, 560), who carefully studied the effect of the 1850 act on Harrisburg, the legislation was initially accepted by most of the 7,834 citizens, who felt compelled to observe the law of the land and were hopeful that it would bring about reduced tensions and increased stability. But following several slave-capture incidents, some fatal and others bloody, the community's attitude began to change. By 1853, most Harrisburg citizens opposed the law, even though, as Eggert points out, the change in attitude did not necessarily reflect a change in attitudes toward slavery. Some citizens remained sympathetic to slavery while recognizing the cruelty and the chaos brought on by the new law.

The 1850 Harrisburg Slave Law Riot (Eggert, pp. 540–545), one of the city's significant slavery confrontations, tells us something of the cruelty of the Fugitive Slave Act and how its implementation affected both black and white citizens of Harrisburg and elsewhere. It illustrates the dogged determination of slave-owners to retrieve their "property" and the fear and desperation of the black population, both free and fugitive. And it shows that some citizens, including people like lawyers Charles Rawn and Mordecai McKinney, demonstrated high moral conviction by representing accused runaways in court proceedings.

The confrontation began on August 17, 1850, just before the September 18 passage of the Fugitive Slave Act. A Harrisburg constable arrested two blacks claimed by Virginia slaveholder William Taylor, and one black claimed by another Virginia slaveholder, Solomon Snyder. On August 23, the three were taken before Judge John J. Pearson, a jurist with a reputation for competence, honesty and professionalism (mentioned earlier in this chapter). Charles Rawn and Mordecai McKinney represented the alleged escapees and presented witnesses who testified that the defendants were working in Harrisburg before the time of their purported escapes. Taylor's lawyers put forth a rebuttal to the defense's testimony by presenting witnesses who testified that they had talked to the accused runaways on August 17, the day of their alleged arrival in Harrisburg. Taylor charged that seven of his slaves, two of whom were on trial, had escaped on horseback, and he was charging the two with horse theft. The trial day's lengthy and tiring proceedings ended with Judge Pearson reserving judgment until the following day.

The early morning of the next day found a large crowd of concerned and excited black and some white citizens gathered on the streets around the jailhouse building at 223 Walnut Street, the site of the hearing. The crowd grew as it was joined by constables, special constables, the sheriff, his deputy and a posse. The sheriff, concerned about the growing crowd, ordered in a company of fifty militiamen who proceeded to clear the street immediately outside the jailhouse.

Inside, Judge Pearson ruled that the charges of horse theft were "only a pretext" to get the slaves back. He released the prisoners "intimating at the same time, that the owners had a right to [take] their property […] provided it was not accompanied by violence." Following the verdict Taylor and his fellow Southerners left the courtroom and waited in the vestibule for the released blacks to appear. Upon their appearance the Southerners attacked and beat them. As the crowd outside grew increasingly hostile, a mulatto, a Joseph Poeple (or Pople), broke from the crowd, forced his way through the iron entrance gate and attacked Taylor and his men with a stick. But he was overpowered and savagely beaten by the Southerners. (*Lewistown Gazette*, Aug. 30, 1850, p. 2)

According to J. Howard Wert, a Harrisburg journalist who later recorded Underground Railroad history in Pennsylvania (Wert, J. Howard, 1998, *Episodes of Gettysburg and the Underground Railroad*, ed. by G. Craig Caba, Gettysburg: G. Craig Caba Antiques, p. 83), Rudolph Frederick Kelker witnessed the bloody melee in the jailhouse. He writes of a conversation with Mr. Kelker including his recollections:

> "How did the field of battle look when the fracas was over?" I inquired of the venerable Rudolph Kelker.

> "Horrible"was the reply. "The floor and walls of the jail vestibule were plentifully besprinkled with blood."

After the bloody melee Taylor and his men were able to gain control of the remaining freed blacks and handcuff them. But at that point the sheriff's posse, acting on court orders, arrested both the runaways and their captors and brought them to Judge Pearson's courtroom. Warrants were also issued to the black leaders in the crowd for inciting a disturbance on the street. Poeple, one of his sons and six Harrisburg blacks were also brought before the bench. Pearson ruled that the runaways were not out of the court's custody when they were taken and shackled by Taylor and his men and that Pennsylvania, unlike Virginia, did not allow brute force in recovering slaves. He therefore charged the Southerners in causing a riot in violation of an 1847 Pennsylvania statute that prohibited the kidnapping of blacks. Taylor, in turn, filed assault charges against the black men to prevent their release. He then left for Philadelphia to obtain a writ that would allow him to take the slaves back to Virginia. The Harrisburg blacks who had been charged with causing a disturbance were released when ten white and two black Harrisburg citizens raised money for their bail.

While these events were going on in Harrisburg the Fugitive Slave Act was moving through Congress. It passed the Senate on August 26 and the House on September 12. President Millard Fillmore signed it into law on September 18. The legislation changed the legal procedures regarding escaped slaves with conditions that greatly favored slave owners, as noted above. To reduce the large number of runaway-slave trials, the new law authorized federal courts to appoint US commissioners who were empowered to decide the status of suspected runaways brought before them. These commissioners presided over expedited hearings where, in the absence of evidence against ownership of the accused slave(s), a simple affidavit, i.e., a testament signed by a claimant, was sufficient to certify ownership. The accused were denied the right to an attorney or witnesses, and they were forbidden to give testimony. Public notice was not required so captured runaways could be rushed immediately from capture to judgment before a commissioner, leaving little time for the defendants to obtain help. [Fugitive Slave Act | American Battlefield Trust (battlefields.org)]

Richard McAllister, a Harrisburg lawyer, was appointed the local slave commissioner, and he took full advantage of the simplified and biased procedures of the act to collect his $10 for almost every black brought before him. In September, on the first day of McAllister's new position, Taylor returned to Harrisburg to recover his slaves. He dropped assault charges against them and took them in manacles from their cells to a hearing before Commissioner McAllister. After signing an affidavit claiming the blacks as his property, and with no comment permitted from the accused escapees, who had no legal representation, McAllister ruled for Taylor, and the owner returned with his captives to Virginia. (Smith, E. L., 2000, *Researching the Underground Railroad in Dauphin County, Pennsylvania*, p. 33)

In November and January, following McAllister's decision, fifty-one white Harrisburg citizens petitioned to have charges dismissed against the people held as rioters. Among the signers were RFK and his brothers Henry Anthony and Immanuel Meister. (Mealy, pp. 134, 135)

But despite the Fugitive Slave Act and whatever support the law had in the Harrisburg community, blacks fleeing slavery were being routed through town throughout the 1840s and 1850s. Harrisburg was, in fact, a major link on the Underground Railroad, with several "stations" or stop-overs sequestered around the town. One of these, in the old Eighth Ward, a community of about nine hundred black citizens located just east of today's Pennsylvania State Capitol Building, was a highly active center on the Underground Railroad. Two Eighth Ward residents, William Jones, a doctor and businessman, and William Bustill, a schoolteacher, hid slaves in their homes and coordinated the movements of runaways entering and leaving Harrisburg. They acted heroically using sophisticated methods of secreting and transporting runaways and devised elaborate schemes to avoid detection. They created a code to disguise their actions and procedures.

Two of Harrisburg's prominent white citizens, neighbors Rudolph Frederick Kelker at 9 South Front Street and Dr. William Wilson Rutherford at 11 South Front Street, hid escaping slaves. (Rutherford, S. S., 1928, *The Underground Railroad*, in Publications of the Historical Society of Dauphin County, pp. 3–8) Both hid arriving runaways in their homes and then sent them off to the next point where they would be picked up for further transport. Rutherford sent his charges to his barn in Paxtang where they would remain until night when they would be picked up by guides and transported to the next station. RFK transported his escaping slaves to his stable located a few blocks from his house at the corner of Barbara and River Streets. (Rutherford, p. 3)

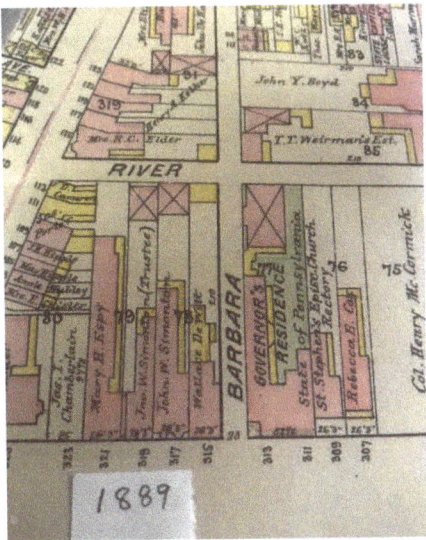

Prepared from maps in the Historical Society of
Dauphin County archives.

Above, an 1889 map of Barbara and River Streets (HSDC archives). Below, a 2018 photo of Barbara
Street looking west where it crosses River. RFK's stables were probably located on River Street just
to the right. Photo by Norman Kelker.

It would be fascinating to have a detailed account of RFK's Underground Railroad activities, to learn more of his efforts with respect to dates, numbers of runaways he assisted and his contacts in the Harrisburg Underground Railroad and beyond. But such records are rare, at best. The Underground Railroad was a clandestine enterprise. To maintain any notes, records, dates and data regarding actions, individuals and hiding places would have jeopardized escaping slaves and their facilitators. Therefore, few records were kept. This very justifiable and essential practice, however, severely limits research efforts. But from what is known Mr. Kelker hid escapees and he helped them along the path to freedom. (Rutherford, p. 3)

People like Dr. William Rutherford, Doc Jones, William Bustill and RFK are shining examples of courage and compassion. Although only fragmentary records of the extent of their activities are known to exist, the numbers of runaways assisted by these men was most certainly large and significant. They were heroes. We remember them and so many others for the high regard in which they held their fellow men and for their heroic acts. (Rutherford, pp. 3–8)

Rudolph Frederick Kelker: His Life. The Kelker family had a long, successful run in Harrisburg beginning with Anthony in his position as the first sheriff of Dauphin County. In 1799, his son Frederick started his business career with the opening of Harrisburg's first hardware store. Frederick moved on to own numerous properties in Harrisburg and its environs. Rudolph Frederick carried on in the tradition of his father, starting in the hardware business and then moving on to the buying and selling of real estate. He profited from his business acumen yet conducted himself all his life in accordance with the teachings of his German Reformed Church and felt the obligation to work for the benefit of the less fortunate.

Rudolph Frederick Kelker lived a long and productive life devoted to business, church and concern for his community expressed through extensive civil and charitable efforts. He left a huge footprint on Harrisburg and the surrounding area from his involvement in Harrisburg Hospital, the YMCA, the founding of Steelton, Kelker Street, the Historical Society of Dauphin County, the Almshouse, Franklin & Marshall College, Ursinus College and numerous other endeavors. Wealth played an important role in his successes both in his business and community efforts, and we can only wonder what his life would have been without that benefit. But though he came from wealth he was not content to live a life of ease that he could have followed by virtue of his father's money. Almost from birth, he was driven to devote himself to his community. The people of Harrisburg and its environs benefitted.

There is no doubt that Mr. Kelker's compelling drive to reach out to his fellow man was driven in large part by his deeply held religious beliefs gained from his adherence to German Reformed Church teachings. From his entry into Sunday school at the age of three to his last breath at eighty-six, he remained an unquestioning believer in the church's admonition to "love thy neighbor." He saw life through a religious lens, and all else followed.

He could be firm and demanding in his business dealings and even his charitable efforts. He recognized that it takes resolve to accomplish things of consequence in the real world, and he had the purposefulness and steadfastness to stay the course through the inevitable problems, frustrations and setbacks. We can see this in his tenure as chairman of the Directors of the Poor during his prolonged struggle over the unbuilt infectious-disease hospital. He could also be stubborn as shown by his reaction to the introduction of Sunday service for the Harrisburg City Passenger Railway Company (see the Henry Anthony Kelker section below for the history of the Passenger Railway Company) when he felt the Sabbath should not be violated, and he showed his disgust by resigning from his position as treasurer.

Rudolph Frederick Kelker dedicated his life to good works that live on long after his passing. Over time, we tend to forget the good done by those who have gone before us. There are many whose achievements have brought a better life to the people of Harrisburg, and Mr. Kelker stands high among them. Thanks to his compassion, caring and devotion, the Harrisburg of today is a better place.

Addenda
Rudolph Frederick Kelker

RFK was an active participant in Harrisburg life. Some of his positions and associations include:

—treasurer and a founder of Harrisburg Hospital
—a director of Harrisburg National Bank
—a director of First National Bank
—trustee of the Pennsylvania State Lunatic Asylum
—chairman of the board of the Almshouse
—trustee of Marshall College
—committee member with seven Marshall College trustees charged with relocating the college from Mercersburg to Lancaster
—trustee of Franklin & Marshall College from the 1850 merger of the two schools until 1869
—trustee of the theological seminary of the Reformed Church in the US
—committee member preparing the Triglott Centenary Edition of the Heidelberg Catechism in 1863
—secretary, treasurer and president of the vestry of the Reformed Salem Church of Harrisburg
—trustee and superintendent of Harrisburg Cemetery
—trustee of Harrisburg Academy
—treasurer of the Harrisburg City Passenger Railway Company
—a president of the American Sunday School Union and a lifetime member
—chairman of the Temperance Sabbath League in Harrisburg
—president of the Dauphin County Temperance Association

Rudolph Frederick and Mary Anne Reily Kelker remembered by their church. Rudolph Frederick and Mary Anne Kelker were devout longtime members of Harrisburg's Reformed Salem Church. The church building, located at Third and Chestnut Streets in Harrisburg, dates from 1791. [History—Salem United Church of Christ (salemuccharrisburg.org)] The plaque noting the couple's service and contributions is displayed in the church sanctuary.

Mary Anne Reily Kelker

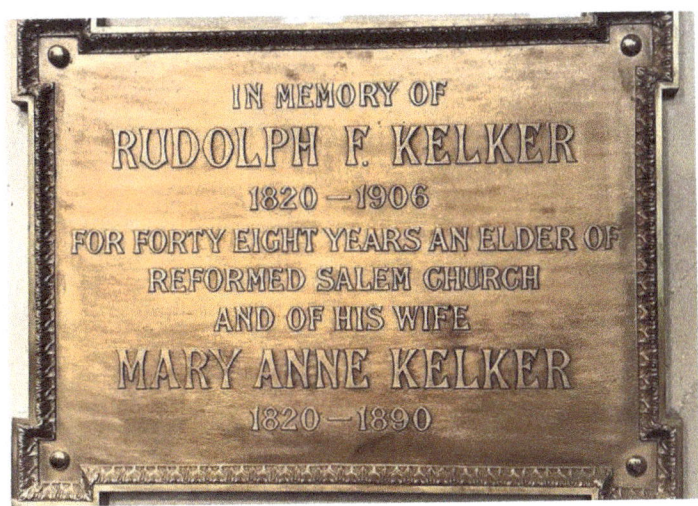

Above, a memorial plaque to RFK and Mary Anne Reily Kelker from the sanctuary of the Harrisburg's Salem United Church of Christ. Below is a portrait of Mary Anne Reily Kelker from the Harris-Cameron Mansion. Photos by Norman Kelker.

Mary Anne Reily Kelker was a source of strength to her family, her church and to the Harrisburg community. She was born in Myerstown, Pennsylvania, on September 20, 1820, to William Reily (1792–1843) and Salome Valentine (1800–1866). Her Reily family in America began when John Reily, Mary Anne's great-grandfather (circa 1765) arrived in Pennsylvania in the early 1700s. He married Mary Millhouse after his first wife died. Their first-born son, Capt. John Reily (1752–1810) was born and raised in Myerstown. Captain Reily was a member of the Pennsylvania bar, attained his rank in the Continental Army and was an original member of the Society of the Cincinnati. (L. R. Kelker, *History of Dauphin County, Pennsylvania*, Vol. 3, pp. 26–28) In 1773, he married Elizabeth Myers, daughter of Isaac Myers, the founder of Myerstown, and they had nine children. Their eighth-born, William (1792–1843), was Mary Anne's father. He served in the Pennsylvania legislature in 1830 and 1831 and was for many years a brigade inspector. At his death he was a brigadier general, having risen to prominence in the military and in business. (Kelker Family Record, p. 95) Mary Anne Reily's marriage to Rudolph Frederick Kelker, on June 17, 1844, brought together two prominent families of the Harrisburg region, and from what we know theirs was a loving and mutually beneficial relationship. Like most women of that time Mary Anne spent her adult life as a wife, mother and homemaker. She and her husband actively supported Harrisburg's Reformed Salem Church (or Old Salem Reformed Church).

Her obituary in the *Harrisburg Telegraph* (August 28, 1890, p. 1) attests to her character:

> [...] in her youth she was beautiful and sprightly. Although retiring and unassuming she was one of our best and most efficient helpers in all good works. In her home she was hospitable and gracious, and the suffering and needy found in her kind sympathy and material aid, and very few persons are as willing to make such self-sacrifices for the benefit of others as our lamented friend. Early in life she professed her faith in Christ and united with the Salem Reformed Church congregation. Mrs. Kelker was energetic and active, looking well to the ways of her household [...] A loving wife, a devoted mother, affectionate friend and kind neighbor [...]

Her 1890 death came after a long illness. Her fine qualities are seen in her sons Luther Reily and William Anthony whose names derive from her Reily family. Luther Reily was named for Mary Anne's uncle, Luther Reily, a prominent

Harrisburg physician and businessman, and William Anthony was named both for her father, William, and her husband's grandfather Anthony Kelker.

Mary Anne Reily Kelker was an important member of the Harrisburg community and a woman of significance in the Kelker and Reily family histories in Harrisburg. Her family name lives on there, with Reily Street named by her husband when he served on an 1860 commission in Harrisburg to lay out streets and roads.

RFK in newspaper gossip. Below are three newspaper items that are of little consequence but show some amusing happenings regarding Mr. Kelker's life in Harrisburg.

Foundling at the front door.

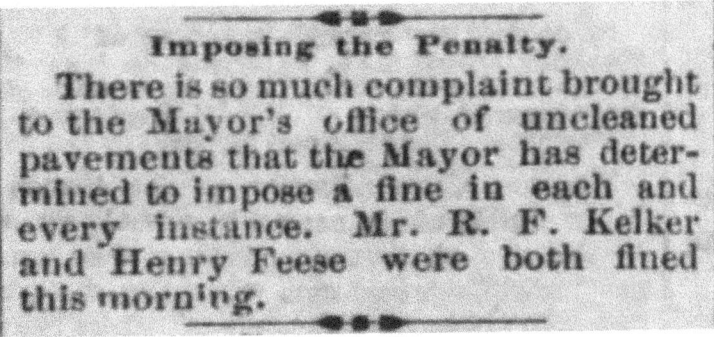

ANOTHER FOUNDLING.—A few minutes before one o'clock this morning Mr. James Garretson, night watchman on Front street, found a female infant, about one week old, on the door step of R. F. Kelker, Esq., Director of the Poor of this county. After calling at the Mayor's office Mr. G. took the child to his residence for the present. Mr. Kelker's family were not aware of the circumstance until about five o'clock.

Harrisburg Telegraph, Oct. 31, 1868, p. 3

Fined for unclean pavement.

Imposing the Penalty.
There is so much complaint brought to the Mayor's office of uncleaned pavements that the Mayor has determined to impose a fine in each and every instance. Mr. R. F. Kelker and Henry Feese were both fined this morning.

Harrisburg Daily Independent, Jan. 2, 1884, p. 1

Rudolph and Mary Anne's Front Street House on fire, almost

> A fire ball from a rocket carried by a number of the Central democratic club last night set fire to the bunting on the residence of Rudolph F. Kelker, on Front street. One of the members of the club tore down the bunting and put out the fire.

Harrisburg Daily Independent, Oct. 22, 1892, p. 8

An 1883 postcard from a John Hesse in Switzerland to Rudolph Frederick Kelker in Harrisburg. The; sender is apparently a relative of Reverend John Hesse who circa 1849 compiled the Swiss Kölliker family record. Reverend Hesse coordinated his efforts with George H. Gounde, the United States Consul at Basel, Switzerland and Mr. Kelker's Swiss agent. The writer expresses his thanks to Mr. Kelker for his kind letter and "the good things you have sent me." He informs Mr. Kelker of some of Reverend Hesse's family and ends with "May the Lord bless you." The postcard arrived in Harrisburg in 1883, the same year that the Kelker Family Record was published and five years after Reverend Hesse's death.

Rudolph Frederick Kelker for mayor. RFK was a community leader active in temperance, charities, business and local politics, as has been extensively noted above. Even though highly qualified he never sought higher office, although he did serve in some lesser positions in city government. In 1883, some fellow citizens placed him on the ballot for mayor of Harrisburg (note point 2 in the political advertisement below).

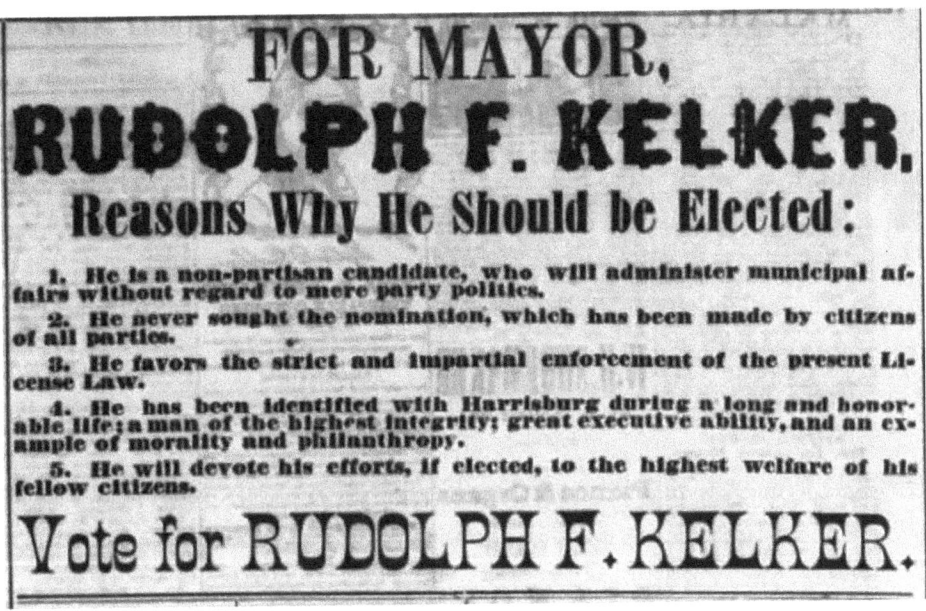

Harrisburg Daily Independent, Feb. 19, 1883, p. 4

A patient rehabilatated at Harrisburg Hospital

NEVER SAY DIE.—We were not aware when we publishe I Giles E. Thurber's letter to the mana ers of the Harrisburg hospital that h · had had his right arm amputated, a d in the last four months had acquired a most striking and beautiful penmanship with his left hand. It is a most remarkable instance of the pursuit of knowledge under difficulties, and we refer to it as an incentive to those laboring under misfortune to overcome an almost crushing evil. Brown Sequard, we belive, has a the ory that man has something like a dual brain, and so our English friend may have been only utilizing his left part of his brain power.

Harrisburg Telegraph, Feb. 27, 1875, p. 4

Immanuel Meister Kelker
Businessman, Religious Leader

Immanuel Meister (1822–1880), the second son of Frederick and Catherine Fager Kelker, was an efficient businessman, a committed member of the German Reformed Church and a devoted family man. He was born at his parent's home at 9 South Front Street. He received what education was then available in the borough's common schools, and then spent a year at Marshall College. In 1843, he joined his brothers Rudolph Frederick and Henry Anthony in establishing the Kelker & Brothers hardware firm and he remained in the hardware business the rest of his life. He married Mary Ann Jefferson Beatty on September 21, 1847, and they had three children: Catherine, born in 1849, George Beatty, born in 1852, and Frederick, born in 1858.

Unlike his brothers, IMK lacked the hard drive and aggressiveness they displayed in their business affairs. He was content to remain in the hardware business and devote himself to his church and his family. His obituary in the *Harrisburg Daily Independent* (March 31, 1880, p. 4) notes that "His life was quiet and retired, never aspiring to public position." He functioned in a low-key, out-of-the spotlight manner. Unlike his brothers his name and activities were infrequently mentioned in the newspapers of his time. Consequently, he left us but few records of his life.

Church, charity and temperance. IMK's life was dominated by his devotion to the German Reformed Church, which he joined at an early age and remained a committed participant throughout his life. He served as a deacon, was a founder of Harrisburg's Second Reformed Church, and served for many years with the church's Sunday school as assistant superintendent and later as superintendent. (*Harrisburg Daily Independent*, March 31, 1880, p. 4) His prominence in church affairs is shown by his selection in June 1877 as a delegate to the Pennsylvania State Sunday School convention in Harrisburg. His service to his church was prominently noted in his obituaries, along with his other good works.

Charitable activities were also noted in his obituaries, showing that in 1877 he was chosen as chairman of Harrisburg Hospital's managers. (*Harrisburg Daily Independent*, May 8, 1877, p. 1) His biography in the Kelker Family Record (p. 101) states that he was active "in providing at his personal expense clothing for destitute ones, and looking after the sick, he was most assiduous. His acts of charity in this direction were mainly unknown to any but the recipients until after his decease."

Immanuel Meister, like his older brother, Rudolph Frederick, was active in the temperance movement. But whereas RFK carried on in a leadership role, as described above, Immanuel Meister played a minor role. We have little evidence of his participation except for a short article in the *Harrisburg Daily Independent* (Feb. 23, 1877, p. 4) where he was reported to have given an "eloquent and effective" temperance speech at a Methodist Episcopal Church meeting. His short biography in the Kelker Family Record (p. 101) relates that he "was a firm and consistent advocate of the temperance reform and did much to warn inebriates and encourage the unfortunate class to abandon the intoxicating cup, and to unite with some christian Church [sic]."

Immanuel Meister Kelker died in March 1880 after a lingering illness. (*Daily Independent*, March 31, 1880, p. 4) The Sunday School Association of Harrisburg met to form a committee to prepare a report recognizing his life and achievements. That such a meeting was called to mourn him and honor his life indicates that his loss was deeply felt within religious community and beyond. Those sentiments were expressed in the committee's report.

> Whereas, God in the exercise of His sovereign will, and in the dispensation of His all-wise providence, has taken from his labors in this world and called to his reward in Heaven, our esteemed friend and brother, Immanuel M. Kelker, with whom we have been associated for years in various ways in Christian work, we believe just to put upon record the expression of sorrow on account thereof, and also to offer our sympathy to the bereaved relatives; therefore, *Resolved*, That while we bow with resignation to the will of God in removing Brother Kelker from us, who, for a period of thirteen years was connected with the Sunday school of the Second Reformed church [...] we feel that we have lost an earnest worker in the church and the Sabbath school; one who was sincere in his endeavors to promote the good of others, and whose great delight was to see the cause of God prosper in the world.

The well-attended funeral took place at his residence at 5 North Front Street. A long line of carriages accompanied the remains to the gravesite.

IMK's life. Immanuel Meister lived his life in Harrisburg as a good and caring citizen. What evidence we have indicates that he was held in high esteem and that he was sincerely concerned for the welfare of the people of Harrisburg. Unlike his business-aggressive brothers who left the hardware trade to pursue other commercial opportunities, IMK was content to spend his career in the hardware business. Hardware, church and family consumed his life. Given his quiet presence and his apparent aversion to the hard knocks and the heated controversies his brothers endured, he was content to live a subdued existence. While his brothers' activities were well covered in local newspapers, IMK received little press coverage. But perhaps it is unfair to compare him to his brothers. He lived a full and active life. His footprint is small, but he was an honest citizen who in his quiet approach to life benefitted those around him.

Addenda

Immanuel Meister Kelker and the Harrisburg Car Manufacturing Company. In May 1874, Immanuel Meister was elected president of the Harrisburg Car Manufacturing Company (*Harrisburg Telegraph*, May 13, 1874, 2). The company was founded in 1853 as the railroad-transport business was growing rapidly. It first produced freight cars but through the years of its existence (1853–1893) it manufactured passenger, mail, baggage, boxcars, cattle, platform, coal and handcars. In 1875, following the discovery of oil and its increasing use, the company produced tank cars. The car-manufacturing company was a major supplier to the railroad industry. In 1881, for example, it produced 3,402 cars and by the end of the year it had received orders for an additional 2,630.

Little is written about Mr. Kelker's time as president. He assumed the office at a time when the company was struggling due to the financial panic of 1873; it had laid off half its workers and was in debt. It did not begin to return to business health until the panic began to ease in 1876. [Harrisburg Car Company (midcontinent.org)] Harrisburg newspapers of that time provide no information about Mr. Kelker's activities with the company. All we know is that he was elected president in 1875, and it seems reasonable to speculate that he didn't last long because of the company's turmoil during that difficult period.

Henry Anthony Kelker:
Businessman, Community Leader

Henry Anthony Kelker (1825–1915) was born to Frederick and Catherine Fager Kelker at the family home at 9 South Front Street. He joined his brothers Rudolph Frederick and Immanuel Meister on Monday, December 16, 1825. He spent his life in Harrisburg as a contributor to his community, a businessman, real estate developer and an active member of his church. He was successful in all his undertakings. His most notable achievements were bringing city railway service to Harrisburg and with his brother Rudolph Frederick founding and developing the town of Steelton. He owned and built residential and commercial buildings in Harrisburg, was active in local politics and supported the Mozart society and other musical groups in Harrisburg. (*Harrisburg Telegraph*, Oct. 2, 1915, pp. 1, 9)

HAK, like his brothers before him, attended the Harrisburg Academy. In November 1842, he entered the preparatory department of Marshall College before its merger with Franklin College. He remained at Marshall until May 1846 when he returned to Harrisburg to set up a partnership with his brothers in the hardware business. After completion of the partnership arrangement, he returned to Marshall with the anticipation of finishing his degree, but when his mother became ill, he left school and returned to help with her care. After her death, on August 15, 1846, he decided to remain in Harrisburg where he embarked on his career with Rudolph Frederick and Immanuel Meister in the Kelker & Brothers firm.

HAK married Ellen Roberts on October 11, 1855, and they had nine children. Tragically, three of the children died before they were reached the age of two: Frederick Anthony, born in 1856; John Roberts, in 1858; and Rudolph Frederick, in 1868. The other six lived to adulthood: Mary Anna, born in 1861; Annie Roberts, in 1864; Henry Anthony, in 1867; Ellen, in 1874; Edith, in 1876; and Katherine, in 1880. All were baptized in the Reformed Salem Church and remained active members. (Kelker Family Record, p. 105) Henry Anthony was an active partner in the hardware firm. In 1851, when Rudolph Frederick retired from the firm, he and Immanuel Meister continued the firm as Kelker & Brother and moved operations from 9 South

Front Street to No. 17 on the southeast corner of Market Square. The business grew in reputation and profitability supplying the hardware needs of farmers, homebuilders and Harrisburg citizens. Then in 1878, Henry Anthony and Immanuel Meister dissolved the business. HAK disposed of a portion of his stock to Rudolph Frederick's sons, Luther Reily and William Anthony, who then operated their business at 6½ Market Square under the name Kelker Brothers. He left the remaining stock to Immanuel Meister, who with his sons George Beatty and Frederick reopened the old 9 South Front Street business as Kelker & Sons and located it at the east corner of Market Square. HAK did not return to the hardware business.

The wealth Henry Anthony derived from his time in the hardware business was not the major part of his net worth. Most of his riches came from his real estate investments in Harrisburg and Steelton and from his role in the City Passenger Railway Company, where he served as president. He faithfully followed his business mantra that investments in the community should benefit both the investor and the community, and his Harrisburg career did indeed benefit both. (Henry Anthony Kelker, Dauphin County, PA, USGenWeb Archives by JAWB)

The Pennsylvania Steel Company and the founding of Steelton. When Frederick Kelker died in 1857, he left two large parcels of land in Baldwin (that would become Steelton) to his sons Henry Anthony and Rudolph Frederick. When the new Pennsylvania Steel Company began its search for the site to build its steel mill (the country's first), Henry Anthony, always alert to a business opportunity, lobbied the steel company to build on the Kelker properties in Baldwin. He enlisted support from US Senator J. D. Cameron and other Dauphin County citizens. Their successful efforts brought the massive steelworks project to Baldwin, with the brothers profiting handsomely from the sale of their lands. Both used their proceeds to buy more Baldwin-area land that they divided into streets, roads and home lots and sold to their properties to arriving steel workers. HAK erected several business buildings there, including the first bank and the first post office. (*Harrisburg Telegraph*, Oct. 2, 1915, p. 9) The Kelker brothers suggested that the growing community should retain the name Baldwin, but the name Steelton prevailed—certainly a most appropriate designation. The brothers rejected a proposal to rename the village Kelkertown or Kelkerville. (*Harrisburg Telegraph*, Nov. 20, 1937, p. 13)

Note: See also the section above on Rudolph Frederick Kelker's role in Steelton's development in RFK's section of this chapter.

Henry Anthony Kelker and Harrisburg's railway transit system. With his brother Rudolph Frederick and three partners, HAK established, managed and expanded the first successful passenger-transit system in Harrisburg. Their company, the Harrisburg City Passenger Railway Company, operated horse-drawn rail service from 1874 to 1891 when it merged with the East Harrisburg Passenger Railway Company. The merger marked the end of horse-drawn cars and the beginning of electric-powered rail service.

The first Harrisburg railway service, the Harrisburg City Passenger Railroad Company, was established in 1861. During the Civil War, it transported soldiers between Camp Curtin, a Union Army encampment at Sixth and Maclay Streets, and the Pennsylvania Railroad Depot, nearly two miles. The company was not successful. It encountered financial difficulties, with lost ridership brought about by the war's end and the closing of Camp Curtin. Unable to find replacement financing and with no alternative, the company was put up for sale.

Henry Anthony, Rudolph Frederick and their partners established a partnership and on May 6, 1873 acquired the struggling company for $5,700. The company was incorporated with a very similar name, the Harrisburg City Passenger Railway Company. HAK became president, RFK became treasurer, and their partners Daniel Eppley and John A. Smith became vice president and secretary, respectively. The company's main office was set up in 1874 on the second floor of a building on South Second Street owned by Henry Kelker. Horse-drawn transit railcars began hauling passengers in 1874.

The new company began business during the 1873 depression and struggled in its early years. The purchase of an omnibus company that ran between Baldwin and Harrisburg helped by feeding passengers into the City Railway line, but financial challenges continued until 1876 when the depression eased. The company then operated profitably, but not without problems, until 1891. Legal struggles with the city over types of rails that could be laid and extension of rail lines, expenses from expanding rail service and expenditures on new equipment had to be dealt with.

In January 1885, City Railway Company stockholders approved the sale of $100,000 in stock to fund an extension of service to areas east of the Philadelphia & Reading Railroad. Allison Hill residents, who were not served by the plan, protested. The company's board responded with planning changes. But the company got diverted from making changes by a dispute with the city over the rail type to be used. In the meantime, Allison Hill residents, impatient for transit service, secured a charter on July 28, 1886 for a new company, the East Harrisburg Passenger Railway, that proceeded with a plan to electrify the new system. Horse transit continued while development proceeded, but in 1888, after successful test runs, electric cars began service on the Allison Hill/Steelton line on August 19. But after establishing electrified service, the East Harrisburg company ran into serious problems. On August 21, the *Harrisburg Telegraph* wrote (as referenced in Steinmetz and Cox, p. 13) "the heavy storm and washouts have left the East Harrisburg Railway in deplorable condition. Three cars are housed for repairs [...] Mud has been washed over the tracks and it is evident that the line should have been built higher [...]" Adding to construction and weather problems, the electrical motors and overhead lighting turned out to be inadequate. So, in April 1890, East Harrisburg Railway gave up on replacement operations and proceeded to build an entirely new electrification system.

Meanwhile, City Railway had been making plans for electrification, and in February 1890 it came up with an ambitious plan to add six new electrified-track extensions. In January 1891, the directors decided upon an electrical system and sought bids to erect overhead lights and secure electrical power from two Harrisburg electric companies, and then began a search for a site suitable for their power plant. But City Railway never carried out its electrification plans.

Merger plans began in 1889 when City Railway was asked by East Harrisburg Railway to enter discussions. Nothing happened until February 1891 when East Harrisburg proposed leasing City Railway for ninety-nine years. East Harrisburg's stockholders approved the deal by a wide margin, and the lease was signed on May 1, 1891.

One consequence of the merger was a dustup over the issue of Sunday service. East Harrisburg Railway had operated its transit service on Sundays from its beginnings. Harrisburg City Passenger Railway Company had not, most certainly because of the strongly held religious beliefs of Rudolph Frederick and Henry Anthony Kelker. They were supported in their opposition by the Ministerial Association of Harrisburg. RFK's view on the matter was certainly predictable. His opposition was expressed in 1888 to a reporter from the *Harrisburg STAR*. When asked if he could foresee the possibility of streetcars operating on Sunday, he emphatically replied, "As long as my name is Kelker, there is not, for we will obey the Lord rather than man. It would be cruel to man and the horses, and I for one would not remain in a company that ran their cars on Sunday." (Historical Society of Dauphin County Scrapbook Collection of Harrisburg newspapers, Z-2006) True to his word, Mr. Kelker resigned in 1891 when East Harrisburg prevailed, and Sunday service began on the newly leased City Railway lines.

Electric-powered transit served Harrisburg until the 1930s when streetcar service ended for good. There could still be some of the old City Railway rails under today's paved streets.

Note: This brief history of Henry Anthony Kelker and Harrisburg transit is taken largely from Steinmetz, R. H., and Cox, H. E. (1988, *Street Railways of Harrisburg*, Harold E. Cox, Forty Fort, Penn, pp. 5–17)

A fight to extend rail service to the community. During its existence City Railway fought a prolonged battle with Harrisburg city authorities over the company's right to lay track on city streets. HAK played a prominent role in the eighteen months of a back-and-forth legal struggle that began in March 1884 and finally ended with the company gaining the right to extend service on designated streets. The company argued that it had the right to extend track based on its charter that it acquired with its 1873 purchase of the original Harrisburg City Passenger Railway Company. The company's rights claim ran into direct conflict with a city ordinance passed on February 25, 1884 that prohibited any street obstruction, such as streetcar rails, unless approved by the city. The battle waged in the courts and the city councils and was extensively reported by the *Harrisburg Telegraph* and the *Harrisburg Daily Independent*. The long controversy that put Henry Anthony against the mayor and city attorneys gives us a glimpse into his character and how it was expressed in business dealings. He was steadfast throughout, adamant in his right to build on the city streets, persistent, bold, unyielding and righteous. He was ultimately successful, but it took those eighteen months of litigation and perseverance to resolve the issue in favor of City Railway. The company finally began laying track in September 1885 and began extended service two months later. Harrisburg at that time had reached a population near 35,000, so the expansion of railway service, when at last legally sanctioned and installed, was a significant beneficial upgrade of city services.

The controversy began at seven in the morning on Tuesday, April 1, 1884, when six City Railway workers arrived at Reily Street and began digging to lay rail ties. The mayor, who had been advised of the construction, arranged for the police to arrive at the same time. The police ordered the workers to stop but they kept digging and laying ties. The police began removing ties and filling in holes. Mayor Wilson then appeared with a summons and the company workers were taken into custody and delivered to a courthouse hearing where each was fined $25.

Near the end of the hearing, the company's lawyers, Mr. Gilbert and Mr. McCarrell, arrived and asked for the case to be reopened, and it was scheduled for 2:20 that afternoon in the mayor's office. Word must have spread fast because the office was filled with anxious and interested Harrisburg citizens. After statements were made by railway-company lawyers and the city's representatives, Solicitor Hargest and lawyer J. M. Wiestling, it was agreed that the information before the hearing was insufficient to address the issue fairly, so a hearing was scheduled for the next Monday at two in the afternoon. (*Harrisburg Daily Independent*, April 1, 1884, p. 1) At the Monday meeting HAK and Samuel Reed, the company's superintendent, were examined. Company lawyers then put forth a plea that the company had been organized before the adoption of the February 1884 city ordinance and that the ordinance was not valid because it was "unreasonable and unconstitutional." City lawyers claimed that the mayor had nothing to do with the validity of the ordinance. All he had to do was decide if it had been violated. Mayor Wilson rejected the company's plea based on what he declared was the only question at issue, and found the six defendants guilty, each of them subject to the $25 fine:

> […] the fact that the ordinance was violated as charged is fully proven and the judgement is as follows, viz.: that the Harrisburg City Passenger Railway Company, [he lists the six fined worker's names] are and each of them are [sic] adjudged guilty of violation of the ordinance of the city of Harrisburg entitled "An ordinance regulating to occupancy of the highways of the city of Harrisburg, approved February 25, 1884, and the said defendants and each of them, viz., the Harrisburg City Passenger Railway Company, [the six defendants are again listed by name] fined in the sum of twenty-five dollars.

Company lawyers exclaimed surprise that the issue was so abruptly disposed of, leaving them no chance to present other evidence, and a lively discussion followed. (*Harrisburg Daily Independent*, April 8, 1884, p. 1)

On April 14, the court granted the company the right to appeal the mayor's decision, and the company put up bail to cover court costs and fines should it lose its case. (*Harrisburg Daily Independent*, April 15, 1884, p. 4) On the evening of April 14, the company served Mayor Wilson with a writ of certiorari, that is, a plea to place the record before the court in the case pending against the company. (*Harrisburg Telegraph*, April 16, 1884, p. 4) On April 17, the *Harrisburg Telegraph* (April 17, 1884, p. 1) published an interview with HAK in which he defended the company's use of its charter to lay tracks on city streets without permission from the city: "It is the wish of the company to exercise the right which its charter gives it in such a way as to disturb the public streets and interfere with travel no more than is absolutely for the constructing of a street passenger railway." The interviewer summed up his impression of HAK's words: "Mr. Kelker talked freely and without hesitation, and evinced great sincerity in his desire to have the question of the rights of the city and company decided by the courts."

The next day's *Harrisburg Telegraph* (April 18, 1884, p. 1) published an interview with the city's attorney, J. M. Wiestling. In response to the reporter's question, "What is the real ground of controversy between the city and the company?" Mr. Wiestling replied:

> It is correctly set forth for the president of the company in his interview, in which he denies the right of the city authorities to be consulted as the manner of extending their lines, claiming the right that under their charter they have authority to construct their lines of railway and occupy any of the streets of Harrisburg, without regard to any regulations of the city. A recognition by the city of such arbitrary and unrestricted powers by a private corporation upon its own streets would be a virtual surrender of its own chartered privileges.

Following much discussion over the rights of the company and those of the city, the issue was taken up by the court in June 1884. (*Harrisburg Telegraph*, June 30, 1884, p. 40) Presiding Judge Simonton rendered his opinion on October 16. He fully sustained the city's argument that it had the right to restrain the City Passenger Railway Company from constructing rail lines on Harrisburg streets. (*Harrisburg Daily Independent*, Oct. 6, 1884, When company attorney McCarrell was asked if the company would appeal the decision, he answered: "I don't think so… although I have not consulted with the directors. I see no reason to appeal. The opinion gives us virtually all we contended for. I say distinctly that the ordinances are not prohibitory, and all we must do is submit to Councils our plans and profiles for approval." When asked what the company might do if the councils did not approve, McCarrell responded: "Then we will go into Court and ask for a mandamus to compel them to do so. Councils cannot prohibit us from occupying such streets as we select providing we submit our plans, as I before stated to them. This the opinion taken by the Court." (*Harrisburg Daily Independent*, Oct. 31, 1884, p. 1)

Mayor Wilson, in his annual message presented on January 13, 1885, included these remarks on the City Railway affair:

> On the first day of April last the company regardless of the ordinances and the warning notices served upon them, proceeded to lay tracks upon Riley [sic] street, whereupon all the parties engaged in said work were promptly arrested, a hearing had, and a penalty imposed. This action on the part of the Mayor was carried by the company into the court upon a writ of certiorari. The case, which attracted great attention throughout the Commonwealth, because of the important questions involved, was ably conducted by City Solicitor Hargest and Joshua M. Wiestling, esq., on behalf of the city. The court in elaborate opinion rendered October 16, affirmed the judgment of the Mayor upon every point at issue and thus secured to the city the rights to all reasonable control of its highways. This decision has been received with the highest gratification by the public, securing, as it does, rights of almost incalculable value in the future progress of the city. (*Harrisburg Daily Independent*, Jan. 13, 1885, p. 1)

On March 26, 1885, a *Harrisburg Telegraph* reporter visited the City Railway office seeking information on the status of the company's ongoing fight with the city. He was told by the treasurer, Rudolph Frederick Kelker, that the matter remained at a standstill and "that the matter would remain in that condition until the councils did something." RFK was referring to a pending ordinance that would give the Highway Committee full authority to grant street-railway permits. Should that ordinance pass, the company would ask permission to extend the line up Second Street and beyond. (*Harrisburg Telegraph*, March 26, 1885, p. 4)

On April 28, at a meeting of the Common Council, a petition was read from City Railway. The document first recounted the history of the litigation and the court's October 1884 decision, and then asked council to pass an ordinance granting the company the right to extend rail construction on certain designated streets. The company said it would accept an obligation to finish the work within twelve months.

At an April 29 meeting of the Highway Committee, company lawyers McCarrell and Gilbert made a plea for construction rights, but the committee failed to approve the plea by a vote of seven to five. At the same meeting a new railway company, the People's Railway, was asking permission to build on Harrisburg streets. Its request to the Highway Committee was approved by a vive-voce vote. (*Harrisburg Daily Independent*, April 30, 1885, p. 1) The appearance of competition placed more pressure on City Railway to move forward with construction of new track. But the competition never materialized. The new entity never began operations, probably for its inability to secure financing. (Steinmetz and Cox, p. 9) Finally, at the June 9 meeting of the Select Council, City Railway was granted privileges to extend rails on certain streets. (*Harrisburg Telegraph*, June 9, 1885, p. 4) The company's request for further extensions was defeated by the council on July 27. But at a meeting of the Common Council on August 10, Councilman Weikert moved to reconsider City Railway's ordinance that was defeated at the July 27 meeting. Weikert said that he made the motion because he believed that People's Railway did not intend to proceed while City Railway was anxious to proceed. (*Harrisburg Daily Independent*, Aug. 11, 1885, p. 4)

On August 31, an amended proposed extension of City Railway tracks was approved in both the Select and Common Council branches. Section 5 of the agreement stated that the extension was to be completed in twelve months. (*Harrisburg Telegraph*, Sept. 1, 1885, p. 4) On September 3, RFK said that work would soon begin but that it would take ten days to two weeks to get delivery of construction material. (*Harrisburg Daily Independent*, Sept. 3, 1885, p. 4) On September 21, the Select and Common branches of the City Council extended permission for City Railway to further extend its lines. Ongoing construction would terminate at Fourth and Market. The new extension continued the track on South Street to Chestnut and beyond. (*Harrisburg Telegraph*, Sept. 22, 1885, p. 1) On November 26, cars began running on the extended lines. (*Harrisburg Daily Independent*, Nov. 27, 1885, p. 4)

So, Henry Anthony and his company finally succeeded. It took eighteen months, many court sessions, legal fees and patience, but City Railway at last got its extensions. The company continued service until 1891 when its operation was leased to East Harrisburg Railway. Rudolph Frederick Kelker then left the company over the issue of Sunday service, but Henry Anthony remained president until his death, in 1915.

The Henry Anthony Kelker family and music. Henry Anthony was a lover of music and a benefactor of musical events in Harrisburg. He shared his love of music with his wife, Ellen, and their son Henry Anthony Kelker Jr., who served as treasurer of the Mozart society in 1884 (*Harrisburg Daily Independent*, Sept. 1, 1884, p. 4) and as its president in 1885 (*Harrisburg Daily Independent*, Sept. 22, 1885, p. 4). Ellen was an active participant but by virtue of her gender was relegated to less responsible duties such as serving as a patroness at musical events, a role she played when distinguished musicians visited Harrisburg. She was one of many patronesses when the Franklin & Marshall College Glee and Mandolin clubs performed in Harrisburg on February 14, 1890. (*Harrisburg Telegraph*, Feb. 11, 1890, p. 1) The family's love of music is shown in a small item that appeared in the *Harrisburg Daily Independent* (Sept. 18, 1886, p. 4), reporting that HAK, Ellen and one of their daughters visited Worcester, Massachusetts, in September 1886, to attend a music festival. That they made the effort to travel 350 miles at a time when transportation was limited to horse-drawn vehicles and slow trains indicates their devotion to music.

Henry A. Kelker Jr. carried on the family's musical tradition as an active participant in Harrisburg's music scene. Unlike his parents he performed in musical productions and lent his tenor voice to numerous choral productions. He sang in a Lenten Cantata at the Market Square Church in 1900 (*Harrisburg Telegraph*, April 9, 1900, p. 1) and sang the tenor part in a *Messiah* performance in 1904. (*Harrisburg Daily Independent*, Jan. 11, 1904, p. 1) The local newspapers praised his efforts. In addition to his performances, HAK Jr. enriched the Harrisburg scene as chairman of the board of governors of the choral society (*Harrisburg Telegraph*, Nov. 5, 1915, p. 8) and as choir director of the Madrigal Club when it was formed in 1915. (*Harrisburg Daily Independent*, Dec. 15, 1915, p. 3)

Deaths of Ellen and Katherine. In February 1893, Ellen Roberts Kelker died at fifty-seven from an illness that had persisted for a year. She was well regarded for her church and charitable work, as noted in her obituary in the *Harrisburg Telegraph* (Feb. 8, 1893, p. 1). "She was a devoted Christian woman, and always engaged in active church and charitable work. She was of a most amiable and cheerful disposition and will be sadly missed in the home circle." Her death left Henry Anthony a widower for the last twenty-two years of his life.

In a stunning blow to his family, Henry Anthony and Ellen's youngest child, Katharine, died at nineteen of "inflammatory rheumatism" on December 14, 1900. Katherine was the fourth child in the family to die, following her three infant siblings' deaths. She was a bright and active young woman who pursued an active social life and was very involved in her Market Square Presbyterian Church and in presenting concerts with the Wednesday Club, a Harrisburg musical society. Her obituary notes that she was "one of the best liked among the younger people." (*Harrisburg Telegraph*, Dec. 15, 1900, p. 1) The loss must have been a crushing blow to Henry Anthony just seven years after Ellen's death.

Henry Anthony Kelker, his life. Henry Anthony and Rudolph Frederick lived lives cast in the mold of their father's life with their devotion to church, community, charity and business. Frederick had set the pattern with his 1805 move to Harrisburg, his hardware business and his real estate dealings. Following in those footsteps, Rudolph Frederick left the biggest footprint with his seemingly endless involvement in church, community, charity and business. Henry Anthony directed his energies largely toward business while at the same time serving his community with distinction.

HAK's legacy, while not as rich as RFK's, is nonetheless significant. In his role as president of the City Railway he brought public transportation to a growing Harrisburg, and along with Rudolph Frederick he established Steelton. He was an active participant in organizations that enriched the life of Harrisburg from the YMCA to the German Society, the Salem Reformed Church, musical societies, numerous charities and others. He also left a large footprint.

Chapter 5 continues with the lives of Rudolph Frederick and Mary Ann Reily Kelker's two sons, Luther Reily and William Anthony.

Addenda
Henry Anthony Kelker

HAK's wealth began with what he inherited from his father and from what he gained from his real estate dealings. Below is a trivial newspaper note about one of his newly built Front Street properties, and a story about a US flag and a little favor for Pennsylvania's Civil War-time governor, Andrew Gregg Curtin.

Mischief in one of Henry Anthony Kelker's Front Street buildings.

> Several small boys gained an entrance to the second story of the new houses being erected by Henry A. Kelker on South Front street at noon to-day, and when a canal boat passed they threw stones at the boatmen.

Harrisburg Telegraph, Nov. 30, 1891, p. 1

Henry Anthony returns Governor Curtin's beloved lost flag.

> Back of the presentation of the flag of ex-Governor Andrew G. Curtin to the Bellefonte post of the G. A. R. by his family the other day is an interesting story of how the Curtin flag came to return to the ownership of the war governor. It seems that when Governor Curtin's term ended he removed most of his goods from the South Second street house, which was for a number of years afterward the home of the late C. A. Spicer, and sold the rest. In some way the fine flag which was always flown from the Executive Mansion on high days and holidays was sold along with the rest. The flag came into the possession of Henry A. Kelker, who, upon meeting Governor Curtin some years after, mentioned the fact. The war governor remarked that he had always regretted the fact that the flag had been disposed of at the sale and very gratefully accepted it when Mr. Kelker offered it to him. The flag was flown many times after that from the Curtin home and when the war governor died it is said to have covered his casket.

Harrisburg Telegraph, July 6, 1915, p.1

CHAPTER 5

Rudolph Frederick and Mary Anne Reily Kelker's Sons
Luther Reily and William Anthony

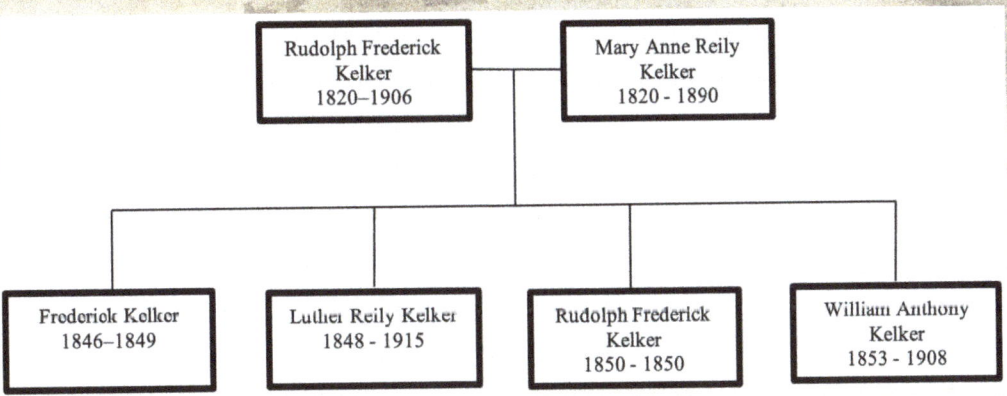

Luther Reily Kelker: Businessman, Historian

Photo from a pentaptych, property of Norman Kelker.

Luther Reily Kelker was born in the family home at 9 Front Street, just like his father and uncles. He spent his entire life in Harrisburg where he became a successful businessman, historian and an active contributor to his community and his church. He was educated in Harrisburg public schools and at Professor Seiler's Academy where he graduated in 1866. LRK did not attend college but went on to a successful business career in real estate, insurance and hardware. He also served as the first state archivist of Pennsylvania. (Kelker, L. R., 1907, *History of Dauphin County, Pennsylvania*, Lewis Publishing Co., New York, Chicago, Vol. I, p. 42; this short LRK biography is from his three-volume county history and thus can be considered autobiography) He married Agnes Keyes Pearsol in 1874 and they had two sons and a daughter, Rudolph Frederick Kelker Jr. who became a traffic engineer and directed construction of Chicago's first subway line; John Pearsol Kelker, who became a thief; and Mary Reily Kelker Sturges, who became a housewife and mother. LRK, like his father, was a shrewd and successful businessman; also, like his father, he accumulated significant wealth. When ill health forced him to retire from his hardware business in 1892, he used his recovery time to pursue his interest in Pennsylvania's pre-Revolutionary War history. Praise for his work was acknowledged by Pennsylvania Governor Samuel W. Pennypacker, who in 1903 appointed him the first chief of Pennsylvania's Division of Records. This position gave him access to a rich archive collection that he used in compiling his massive three-volume *History of Dauphin County* in 1907. He died on October 24, 1915. (*Harrisburg Telegraph*, Oct. 25, 1915, p. 1) Numerous obituaries praised his life.

Luther Reily Kelker as a young man. Photo from The Historical Society of Dauphin County's Kelker Archive Collection AL59

Young LRK's brush with history: Abraham Lincoln's Funeral Cortege.

Luther Reily Kelker was seventeen years old and a student at Professor Seiler's Academy when President Abraham Lincoln was assassinated on April 14, 1865. The country paid an extended tribute to the fallen president that included a long slow funeral procession that traveled by rail from Washington to Springfield, Illinois. The train moved at a pace never exceeding twenty miles per hour, and it retraced the path Lincoln took four years earlier when he traveled from Springfield to Washington for his first inauguration. The funeral cortege left the nation's capital at eight in the morning on a wet April 21st and arrived in Baltimore at ten. There the presidential coffin was removed and taken to the Merchant's Exchange Building for three hours of viewing. The train then left Baltimore for the fifty-eight-mile trip to Harrisburg, making short stops along the way. At New Freedom, Pennsylvania, just over the border from Maryland, Pennsylvania Governor Andrew Gregg Curtin and his party joined the funeral train. Governor Curtin oversaw arrangements for the state's observance of the dead president, and in preparation for the Harrisburg visit, he notified every Harrisburg minister two days before the event. (*Harrisburg Telegraph*, Feb. 12, 1909, p. 9)

> The remains of the murdered patriot Abraham Lincoln, President of the United States, will arrive in this city on Friday evening next on their way to the place of internment in Illinois. They will come from Baltimore to Harrisburg—thence will, on Saturday, be conveyed to Philadelphia, and thence, on Monday morning to New York. I shall meet them at the State line, and take charge of them while in the Commonwealth. I recommend that all business be suspended during the passage through this State, and that the local authorities and people everywhere, join the State authorities heartily in paying honor to the memory of the martyred statesman, who has fallen victim to the savage treason of assassins.
>
> By the Governor,
>
> A. G. Curtin
>
> Secretary of the Commonwealth,
>
> Eli Slifer.

The train arrived in Harrisburg just after eight in the evening. The coffin was taken to the Pennsylvania House of Representatives and public viewing began soon after at 9:30 pm and continued until ten the next morning. A long line of forty thousand people formed along the streets to observe the coffin before it was returned to the train, which then set off for Philadelphia where it arrived at the Broad Street Station at 4:30 in the afternoon (Abraham Lincoln's Assassination. (https://rogerjnorton.com/Lincoln51.html)

Lincoln's funeral train at Harrisburg's railway station. Photo: http://www.post-gazette.com/ news/ nation/2015/04/19/Harrisburg-to-observe-Lincoln-funeral-train-on-Tuesday/stories/201504190067.

Citizens of Harrisburg and its surroundings, like most Northerners, were stunned by Lincoln's assassination, and reacted by lining the city streets as his coffin was transported to and from the capitol building. Young Luther Reily joined in the mourning by marching to the capitol building with his fellow YMCA members and the huge throng of Harrisburg citizens, and he waited in the long line to observe the president's body. Forty-four years after the assassination and six years before his own death, he recounted his experience to the *Harrisburg Telegraph*. (Feb. 12, 1909, p. 9)

> The night of Friday, April 21, was one of the worst in the city. It had rained all day and the storm continued without abatement during the evening. The funeral train backed alongside the old Pennsylvania station between 7:30 and 8 o'clock in the evening, and the President's remains were immediately transferred to a waiting hearse.
>
> The city was crowded with thousands of people from the surrounding districts. The news that the body would be placed in state at the Capitol had spread broadcast and many took this opportunity for their last view of the well-known countenance. In his honor all the organizations of the city had turned out in a body: fire companies, secret societies and military orders alike determined to pay their respect to the martyr.

The hearse proceeded out Market street to Market Square and the marching bodies fell in line following it. We (the Y.M.C.A.) were some distance in the rear. The sewer along Market Square had become clogged and in some places we had to wade through a foot and a half of water.

The cortege turned up to second street to State and in State to the Capitol. Here all arrangements had been completed to receive the body. The Speaker's desk in the House of Representatives had been draped and a somber black cloud of folded cloth covered everything in the vicinity. Directly above the dais upon which the body was to rest was a painting of the President.

The body was laid in state and shortly afterward commenced the long, seemingly unending, line of citizens, who viewed the remains. Undeterred by the storm, the residents of Harrisburg and vicinity turned out *en masse*.

The crowd entered by the main doors into the rotunda. Here a guard of officers and soldiers formed them into two lines and thus they proceeded down the central aisle in the House of Representatives. At the bier the lines divided, one passing to the left and the other to the right of the coffin. A guard of soldiers surrounded the remains. The line was not allowed to stop, but, like a long snake, crawled slowly along. As the lines divided, they passed on either side of the Speaker's chair to the windows in the rear of the room. From these windows broad wooden steps had been erected to the ground and down these the people passed.

Far into the night the vast line of mourners continued. The next morning also the crowd was large and continued so until preparations were made about noon to convey the remains to Philadelphia. The manner of departure was similar to the arrival and the pleasant homely face of Abraham Lincoln, the martyred President, disappeared for all time from the sight of the citizens of Harrisburg.

In 2015, a hundred and fifty years after President Lincoln's body passed through Harrisburg, the Historical Society of Dauphin County held a program to commemorate that event. An announcement for the commemoration contained this statement: "On April 22, 1865, the tremendous outpouring of emotion from Pennsylvanians generated the hushed and reverent event. Their voices were silent! We speak for them now!"

Luther Reily Kelker, Businessman . Like his father, uncles and grandfather, LRK was a successful businessman. And, like them, his career began in the hardware business. As young men he and his brother William Anthony were employed in the Kelker & Brother hardware store owned by their uncles Henry Anthony and Immanuel Meister. That business, located at the southeast corner of Market Square, was dissolved in 1878 and Henry Anthony disposed of his stock to his two nephews and to his brother, who with his sons George Beatty and Frederick opened a new hardware business, Kelker & Sons, at the same location. LRK and William Anthony then operated Kelker Brothers, a second hardware business at 6½ Market Square. William Anthony left the business in 1883 and LRK continued operations as the sole owner. He renamed the business Luther R. Kelker and ran it on Market Square until 1892 when he became ill and was forced to retire at forty-eight.

An 1882 photo of a circus parade passing the Luther R. Kelker Hardware store on Market Square. Photo: courtesy of Erik Fasik.

The Luther R. Kelker firm dealt in a wide variety of goods. Searching through copies of newspapers of that period reveals advertisements for almost anything a farmer, homebuilder, bicyclist, winter-sports enthusiast or almost anyone would want or need, from building supplies to saddlers' and coach hardware, mechanics' tools, paints, oils, glass, iron, steel and other merchandise. (*Harrisburg Daily Independent*, April 11, 1883, p. 4) An advertisement from the *Harrisburg Daily Independent* (Nov. 23, 1888, p. 2; see below) gives an idea of the broad inventory and an emphasis on bicycles.

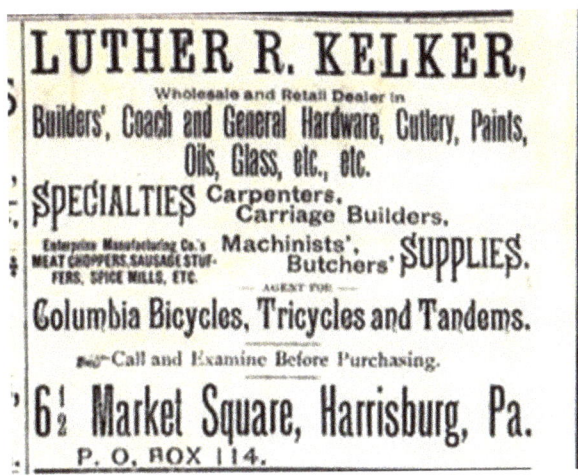

Bicycles and Toboggans. LRK jumped into the "wheeling" market when bicycling was becoming popular, and into the winter-sports market when sliding down snowy hills became the rage. He sold bicycles in the summer and skates, sleds and toboggans in the winter. An article from the *Harrisburg Telegraph* (April 23, 1890, p. 4) shows his marketing of bicycles.

> Mr. Luther R. Kelker [...] informed a Telegraph representative that this is the biggest bicycle season he has ever had, and the demand increases every day. There is no cause for special wonder in this because Mr. Kelker keeps the best bicycles on the market, and the rule in purchasing a bicycle is—"get the best." Mr. Kelker is agent for the Pope manufacturing company and numerous other manufacturers, and has bicycles, safety and high wheel, for from $12 to $200 each, singles and tandems. Of the safety wheels he has a very large stock, in fact his assortment of wheels cannot be excelled outside of New York and Philadelphia, and he invites people to visit his place just to see what a magnificent lot of machines he has. One side of the big room is lined up with handsome bicycles like horses in their stalls. Particular attention is paid to ladies' safety bicycles of the Columbia make, which are as finely finished as those for gentlemen, and are perfect beauties. There is also a large stock of wheels for little folks [...]

A cynical reader might wonder if LRK planted the article or even wrote it himself. But there can be little debate about his smart business sense and his readiness for having supplies to meet demand. The 1885 development of the safety bicycle revolutionized cycling with its chain drive, equal-sized wheels and with the front wheel more easy to steer and free of pedals. On their way out were the oversized front-wheel boneshakers with pedals on the big front wheel (History of the Bicycle, Wikipedia). Luther Reily rode that wheeling wave and promoted sales by organizing a wheel club of biking enthusiasts who made excursions to distant places (see photo below).

Harrisburg Wheel Club, circa 1886 to 1888, at Natural Bridge, Virginia. Photo from the Historical Society of Dauphin County.

LRK was also an active participant in the cycling craze. And why not—his participation in the Harrisburg Wheel Club was good for sales, and he probably enjoyed it. In August 1892, he and his sons Rudolph Frederick Jr. and John Pearsol took a bicycle tour of Lebanon and Bucks Counties. (*Harrisburg Telegraph*, Aug, 25, 1892, p. 1) The *Harrisburg Telegraph* (July 2, 1891, p. 1) reported that he was to ride with about forty fellow Wheel Club members to Hagerstown to participate in a Fourth of July meet. He was elected secretary and treasurer of the Wheel Club in 1886 (*Harrisburg Daily Independent*, Dec. 24, 1886, p. 4) and president in 1890 (*Harrisburg Daily Independent*, July 9, 1890, p. 4). "Wheel Notes," an article in the *Harrisburg Telegraph* (Sept. 18, 1886, p. 6), gives us an idea of the city's cycling scene at that time. A series of separate comments relates that:

The long-talked of run to Lebanon which was to have been taken to-day by the Harrisburg Wheel Club was postponed on account of rain.

Mr. Henry Kelker is a believer in the healthful results of wheeling. He purchased three tricycles last week, one for each of his daughters.

Mr. James McCormick received his tandem tricycle this week from the factory, where it had been sent for repairs.

The number of wheelmen is steadily growing.

Keen to the market year-round, LRK also focused his sales efforts on winter-sports items. When a toboggan slide was built in Harrisburg, he was ready with a supply of toboggans, and when another was proposed for Lebanon, he got the contract to build it. (*Harrisburg Telegraph*, Jan. 1, 1887, p. 6) His winter inventory included a large supply of toboggans, sleds and skates.

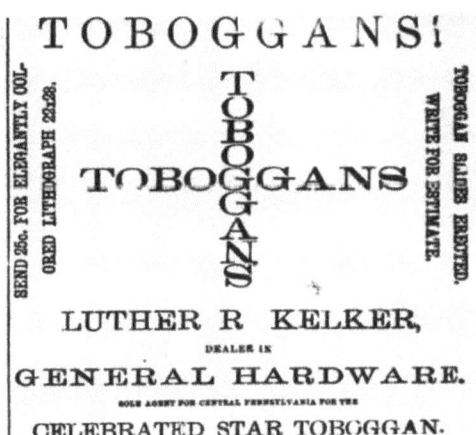

Toboggans for sale—and LRK will build the slide. *Harrisburg Telegraph*, Feb, 16, 1887, p. 4.

In December 1886, work began on a toboggan slide at Third and Reily Streets. A group of "men interested in the enterprise," actually stockholders, met on December 23 at LRK's hardware store to hear a report and "to transact other important business." (*Harrisburg Telegraph*, Dec. 22, 1886, p. 1) LRK was elected secretary and treasurer. The name chosen for the association was Harrisburg Toboggan Club. Rates for single rides, coupons and season tickets were established, and it was reported that twenty toboggans had been ordered. The article describes the slide's design:

They will be of the latest and improved style, cushioned for comfort and strong for safety. The slides or chutes will be divided, thus rendering it impossible for collisions to occur. In case the fall of snow is scant, an ice track will be made and kept in condition by frequent flooding. A loaded toboggan over such a surface and at the angle upon which the regulation slide is constructed, will attain a marvelous rate of speed, which in the majority of instances, and with all conditions favorable, *reaches a mile a minute*. All Harrisburg is waiting to take a slide. [Italics added.]

We can only imagine what it would be like to speed downhill on a crowded toboggan at sixty miles per hour.

Luther Reily Kelker, Historian. LRK's hardware career came to an end when he became ill and was forced to close his business at age forty-eight. While recuperating he used his time to pursue his interest in early America before independence. Recognition of his research efforts led to his appointment as the first Pennsylvania State Archivist. He began a new life.

LRK's illness that ended his career in commerce in 1892 turned out to be a most fortunate turn for him and for Pennsylvania. His recovery period afforded him time to pursue his lifelong interest in history, and he soon acquired a reputation for his work on early Pennsylvania history. He was asked by the state to examine some long-ignored archives, some of them stored in the capitol building for more than a century. A historian from the American Historical Association who studied LRK's work on the documents "warmly praised his systematic and thorough methods." With his reputation growing, his work was brought to the attention of Pennsylvania's governor, Samuel W. Pennypacker, who established the Division of Public Records at the state library in 1903 and appointed LRK its first superintendent. The new entity was the first of its kind, and according to the *Harrisburg Telegraph* (Oct. 28, 1915, p. 7) it "attracted considerable attention from other commonwealths and was highly praised by scholars and commended" by the state librarian. After establishing and organizing the new entity, he continued what was to become a very productive second career, now aided by his facilitated access to historical records. His success was impressive. He collaborated with other historians in the editing of twenty-two volumes of Pennsylvania archives while developing Pennsylvania's Division of Public Records as a recognized, authoritative source on government, business and family histories of colonial America. He deciphered and made available many old records, some of which greatly aided counties in establishing their history, with others used to establish boundary lines.

Among other valuable records that he and his staff published were muster rolls of soldiers from the French and Indian Wars, lists of early colonial inhabitants, the Whisky Rebellion, the Revolutionary War, the War of 1812 and others. (*Harrisburg Telegraph*, Oct. 28, 1915, p. 7; Kelker, L. R., *History of Dauphin County*, Vol. 3, pp. 42a–42f)

Mr. Kelker's best-known historical work is his three-volume, 1,500-page *History of Dauphin County* (1907). It contains biographies of prominent citizens, lists of village, town, city and county officials, and histories from the earliest settlers up to the time of publication. It serves as a key resource for historians.

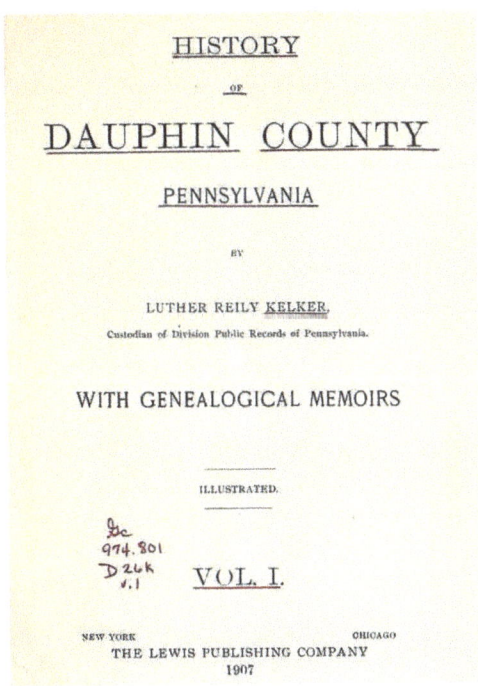

History of Dauphin County, Vol. 1

LRK accused of lying and conspiracy. I find it difficult to understand how someone as highly principled as Luther Reily Kelker could find himself answering to charges of jury tampering and conspiracy. But it happened. Even more curious is that the accusation came from a lawyer representing a prominent, respected Methodist minister. It all had to do with spending practices of the state government, an 1897 fire that destroyed the Pennsylvania State Capitol building and accusations by the Reverend Silas Comfort Swallow (1839–1930).

Dr. Silas Comfort Swallow: https://images.fineartamerica.com/images-medium-large/silas-swallow-1839–1930-granger.jpg

Reverend Dr. Swallow was by any measure a colorful character: religious, proud, unflinchingly righteous, stubborn, fearless, outspoken and controversial. Raised on a backwoods farm in northeastern Pennsylvania by devout Methodist parents, he rose to high office in his church and ran for president as the 1904 nominee of the Prohibition Party. Swallow's career began not in religious service but in the secular practice of law. He made his start as an employee in a Wilkes Barre attorney's office. But his strong and unshakable religious faith ("Woe is me, if I obey not the call") led to a path to the ministry. In 1860. Swallow was working as a preacher and as a teacher at a country school near Hazelton, Pennsylvania. But when school closed for the year, he moved on to Binghamton, New York, where he studied at Binghamton Seminary and continued to preach. His natural talent for public speaking lent forcefulness and conviction to his sermons as he railed for his three favorite causes: women's suffrage, prohibition and abolition of slavery. As a sign of his commitment to abolition, Swallow joined the Union Army in 1862, where he performed ministerial duties. Following the war he served at numerous churches, and in 1888 he was awarded a Doctor of Divinity degree from Taylor University in Upland, Indiana. (Steinmetz Sr., R. H., 1885, Silas C Swallow: Reformer,

Cumberland County History, vol. II, no. 2, pp. 17–20) Thereafter he was almost always addressed as Dr. Swallow.

Swallow's commitment to the elimination of alcoholic drink, aided by his commanding and persuasive oratory, gained him a leading role in the prohibition movement. He is probably most remembered today for his unsuccessful political campaigns. He ran on the Prohibition Party's 1897 ticket for Pennsylvania state treasurer, for governor in 1898 and 1902 and as candidate for president in 1904 against Republican Teddy Roosevelt and Democrat Alton B. Parker. He never received more than 16 percent of these votes, and in his presidential bid he won only 1.9 percent. (Our Campaigns—Candidate—Silas C. Swallow)

Dr. Swallow's campaign pin, Prohibition Party Presidential candidate, 1904 campaign button, From the HSDC collection.

Swallow's fearlessness, forcefulness and irascibility may never have been more on full display than in 1897 when, through his attorney, he made accusations of graft and bribery against state officials and, through his attorney, accused Luther Reily Kelker of conspiracy and witness tampering. It began on February 24 when the *Pennsylvania Methodist*, the organ of the Central Pennsylvania Methodist Conference—Swallow was its editor—published an editorial accusing statehouse officials of theft and of responsibility for the February 2nd fire that destroyed the capitol building. The accusations set off a firestorm, and every newspaper in central Pennsylvania and many beyond printed front-page articles. It very much appears that Swallow, as the paper's editor, wrote the piece, although he never acknowledged doing so, claiming that it was dictated to him.

In the article, he referred anonymously to the source—most likely Swallow himself—as "A resident of Harrisburg who is responsible for what he says." And he then went on to list the accusations, claiming that fees were paid from the state treasury for services that were not carried out, that people performing services for the state were forced to sign receipts for "two, three and even four times as much money as they were actually paid," that materials furnished for the Soldiers' Orphan Schools cost the state eight times their value, and that the state lost "many thousands of dollars" in materials, alterations and repair of capitol buildings due to a rigged system of competitive bidding. His most shocking claim, though, was that criminal intent was responsible for the 1897 fire that leveled the state capitol building.

> That the burning of the capitol building by which the state lost over one million dollars-worth of valuable property, if at all accidental was also in a sense incidental. That the possibilities and even probabilities of a fire had been for some time discussed by employees of the state, and that it was a logical sequence of having exhausted excuses for expending public money. And further that there is convincing evidence of criminal carelessness and neglect on the part of the state house custodians, and, presumptive evidence of criminal intent. (From the editorial in the *Pennsylvania Methodist*, reported in the *Daily News*, Mount Caramel, Pa., Feb. 24, 1897, p. 1)

Swallow claimed that he had received damning information from sources he would name only after the legislature appointed a committee of twenty-five mayors and public officials to carry out an investigation, something the legislature refused to do. (*Daily News*, Mount Caramel, Pa., Feb. 24, 1897, p. 1)

His accusations brought immediate and resounding blowback from the accused parties. On Thursday, February 25, the day after the Daily News article appeared, enraged state officials met in the executive chamber to discuss legal action against Swallow. Among those present were Gov. Daniel Hartman Hastings, Auditor General Mylin, Treasurer Haywood, Capt. J. C. Delaney, Superintendent of Buildings and Grounds, Gen. Thomas J. Stewart, formerly on the Soldiers' Orphan School Commission, and two attorneys. The matter was discussed, and at a meeting the following day, two warrants were issued for Swallow's arrest. (*Harrisburg Telegraph*, Feb. 26, 1897, p. 1)

Swallow was taken into custody, paid $500 bail for each of the two charges and was ordered to appear for a hearing the next Tuesday evening. However, he waived the hearing appearance, and the case went directly to trial. After a long parade of witnesses, the jury was charged on March 25, the day LRK was put on the stand. He had been called to testify earlier but had unsuccessfully pleaded to be excused due to other commitments. But the day before he was to appear as a witness, he read in the *Harrisburg Daily*

Independent that one of Dr. Swallow's attorneys made the accusation that "Mr. Luther R. Kelker had been tampered with." Infuriated, he immediately sent a letter to John W. Simonton, the presiding judge:

Harrisburg, Pa., March 24, 1897

To the Honorable John W. Simonton,

President [sic] Judge

Dear Sir:

On reading the Star-Independent of this evening the account of the libel case now being tried before your honor, I was greatly surprised to find stated therein the E. W. Jackson, esq., one of the attorneys for the defendant announced to the court that as a witness in the case "Mr. Luther R. Kelker had been tampered with." It is due to myself, as well as to all concerned, that I should declare any such statement, whether made by Mr. Jackson or any other person, as absolutely untrue, and my deep regret that Mr. Jackson should either of his own volition or at the instigation of any other person make an assertion so utterly devoid of truth.

Yours with profound respect,

Luther R. Kelker

The matter was brought up early on the last day of the trial, March 25, when one of the prosecuting attorneys asked that the charge against Mr. Kelker be examined. The *Harrisburg Daily Independent* (March 25, 1897, p. 1) reported on the proceedings:

At the opening of today's session Mr. Graham [an attorney for the prosecution] informed the court that he and his colleagues decided that the Kelker matter be inquired into. Mr. Kelker was called and the defence [sic] was asked if they had any questions to ask the witness. Mr. Jackson [an attorney for the defense] said that the prosecution called him and it should go on ahead. Mr. Murray [for the prosecution] then asked Mr. Kelker when he was subpoenaed. He said about the 15th of March. He was then asked if he did not call on Mr. Jackson and say he would not attend court under any circumstances. His answer was that he did say that in part and told Mr. Jackson that he did not want to lose the time to attend. He denied having an interview with any person in behalf of the prosecution. Mr. Jackson then asked the witness whether he did not say to him "you had better say nothing about the case to anyone." Mr. Kelker denied this. He was then asked whether he did not say he would suffer any penalty than attend court. "No, I did not know what they wanted with me at court."

He said to Mr. Jackson: "You have made a charge that I was tampered with and I want you to prove it." He further stated that the statement of his being tampered with was an infamous falsehood. Mr. Kelker was then excused.

Attorney Jackson for the defense was then called to the stand and questioned by Mr. Graham of the prosecution about his contacts with Mr. Kelker. George Kunkel, attorney for the defense, was then called and testified that Mr. Kelker had come to him and questioned the serviceability of his subpoena, and that he told him that as a council for the defense he could not discuss the matter. At this point Judge Simonton had heard enough. He dismissed Mr. Kelker and declared the matter a "tempest in a teapot" and moved on with the proceedings that ended that day. The jury was then charged and was in deliberation until ten in the evening, when it reported that it had reached a verdict. (*Harrisburg Daily Independent*, March 25, 1897, p. 1) When the sealed verdict was opened the next morning, Swallow was found guilty on one charge and not guilty on the other. His attorneys immediately set about preparing an appeal, but at a hearing in November, the verdict was upheld. Swallow continued efforts for repeal, and in November 1898 the State Supreme Court reversed the verdict on the basis that his words were not libelous and were protected by his right to free speech. (Beers, Paul, 1965, *Preacher, Politician, Prohibitionist: Here Was a Colorful Pennsylvanian*, Lycoming College, p. 82, https://www.lycoming. edu/umarch/chronicles/2001/8.swallow.pdf)

What did Dr. Silas Comfort Swallow gain from his public accusations of government wrongdoing? Apparently, nothing, except possibly for bolstering his political ambitions by keeping his name in the news. He played fast and loose with peoples' reputations without producing credible evidence of their guilt. Those he accused had to expend time, money and effort and suffered major disruptions in their lives. But Swallow's reputation barely suffered despite all the unfounded accusations and obvious fabrications. He went on to represent the Prohibition Party as nominee for the offices of Pennsylvania governor and for the US presidency, as noted above. Those races, like all his attempts, ended in resounding defeats. Luther Reily Kelker suffered nothing from the affair but discomfort brought on by Dr. Comfort. LRK went right on with his life.

Hohenheim, Mr. and Mrs. Luther Reily Kelker's Steelton home

Luther Reily Kelker builds a Steelton home and donates parkland. Mr. Kelker's real estate portfolio included an undeveloped plot of approximately sixty-two acres in Steelton. Then, on April 19, 1910, he and Mrs. Kelker moved into a magnificent newly built house on that Steelton property. (*Harrisburg Daily Independent*, April 18, 1910, p. 7) They named their new home Hohenheim (High Home), and on at least one occasion it was the site of a grand social occasion. In February 1911, Mrs. Kelker hosted an at-home dinner reception to honor Mrs. John Kinley Tener, the governor's wife, who was present with the governor. A reporter for the *Harrisburg Telegraph* wrote that the event was "Thronged with Guests to Greet Mrs. Tener." (Feb. 7, 1911, p. 3)

On May 9, 1910, just days after moving in, Mr. Kelker completed a gift transfer of ten acres of property adjacent to Hohenheim to the village of Steelton for development of a public park. (*Harrisburg Daily Independent*, May 9, 1910, p. 7) The gift was gratefully accepted by the village council (*Harrisburg Daily Independent*, May 10, 1910, p. 7), but due to a lack of funds the village council could do nothing to develop the park. For the next four years the neglected land became an "untamed wilderness" covered with brambles, weeds and untrimmed trees. (*Harrisburg Telegraph*, Oct. 22, 1915, p. 16) Finally, in 1914, at the urging of the municipal league, an organization of public-spirited men, the first few steps toward park development were taken. The village council authorized its finance committee to confer with Warren

H. Manning, a well-known Boston landscape architect who had designed Harrisburg's parks system, to develop plans for the new park. (*Harrisburg Telegraph*, May 5, 1914, p. 7)

What remained a challenge was the problem of how to build a park without a means to finance the effort. The only alternative was to call upon Steelton citizens to volunteer their time and effort. So, on May 8, 1915, the municipal league organized a field day under the direction of Manning, the landscape architect, to clear brambles and brush, grade walks and drives, and trim trees. More than two hundred school children of various nationalities and men from all levels of village society took part. (*Harrisburg Telegraph*, May 11, 1915, p. 8) Groups of volunteer laborers with relevant expertise, working under Mr. Manning's supervision, were directed by the borough engineer, the highway commissioner, a labor boss from the Pennsylvania Steel Company and the company's real estate manager. The work force was made up in significant part by a large delegation of grammar school boys and a group of twenty-five little girls from a parochial school. The *Harrisburg Telegraph* (May 8, 1915, p. 9) wrote that "Kelker Park was transformed from a wild tangled woodland, covered with dense, thorny underbrush, to a beautiful park."

When the Municipal League met after a three-month summer hiatus, it set about organizing a second field day for further Kelker Park improvement, and again a large number of citizens responded. But Kelker Park no longer exists, and nothing but a grassy field remains at the site.

Luther Reily Kelker died at Hohenheim on October 5, 1915 at age sixty-seven after suffering a long illness. He was buried in Harrisburg Cemetery among his Kelker family. Numerous obituaries noted his work as a businessman and historian.

Luther Reily Kelker, his life. Luther Reily Kelker lived a good life remarkable for success in two careers, as a businessman and as a historian. His lasting legacy is his exhaustive and extensive recording of the histories of Dauphin County and Pennsylvania that left us valuable history that may otherwise have been lost or only partially reported. His magnificent *History of Dauphin County, Pennsylvania* is a detailed record that remains a valuable source for historians.

LRK and Agnes' son Rudolph Frederick Kelker Jr. continued the family tradition of professional success. He became a traffic engineer in Chicago where he and his consulting firm designed and oversaw the construction of the city's first subway system. Their son John Pearsol Kelker embarrassed the family by becoming a criminal who cheated family members and friends and spent time in prison. Their daughter, Mary Ellen Kelker, married Roscoe William Sturges in 1906 and moved to Mansfield, Ohio, where she spent her adult life as a wife and homemaker.

Addendum
Luther Reily Kelker

LRK's Affiliations
—trustee of First National Bank of Harrisburg
—created the Pennsylvania Division of Public Records of the State Library, from 1903
—member of the American Historical Association, the Historical Society of Pennsylvania, and historical societies in Pennsylvania counties including Dauphin, Schuylkill, York and others
—as head of the State Division of Public Records, collaborated in editing of twenty-two volumes of Pennsylvania archives
—compiled te three-volume *History of Dauphin County, Pennsylvania*
—member of the American Literary Association
—member of the Robert Burns Lodge of the Masons
—Knight Templar of Pennsylvania
—member and officer of the Market Square Presbyterian Church
—secretary-treasurer and president of the Harrisburg Wheel Club
—stockholder in the Harrisburg Toboggan Slide
—Harrisburg agent for the Massachusetts Mutual Life Insurance Company
—Harrisburg hardware merchant and businessman
—appointed to the Board of Trade legislative committee.

Governor Pennypacker takes time from his summer vacation to appoint LRK State Archivist. An interesting bit in the *Reading Times* article below is that in 1903 the governor took the summer off and retreated to his farm in Montgomery County in the state's southeast corner over a hundred miles from Harrisburg. He returned to the capital weekly for two days to take care of business. And one of those items of business was appointing LRK to the newly created position of State Archivist.

STATE ARCHIVIST APPOINTED, AND A NEPHEW OF COOPER GETS A PLACE—FACTORY INSPECTORS.

Harrisburg, Pa., May 28.—Governor Pennypacker and family have gone to his farm at Pennypacker's Mills, Montgomery county, to spend the summer. The Governor will, however, divide his time between his farm and Harrisburg during the summer. He expects to spend two days a week here answering his private mail and attending to such official duties as require his presence in Harrisburg. The Executive Mansion will remain open, although some of the servants have gone along with the Pennypacker family to the farm.

The Governor has appointed Luther R. Kelker, of Harrisburg, State Archivist, and Helen Boyd, of Harrisburg, a clerk in the State Archivist Bureau. This office was created by the last Legislature to classify and preserve in the State Library the public records of historical value. Mr. Kelker is a member of the Pennsylvania Historical Society and several kindred organizations with which the Governor is also actively con-

Reading Times, May 29, 1903, p. 1

William Anthony Kelker
Historian, Collector, Astronomer, Weather Clerk, Good Citizen

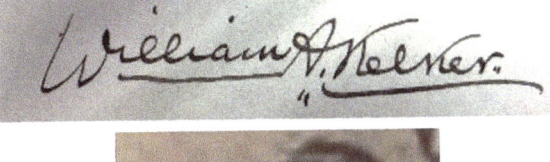

The young William Anthony Kelker on April 15, 1877. From the Kelker Archives at the Historical Society of Dauphin County

Brief Bio. William Anthony Kelker (1853–1908), like his brother, father and grandfather, was born in the family home at 9 South Front Street. He was educated in the Harrisburg public schools and at Harrisburg Academy. He spent his entire existence in Harrisburg where he continued the family tradition of business, devotion to church and community service. But most enduringly he was a historian, collector and observer of nature. He studied, befriended and wrote about the Native Americans of the Susquehanna Valley, collected their relics, kept daily weather records for more than twenty years, and was active in the Historical Society of Dauphin County and the Pennsylvania German Association and many other groups. Upon his death the Harrisburg Telegraph (Feb. 17, 1908, p. 7) remembered him as a "Local Historian, Relic Collector and Weather Observer." His life came to a sudden and tragic end in 1908 when he collapsed and died while on a nature hike at the age of fifty-five.

William A. Kelker's intense curiosity, attention to detail and broad interests were apparent early in his life. At fifteen he was reading as many as fifteen books a month and he maintained a record of each one. He assembled his 1868 reading record in a small booklet that listed all 124 books, but he left room for doubt: "Any person that does not believe this they need not."

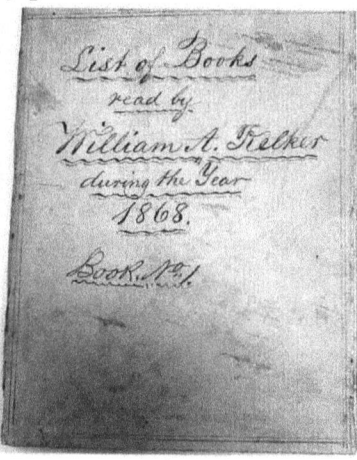

WAK's 1868 reading record. From the Kelker archives at the Historical Society of Dauphin County, Box 4.

In other comments he noted that he was born on September 20, 1853, and that on September 7 he moved into his new home at 9 South Front Street that was built by his father, Rudolph Frederick Kelker, to replace the previous home that stood there. He added that he lost the use of his right eye on January 24, 1866, and that he grew eight inches in thirty months. William Anthony's booklet gives us a peek into his character: detail oriented, blunt, curious, honest and bright with a strong penchant for collecting and keeping records. Those traits drove his active and productive life, and he left behind a treasure trove of valuable records and collections for historians to study and appreciate.

Early business experience. WAK spent five of his early career years in the world of commerce. At twenty-four, he entered the family hardware business when in 1878 his uncles Henry Anthony and Immanuel Meister dissolved their Kelker and Brother hardware firm. Henry Anthony disposed of his stock to his brother and his nephews William Anthony and Luther Reily.

Then WAK and his brother operated their new Kelker Brothers business at 6 1/2 Market Square until 1883 when William Anthony retired, with Luther Reily continuing business under the name Luther R. Kelker until 1892. WAK never returned to commercial endeavors. He had other interests, and from that time on he fully devoted himself to his love of history and nature. He was not burdened with the need to provide for his existence. With his wealthy father's support, he was free to pursue his interests.

Historian and collector. William Anthony Kelker delighted in recording the histories of Harrisburg and the Susquehanna Valley. He studied and wrote about native nations of the region, Civil War events in Pennsylvania and bridges that spanned the Susquehanna River. His recorded observations are enlivened by the fact that he lived in close proximity to much of the history that he wrote. He befriended local Native Americans and their leaders, he acted to preserve historical landmarks and he closely followed and recorded the construction, operations and destructions of the Susquehanna bridges of his time.

Like his brother he had a passion for detailed accounting of Dauphin County's past. He gathered and left behind a huge collection of Native American stone tools and arrowheads discovered on his many treks through fields and forests of the Susquehanna Valley. He coauthored a book that described stone artifacts found in the region. (Bashore, H. R., Kelker, W. A., O'Connor, J. H., 1898, "Contributions to the Indian History of the Lower Susquehanna Valley," Annual Report of the Committee on Archaeology of the Dauphin County Historical Society, Harrisburg) He also accumulated an impressive collection of artifacts of historical, social and political interest. Many of these are preserved in the Kelker archives at the Historical Society of Dauphin County.

WAK's passion was not confined to collecting and recording. He was fascinated by nature, and he possessed a vast knowledge of the region's plant life that he acquired from an untold number of excursions through wetlands, forests and lakes observing and recording the local flora. In a sad twist of fate, he collapsed and died while examining the flora at a local swamp, as described below. He also possessed a passion for the weather, and he unfailingly kept a daily log of Harrisburg's weather that was published monthly, quarterly and semi-annually in the *Harrisburg Daily Telegraph* for more than twenty years (the *Telegraph* referred to him as the "weather clerk"). And he was a self-taught astronomer who owned and used what must have been for that time a sophisticated telescope.

Note: The histories below of the Camelback and Cumberland Railroad Bridges, unless otherwise cited, are taken from WAK's lecture at the Historical Society of Dauphin County on March 9, 1899, and from an article published in the *Harrisburg Daily Telegraph* on Jan. 16, 1891.

A look at WAK's fascination with Harrisburg's bridges. WAK held a special fascination with Harrisburg's bridges. He closely observed and faithfully recorded their history of flood damage, fire damage and rebuilding. He traveled them, and on a personal level he made good friends with the toll collectors. He in fact mentioned every one of those toll takers at his 1899 Historical Society of Dauphin County lecture, and he designated one of them, a Mr. James Dougherty, as executor of his will. He also presented his bridge observations in the record he made of that lecture.

During William Anthony's time four local bridges spanned the broad Susquehanna, the longest river along the East Coast. They are shown in the 1916 photo below.

Birds eye view of Harrisburg's Susquehanna River bridges in 1916. From left to right (Northeast to Southwest) are the Walnut Street Bridge completed in 1890, the Camelback Bridge, the Cumberland Valley Railroad Bridge (completed in 1839) and the Philadelphia & Reading Railroad Bridge (opened in 1891). The photograph was taken by an unknown photographer from the Pennsylvania Capital Building looking southwest. (From the Historical Society of Dauphin County's archives general collection)

The four bridges exist today, The Walnut Street bridge is a pedestrian crossing between Harrisburg and City Island. Its western span no longer exists because of destruction from the 1996 flood. The Market Street Bridge that succeeded the Camelback was last reconstructed in 1926. It serves automobile traffic. The Cumberland Valley Railroad Bridge has been unused for many years. Possible uses for the bridge have been discussed but it now sits idle. The Philadelphia and Reading Bridge is in use for train traffic. Two more recent bridges, the southernmost John Harris Memorial Bridge, that opened in 1960, carries Interstate 83 traffic over the Susquehanna, and the northernmost M. Harvey Taylor Bridge, that opened in 1954, supports automobile traffic. (References from Wikipedia)

Nineteenth-century Harrisburg's economy and its growth as a commercial center depended on the flow of goods and people to and from the city, and a significant part of the city's commerce depended on getting goods and people transported across the very wide Susquehanna River. Before 1816, the only way to cross was by ferry or private boat, and that often meant that traders, merchants and others experienced long delays waiting for transport. The problem was solved by the construction of Harrisburg's first river crossing, the Camelback Bridge, so named for its arching span. The humpbacked bridge was a two-lane, covered wood structure that accommodated pedestrians, bicycles, horses, wagons, animal herds and flocks. Throughout its time it underwent repeated rebuilding following damage from floods, ice floes and fires. Construction and maintenance costs were paid from toll collection on each human, animal and vehicle that passed through.

western section commonly called the old camelback - showing original size of windows. 1812- 1902.

The western span of Camelback Bridge, in place from 1817 to 1902. Note the curved arch that gave rise to its name and the windows that provided light for the enclosed structure. Photo: the Dauphin County Historical Society, ALB 9.

Work on the original Camelback began in 1812. It was designed by Theodore Burr, a master bridge builder of the period and, interestingly, a cousin of Aaron Burr, Thomas Jefferson's vice president who killed Alexander Hamilton in their 1804 duel. (Rick Dapp, March 14, 2017, https:// harrisburgmagazine. com/community/did-you-know/did-you-know-camelback-bridge/) Burr designed the bridge's roadway to pass through City Island located midway between Harrisburg and the western shore at Cumberland County. The complete structure consisted of an eastern span connecting Harrisburg and City Island, a western span connecting City Island and Cumberland County on the west and the stretch of roadway on City Island that connected the two spans. Construction was completed in 1817, though the unfinished bridge was open for traffic in October 1816. The first toll was paid by a US Mail stagecoach.

Camelback's eastern span lasted until March 15, 1846, when a flood washed it away. A replacement was completed, and it opened to traffic on September 20, 1847. But the rebuilt section was destroyed by an 1866 fire that started from City Island. A second replacement was completed and reopened on November 1, 1867. It lasted until 1902 when the bridge was again destroyed by a flood the ended the era of wood bridges that spanned the river in Harrisburg. (Camelback and Market Street Bridges—Harrisburg—PA—US—Historical Marker Project)

Construction and maintenance of the Camelback bridge was financed by toll collection. To assure compliance a toll taker was stationed to collect fees from pedestrians, bicyclists, carriages, wagons, carts, animal herds and any others passing through the station. The tollkeeper's job was not always easy. It got more burdensome when he had to deal with herds, especially large ones, as a per-head fee was charged. To get an accurate count, the animals passed one by one through a gate with the collector standing by and recording. Sheep, goats, cows, horses, mules and pigs filed through.

The Camelback Bridge:: interior view of the western section and gate where animals were counted. (Historical Society of Dauphin County, ALB 9)

An excited herd (or drove) could make things even more difficult. In his 1899 lecture, WAK relates an incident with a drove of mules that took place while he and his father were crossing east to west on the old Camelback:

> Mules also were brought over in great numbers and in nearly every case the person leading the drove rode a sorrel horse. This leader greatly amused the youngsters by continually calling out "Come boys, come boys!" to the mules following him. The drove was usually rounded up by a couple of mounted drivers who knew how to use the long-lashed whips they carried with them. The writer remembers crossing the bridge with his father on an errand into Cumberland county during the Civil War. On the way over a small drove of seventeen mules were being brought to Harrisburg. By the time we reached the center of the old "camel-back" bridge, we heard great cries of "Drive on, drive on!" from a couple of teamsters back of our carriage. The old bridge was doing its best not to jump off the piers, so greatly was it swaying, and it was all caused by those seventeen contrary mules, who had turned on their drivers and recrossed the bridge at a break neck speed, terrifying everyone who they overtook during their mad charge. Not being able to quiet our team, we jumped out of the vehicle and got into the footway and took the horse by the head, but he soon got the better of us and went along with the runaway mules,

who passed out the gateway with a grand rush, leaving our team to be captured by a soldier who was doing guard duty at the western end of the bridge.

The toll collector had to be constantly on high alert for gatecrashers who used a variety of ploys to avoid paying. WAK relates in his lecture several clever tricks employed to get by the gatekeeper who often reacted with fits of anger and an urge to retaliate. Some tried to pass non-negotiable currency, and others, mostly young boys, resorted to a variety of often-successful strategies. He relates two instances probably best told in his own words:

> About 2 o'clock one August morning in 1840 two men from the Cumberland County side awakened Mr. Fager (the toll collector) by their loud cries of "Open the gates, we want out," adding a great deal of profanity to their request. They continued in their rough language while he pretended to open the padlock at the gate. He then asked them in his usual quiet manner "If they were done." They replied, "We are." He in turn replied "So am I, gentlemen." With this remark he relocked the gates and went into the toll-house and would not let them through. They had nothing else to do but to return to the Cumberland shores […]

One tollman, a Mr. Steiner, employed the following strategy:

> Another mode adopted by Mr. Steiner to stop the gate runners was to stone them, and for this purpose he kept a stock of stones on the frame work just inside the bridge, and woe to the boy who made the dash through the gates in the presence of Mr. Steiner, for the volley of stones that was to follow him would do credit to the Gatling gun of the present date.

The Camelback was an immense boost to the growth and prosperity of Harrisburg and the surrounding community, but its susceptibility to floods, fires and ice floes, along with the arrival of motor vehicles, rendered it obsolete. The bridge met its end in 1902 when a flood destroyed both the east and west spans. It was not rebuilt. The era of wood bridges had passed, and they were being replaced with stone and iron structures designed for automobile use. A new stone two-lane bridge over the old Camelback route was completed in 1904. Placed at its Harrisburg entrance were two stone columns recovered from the burned wreckage of the state-capitol building. They added a touch of graceful majesty to the structure, and still do. The new bridge served as the forerunner of the present-day Market Street Bridge.

The problem of increased automobile and truck traffic was addressed in 1926 by broadening the bridge's roadway from two to four lanes. The widening was accomplished using a unique engineering feat. The eastern Harrisburg–City Island two-lane span was removed in its entirety, transported to the western side and placed alongside the western span. This was accomplished by section-by-section removal of the eastern span, with each section transported by boat to the western span where the removed sections were arrayed alongside the existing structure to form a four-lane roadway. The eastern span was replaced in its entirety. (Frew, K., 2009, *Building Harrisburg: The Architects and Builders, 1719–1941,* The Historical Society of Dauphin County, Harrisburg, p. 248) The splendid engineering feat was carried out by Polish-born Bridge builder Ralph Modjeski. He built more than forty major North American bridges including Philadelphia's Benjamin Franklin bridge and the San Francisco-Oakland Bay Bridge. A plaque on the Market Street Bridge's east entrance recognizes his contribution. (Bridgehunter.com | Ralph Modjeski)

Weather Clerk. William A. Kelker's compulsive need to observe and record was never more on display than with his consuming fascination with the weather. Throughout his adult life he kept daily records of Harrisburg's weather conditions that he compiled into monthly, quarterly and yearly reports published in the *Harrisburg Telegraph*. A short piece from the newspaper (Jan. 4, 1879, p. 4) gives us an idea of his tenacity, the magnitude of his efforts and how much his work was appreciated:

> Our readers have had ample time, at least those scientifically inclined, to study the elaborate table published on the 1st instant, of meteorological statistics prepared by William A. Kelker, Esq. These reports are made monthly, quarterly and annually, and are the results of all observations made three times every twenty-four hours. Some idea for the labor involved is had by a critical examination of the tables, the exactness and regularity with which the observations must be made, and the absolute correctness of every record, all of which involves method, peculiar adaptation of the man engaged in the service, with a thorough appreciation and love of the science pursued. Mr. Kelker has all these, and like all scientific men engaged in a work for the benefit of the public, his labor is one of love, in which there is no profit beyond the satisfaction of knowing that he respects and instructs his fellow citizens. We

thank Mr. Kelker for his disinterested service, and we are assured that the public also feel grateful to him for the valuable information he places within its reach.

THANKS TO WHOM THANKS ARE DUE.

MR. EDITOR—The thanks of the community are due to our young friend, Mr. Wm. A. Kelker, for the very reliable and regular meteorological register, which is so satisfactory and useful. Many of our intelligent agriculturists value it most highly and carefully preserve it for reference.   M. L. T.

Harrisburg Telegraph, July 10, 1879, p. 4.

WAK's predisposition for things historical influenced his weather reporting. He frequently published retrospective summaries of various aspects of Harrisburg's weather. For example, he published a compilation of the city's March weather from 1874 to 1896 (*Harrisburg Telegraph*, April 1, 1896, p. 1), noting clear days, cloudy days, rain or snow days and lowest, highest and average temperatures. In the *Harrisburg Telegraph* (June 1, 1885, p. 1) he published a summary from 1874 to 1885 of the "Decoration Day Weather for Twelve Years." In the paper's edition for April 2, 1885 (p. 4), he published a fifteen-year record, from 1871 to 1885, of openings and closings of the Susquehanna caused by ice. He published a report (*Harrisburg Telegraph*, Feb. 12, 1885, p. 4) of city weather conditions for the first twelve days of February from 1881 to 1885, and in the *Telegraph*'s edition for June 30, 1884 (p. 4), he published "The Five Hottest and Coldest June Days in Five Years," spanning 1880 to 1884. He published on "High Water in Ten Years" (*Harrisburg Telegraph*, Feb. 8, 1884, p. 4), on "The First Snow" from 1874 to 1884 (*Harrisburg Telegraph*, Oct. 29, 1884, p. 1) and on "A Comparison of Christmas Day Weather for the Past Fourteen Years" from 1874 to 1888. (*Harrisburg Telegraph*, Dec. 26, 1888, p. 1) He just could not keep himself from examining, analyzing and presenting his weather data in various contexts.

Each year WAK presented a comprehensive and concise summary of weather conditions for each day of the year. His 1889 report is shown below. He copyrighted the reports and made copies for distribution.

1889. A Year of Remarkable Weather.

Month	1	2	3	4	5	6	7	8	9	10	11	12	13	14	15	16	17	18	19	20	21	22	23	24	25	26	27	28	29	30	31	Cloudy	Rain	Clear	Rain Fall
January,	O	O	O	C	R	R	C	O	R	O	C	O	O	C	RS	R	R	O	O	S	O	O	O	C	O	R	RS	S	O	R	R	5	12	14	2.86
February,	O	C	S	S	RS	C	O	S	S	S	S	S	O	O	O	O	C	R	C	C	R	CRS	C	O	O	C	O	R	R	O	RS	5	16	7	1.48
March,	C	R	R	R	C	O	C	S	S	O	O	C	O	R	C	O	C	R	R	C	O	R	O	O	R	R	R	R	R	R	R	6	16	8	3.96
April,	R	R	C	C	S	S	O	O	C	O	R	C	R	R	O	O	O	O	R	R	R	R	R	C	R	O	C	R	R	R		7	14	10	9.51
May,	C	R	C	C	O	O	O	O	R	C	R	R	O	O	O	R	R	R	R	R	R	C	R	O	R	R	R	R				8	19	3	7.18
June,	C	C	R	R	C	C	R	R	R	R	R	C	R	R	R	R	C	R	O	R	C	O	R	R	O	R	R	R				4	19	8	8.68
July,	R	R	R	R	O	O	O	O	O	R	R	R	O	R	R	C	C	O	R	R	C	O	R	R	O	R	R	R	R	R	R	13	9	9	3.38
August,	R	C	C	R	R	R	O	O	R	R	C	O	R	R	C	C	C	O	C	C	C	R	C	C	O	O	O	O	O	O		7	19	4	4.53
September,	C	C	C	R	C	R	C	O	R	O	R	R	R	R	C	O	O	C	O	R	RS	O	C	R	R	C	C	C	R			11	12	8	3.33
October,	R	C	C	O	O	C	C	C	R	O	R	R	R	C	RS	O	R	R	R	R	R	R	C	C	R	C	R	RS	S	S		5	19	6	6.59
November,	O	R	R	O	O	C	O	R	R	O	R	R	C	R	C	R	R	R	R	R	R	R	O	C	R	C	R	O	O	R	C	O	6	18	7	2.11
December,	O	O	RS	S	R	C	O	R	C	R	C	R	C	R	R	RS	C	R	R	RS	C	R	R	R	R	R	O	R	O	R	C	O	6	18	7	2.11

C–Cloudy.	Earthquake,	Rain fall 8 in,	Flood,	Greatest Wind Velocity,	86	186	93	57.07
R–Rain. O–Clear.	6.40 P. M.,	May 31–June 1, 6 A.M., June 2d,	Noon, Dec. 26th,					
S–Snow.	March 8th.	in 18 hours,	26 ft., 2 in.	66 miles per hour, N. W.		**TOTAL.**		

Compliments of

Wm. A. Kelker.

One of WAK's annual reports for 1889 that he had printed for distribution. It also appeared in the *Harrisburg Telegraph*. From the Kelker archives at the Historical Society of Dauphin County, Box 4.

WAK's weather reporting received gratitude and recognition from the Harrisburg community and beyond. When the new state-capitol building was dedicated in 1904, its cornerstone was laid by Governor Pennypacker and in it were sealed various articles including his Harrisburg weather reports from 1869 to 1903. (*The News*, Frederick, Md., May 6, 1904, p. 1) He was appointed along with Dr. W. H. Egle and Dr. H. Hamilton to a Board of Trade committee to work with Harrisburg's observer of the signal service to secure "first-class weather service in this locality." (*Harrisburg Telegraph*, Oct. 6, 1888, p. 1) When Gen. A. W. Greeley was head of the US Weather Bureau in the nation's capital he learned of WAK's weather reporting and requested records, which WAK duly sent. In his thank-you letter General Greeley wrote that "they were the best amateur records, and I have examined many, that I have ever seen." (*Harrisburg Telegraph*, Feb. 17, 1908, p. 7)

Death on a nature hike. William A. Kelker died suddenly and unexpectedly while on a nature hike. His death was a shock to his many friends in the Harrisburg community and beyond. The statement below was made by his friend Theodore B. Klein at the memorial service at the Historical Society of Dauphin County, and reported by the press:

Sad, indeed, and startling was [sic] tidings that spread rapidly through the city, and the community was deeply stirred, for the event betokened the loss of a man so well and favorably known, whose departure left an aching void in the hearts of many, very many, who numbered him as a dear friend. (*Harrisburg Telegraph*, March 13, 1908, p. 11)

Just a month earlier, on Saturday afternoon, February 14, William and his good friend Dr. John Fager had gone for a hike to examine plant life in the Wetzel swamp near Rockville. After visiting the swamp and hiking back toward Harrisburg, William was struck down, apparently by heart failure, and fell dead almost at Dr. Fager's feet. (It appears that heart disease caused his death, although no autopsy was done for confirmation.) Dr. Fager, shaken and saddened recounted the tragic event in the *Harrisburg Daily Independent* (Feb. 17, 1908, p. 1).

I told Mr. Kelker I was going for a walk last Saturday through the swamp and he, being ever ready for a walk into the country, met me on the 2 o'clock car for Rockville. He was in high spirits. We got off the car at the Linglestown road and as the water and mud were deep and we were wading he said he was afraid the dust was going to trouble us.

We entered the swamp, looking for plant life as shown in the early beds of chickweed and the green color of the dandelion plant. We walked leisurely, he frequently suggesting a brief rest. We waded and walked, stopping to get on a big cake of ice once, and this we poled over some of the deeper water. We found a field mouse and several muskrats and he stopped several hunters in a conversation with them said he would never kill anything for pleasure.

At last we came to Paxton creek in one of its wild rampages. We tries [sic] to cross, but the first bridge we came to was entirely surrounded by water. Another could not be reached either and at the third bridge we met two men who told us the nearest way to Harrisburg was by way of the hills to the Linglestown road. We walked along slowly, he saying he was going as fast as he could. Our conversation turned to death. I said that I believed a man could be brave in death, citing a case of a patient who facing death is as brave as a lion. He told me of an old darkey [sic] friend who, upon being asked if he was afraid to die, said: "No indeed, I'm perfectly willing to go."

"And why should we be afraid, why shouldn't we be brave?" Mr. Kelker said to me. We had just come in sight of the Linglestown road when I heard a peculiar sound back of me, and looking about saw he had fallen. I jumped to his side and found him unconscious and his pulse gone. He was dead. I spread the alarm to some people who kindly did all they could. Harvey Hocker brought the body home. I feel I have lost one of my best friends, one who compelled me to do my best. I know many people are the better for knowing William A. Kelker.

William A. Kelker's sudden death was reported in newspapers in and around Harrisburg. The *Harrisburg Telegraph* (Feb, 17, 1908, p. 7) remembered him as a "Local Historian, Relic Collector and Weather Observer" and described his conversation about death with Dr. Fager in the moments before he collapsed. The March 13, 1908, issue of the *Telegraph* (p. 11) reported one of the many tributes paid to William A. Kelker at a meeting of the Historical Society of Dauphin County where the HSDC member Theodore B. Klein heaped further warm praise on his life:

> No words of mine are adequate to render a fitting or worthy tribute to the memory of our late associate, William Anthony Kelker, who departed this life so very suddenly on the 15th day of February, 1908. His call came without a moment of warning, the bolt of death falling upon him as the red flow of the setting sun tinted the western sky beyond the ice-bound river. So suddenly that there was not a moment of time to murmur a whisper of a good-bye or a farewell message for any one.

Mr. Klein went on to acknowledge the warm and nurturing relationship WAK enjoyed with his parents, and he notes that his father, Rudolph Frederick, had passed away only two years earlier.

> Words of mine will not suffice to express the measure of his goodness and kindness of heart, which was inherited and cultivated in his whole life's work. It began at the foot-stool by his mother's side and at the right hand of a loving and indulgent father, and was continued until the last moment of his life. The patriarchal sire was called away (full of years and honor) but a short time ago, after a long period of infirmity, which was rendered in a measure supportable by the watchful and tender ministrations of our late friend.
>
> This service stamped the mark of the true and devoted son upon his character, and called forth unlimited praise from his many friends.
>
> The sleepless hours, the self-sacrifice, the untiring vigilance, the continued patience of the faithful and affectionate son and attendant of the plaudits of the recording angel and of this community.

Most published remembrances acknowledged WAK's love of collecting, his historical works, his devotion to climate study and his many acts of community involvement. But his footprint in the Harrisburg community did not end with his death. He departed as a man of wealth, and there was a natural curiosity about how and to whom he would bequeath his property. The *Harrisburg Daily Independent* (April 9, 1908, p. 1) published a piece headlined, "CURIOUS TO KNOW WHAT WILL CONTAINS, An Intimate Friend of Late W.A. Kelker Tells of Its Contents." The unidentified intimate friend had gained access to the contents of the will before it was to be sent for probate, and seemed anxious to reveal the information to the public.

The key question stirring the public's curiosity was what would become of his 9 South Front Street house. The intimate friend claimed that the house would go to the Historical Society of Dauphin County where WAK had been an active member and son of a founder, and that he had placed conditions on the society's acceptance of the donation. The building would have to be maintained properly, the society could not sell the building or use it for any other purpose except as its home. Apparently he had considered that the society might have difficulty meeting these terms as its only income came from members' dues. So, he set as a fallback plan that if the society declined the property it would go to Harrisburg Hospital.

William A. Kelker's will was filed for probate on about April 10, 1908. The full text of the will was not released, but a significant amount of information was made public. His estate was valued at $100,000. As expected, he left his South Front Street house and all its contents to the Historical Society of Dauphin County (with the stipulations mentioned above). He left $20,000 to be divided among his friends, and he remembered his housekeeper. (*Reading Times*, April 11, 1908, p. 3) He left a piece of his farm to his brother, Luther Reily, and his two sons. (*Harrisburg Daily Independent*, April 13, 1908, p. 1) He left nothing else to his brother.

On April 13, a few days after the contents of the will were revealed, his brother Luther Reily through his lawyer challenged the validity of the will. Newspaper articles of that time do not reveal Luther Reily's motive, but it seems reasonable to assume that the brother found it hard to see $100,000 pass him by. He may also have been interested in the South Front Street house. In a court hearing on that Monday, he argued that the document was

"Not Properly Drawn" based on the status of the two men who witnessed the signing of the will. The hearing was called to hear evidence of the competency of the two witnesses, David W. Cotterel, a bookseller and stationer, and his brother James K. Cotterel, a photographer. The two brothers testified that they had indeed witnessed William A. Kelker's signature on September 9, 1907, and that there was a codicil of February 8, 1908. They stated that they did not know the contents of the will.

Following the Cotterels' testimony Mr. Snodgrass, Luther Reily's lawyer, put into the record that on behalf of his client he was registering a protest that the witnesses were not competent as they were interested parties designated to receive inheritances from the deceased. The hearing was adjourned until the next Thursday morning, April 16, at 10:00 when the will was to be probated and read in its entirety.

At the April 16 hearing the long document written in WAK's hand was read. Mr. James Dougherty, the night collector of bridge tolls, was named executor. The house at 9 South Front Street was left to The Historical Society of Dauphin County. Following the reading the Register of Wills ruled that the Cotterel brothers were competent witnesses to the signing. The will was thus legal and could be executed according to the wishes of the deceased. Luther Reily lost his challenge. His attorney, when asked what his next move would be, replied, "We have not decided what we shall do." Nothing further was done, however, with Luther Reily making no further attempts to challenge his brother's will. (*Harrisburg Daily Independent*, April 16, 1908, p. 1)

This words below address the key concern:

> I give and bequeath the homestead, No. 9 South Front Street, to the Historical Society of Dauphin County of Pennsylvania, with all its contents (except for the books of my father's library, books, curios, and relics of whatever nature they may be: the property to belong to said society as long as it [the society] exists. Should the society dissolve, then the property shall go to the Harrisburg Hospital as a home for its nurses. In memory of my dear parents is this bequest made.

The complete version revealed that he did indeed leave a portion of his farm to his brother and his brother's sons Rudolph Frederick Jr. and John Pearsol. The farm's other portion went to Edward M. Hawkins, chief engineer of the

Pennsylvania Steel Company. But William Anthony added that "no portion of the farm to be sold unless each share in the proceeds of the sale."

He distributed a number of thousand-dollar bonds of the Harrisburg Gas Company to the Reformed Salem Church in memory of his parents; to Dr. William M. Irvine, principal of Harrisburg Academy where William had studied; to his godchild, Caroline Davenport Gardner; to the Home for the Friendless and the Children's Industrial Home who were to divide the proceeds after the sale of the bond; and others to friends and institutions. Provisions were made to pay his taxes, and he left the remainder of the estate to Harrisburg Hospital. (*Harrisburg Daily Independent*, April 16, 1908, p. 10) He directed his executor to pay $500 to a Mr. William J. Crawford, a sculptor, "for which he will erect in the river park opposite the Kelker residence a rock faced boulder of Barry granite with the following inscription:

In Memory of
J. CONRAD WEISER
1696–1764
Provincial Interpreter,
and his friend,
SHIKILLINY
1683–1748
an Oneida Chief

Weiser was an immigrant from the Palatinate who arrived on American shores in 1710 at fourteen and gained proficiency in the Mohawk language while living among the Mohawks at sixteen. His language skills and his friendship with some native Pennsylvania groups were of great service to the British in treaty negotiations with Native Americans. It is easy to understand why WAK, himself a student and friend of local native nations, would have great admiration for Weiser. (Johann Conrad Weiser Sr., Wikipedia)

Note: While the inscription notes that Weiser died in 1764, other sources list the year as 1760.

William Anthony Kelker's life. William A. Kelker lived a fascinating life. While perhaps a bit odd in his compulsive pursuit of things that interested him, e.g., history, the weather, Native American life and collecting, he left us valuable historical records. His early life provides some insight into his personality. His account of books read as a fifteen-year-old then carefully recorded in a neatly prepared booklet indicates how the adult WAK approached his many projects. He diligently collected, investigated and recorded. There was more than a bit of hoarding trait in his psyche, but that worked to his benefit and ours. He left us significant historical accounts and a valuable collection of related artifacts.

WAK did not fit the family mold. Unlike his father, brother, uncles and grandfather Frederick, his instincts did not lead him to a career in business. Although he participated in the family hardware business in his young years, he was more attracted to pursuing interests in history and nature. Had he been born to a family of lesser means he likely would not have had the freedom to spend his time studying and collecting, and we can only wonder what his life would have been under those circumstances. But with the freedom of a single man, he devoted his time to his passions. Perhaps describing him as a dilletante or, in today's parlance, as perhaps a "nerd" is too harsh. But what he pursued, his exacting weather reporting, his investigations into the indigenous populations' history in the area, his historical observations on the Susquehanna's local bridges, his compulsive collecting of historical objects, were all done with care and professionalism that resulted in a fine finished products, e.g., his detailed and clearly presented weather reports. WAK's intriguing life provided us with valuable histories and remarkable objects of that time. We can look at his life and acknowledge his uniqueness with appreciation for what he accomplished and left to us.

Chapter 6 continues with the lives of Luther Reily and Agnes Keyes Pearsol Kelker's son, Rudolph Frederick Kelker, Jr., a traffic engineer in Chicago who dealt with the traffic problems and politics in fast growing Chicago.

Addendum
William Anthony Kelker

WAK, obsessive collector. William Anthony, an obsessive collector by nature, eagerly sought out items of historical interest. He was aggressive in his search for memorabilia, and used his many personal connections to gather more items (one might term them "junque") for his massive collection. He was a true, honest pack rat, in the most respectable sense. And his obsessiveness has left us valuable historical records of Harrisburg. Much of what remains of his collections is now archived at the Historical Society of Dauphin County.

Commemorative collage of the Pennsylvania's Electoral College's signing of election results in 1888. The framed collage is on display in the Harris-Cameron Mansion in Harrisburg. Above left and right are signatures of president-elect Benjamin Harrison and his vice president, Levi P. Morton. Below these are their signed photos, below which are boxes with statements of their titles and names. The pen was used by Pennsylvania's electors in signing to confirm the state elector's vote. Written under the pen by William A. Kelker are the following words:

> The Likeness, the Seal and the Flag are part of the Souvenir Ball held at Washington City, March 4, 1889. The autographs were received from the invitees. The ballots are two of those actually cast by the Pennsylvania Electoral College in the Senate Chamber of Harrisburg Pa January 14, 1889, and the pen is the identical one used by the members thereof in signing the Official Returns of the Election, and also by

Harrison and Morton, in writing their Autographs for the Cities of Indianapolis and New York, their respective homes. The pens are received from Capt. John C. Geaney Senate Librarian and the ballots from M. William McHarney Esq one of the Electors.

Harrisburg Pa. March 8, 1889   William A. Kelker

He had made considerable effort to create the collage. An 1889 *Harrisburg Telegraph* article (Feb. 5, p. 4) describes those efforts.

> ### An Interesting Souvenir.
> When the Electoral College of Pennsylvania met in the Senate Chamber a few weeks ago Mr. W. A. Kelker, of this city, who is a great relic hunter, secured the steel pen with which all the electors signed the certificate which was forwarded to Washington. Then Mr. Kelker sent the pen to General Harrison and secured his autograph, which was returned with the pen. Next it was forwarded to Mr. Morton, who will also write with it. Then Mr. Kelker will place the pen in a neat case and preserve it.

William Anthony kept the collage in his collection, where it remained there until his death, when it passed to the Historical Society of Dauphin County.

William Anthony, autograph seeker (gets Vice President Levi Morton's signature).

> Mr. W. A. Kelker has received the autograph and also a photograph of Hon. Levi P. Morton.

Harrisburg Telegraph, Feb 8, 1889, p. 4

A letter sent 'round the world. William's addiction to recording and collecting unique and often obscure artifacts together with his delight in whimsy are shown in an 1888 article from the *Philadelphia Ledger*. The piece notes the existence of a letter he sent that went around the world. "Gossip remembers the experience of a letter sent around the world a few years ago by Mr. W. A. Kelker, of Harrisburg […]." The letter went from Harrisburg to San Francisco and on to Yokohama, and from there to Singapore, Alexandria, Liverpool, New York and finally to Harrisburg 107 days after it left. The article notes that the "This was the fourth that had been sent around the world in this manner, the Postoffice [sic] Department soon after adopting a regulation which discouraged the practice."

William Anthony, pigeon racer. Two short 1891 pieces in the local press tell us that this man of many interests participated in pigeon races:

> A pigeon match comes off this morning in Kelker's field, near Mohn street, East Steelton. The contestants are Messrs. John Hepsch and S. O. Thumma—ten birds; stakes $10 a side.

Harrisburg Daily Independent, Jan. 10, 1891 p. 1

> W. A. Kelker released a lot of homing pigeons yesterday afternoon and they at once started for their cotes in Philadelphia.

Harrisburg Telegraph, Aug. 22, 1891, p. 6

William Anthony, scavenger.

> **A Neat Relic.**
> Mr. W. A. Kelker had made for himself a neat souvenir of the old market sheds that are no more. He got a piece of the timber and made from it a butcher's block. with rack containing hooks and all complete.

Harrisburg Telegraph, Feb 18, 1889, p. 1

William Anthony is accused of being an Irish deserter and held in an immigration center. WAK was an explorer and adventurer who, thanks to being born into a wealthy family, was able to venture beyond Harrisburg far more extensively than most of his fellow citizens. On an 1883 tour of New York City, he and traveling companion Harry Ross entered Castle Garden, then a busy landing site and immigration center for the many Europeans entering the US. What remains of Castle Garden can be seen at Manhattan's southern tip in what is now Battery Park. It had been the first official immigration center, and over a hundred million US citizens today have ancestors who passed through the facility. It operated from 1820 to 1890 and is now a historic relic, with only a few walls still standing (castlegarden. org). The friends' adventure is described in this *Harrisburg Daily Independent* article. (March 1, 1883, p. 4) Note the misprint in the headline:

A visit to Castle Garden, New York.

A HUGH JOKE.
Two Citizens of Harrisburg Taken for Escaped Irish Deserters.

Will Kelker and Harry Ross, two of the most amiable and conscientious young men in the country and among Harrisburg's most popular citizens, were in New York last week. In their rambles the tourists got down to Castle Garden. Curious to see the sights of that wonderful ingress of the world's population, entered the famous grounds and began a study of the situation, and before they were aware of it found themselves locked in with eight hundred emigrants, in an atmosphere ladened with aromatic odors, the exhalations of foul clothes and the vapor of almost as many execrable pipes. The guard on duty regarded the well dressed gentlemen with suspicion and when it was ascertained that they were American citizens, come to look at the swarms of foreigners, the guard shook his head and frankly said, "It can't be possible." It was possible and it was proven to them and our fellow citizens iterated and re-iterated that they were not foreigners, nor escaped Irish assassins, but had come to look at the sights, to all of which the guard replied, politely but firmly, "You must be examined, gentlemen, before you can go out." It was a moment of extreme embarassment to both Harrisburgers to hear that they were suspected, but they were released and the incident has its moral.

A telescope received from his father on May 1, 1868.

In 1868, at the age of fourteen, William Anthony's father presented him with what for that time must have been a sophisticated telescope. It seems an entirely appropriate gift for the scientifically curious William who, we can reasonably presume, spent much time exploring the stars and planets. The telescope at some point disappeared from the Kelker family collections, and it's not known how it happened. It came into the possession of an individual in California, and sometime thereafter into the possession of James W. Dougherty of Penobscot, Maine. Mr. Dougherty was able to locate and contact Ken Frew, the HSDC librarian, and generously donated the telescope to the historical society, where it is now maintained among the archives.

The inscription reads:

Presented May 1, 1868 To

William A. Kelker

by his Father

Rudolph F. Kelker

Harrisburg, Pa

CHAPTER 6

Rudolph Frederick Kelker Jr.
Chicago Traffic Engineer

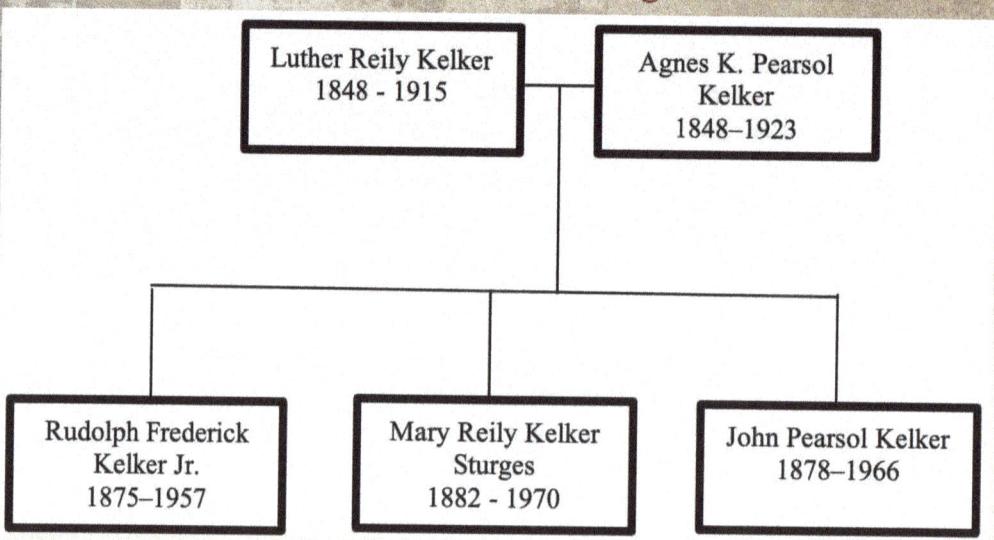

A **brief biography.** Rudolph Frederick Kelker Jr. was the first Harrisburg Kelker in five generations to seek his fortune beyond the city of his birth. Unlike past Kelkers, he showed little interest in the traditional family pursuits of business and local history. He chose a career in engineering that took him to Chicago and other major cities, where he developed transit systems to meet the challenges that rapid urban growth was bringing at that time.

RFK Jr. was born in Harrisburg on August 5, 1875, to Luther Reily and Agnes Keyes Pearsol Kelker. As with previous generations of Kelkers he attended Harrisburg Academy where he graduated in 1891. He then studied at Pennsylvania State College and received a degree in electrical engineering in 1896. After a year of postgraduate study there he took a position in Steelton in the drafting department of the Pennsylvania Steel Company. He remained there for nearly a year before becoming a maintenance-of-way engineer for streetcar traffic in Buffalo, New York. His career got a modest upward boost when he took a similar position with more responsibility in Brooklyn with the New York Rapid Transit System.

In 1907 RFK Jr.'s career took a significant upward bounce when Chicago hired him as an engineer to represent the city in transportation matters. The hiring process required all applicants to pass a civil-service exam. He was the only one of the twenty-seven applicants who passed and thus became the de facto choice to take charge of planning, construction and operation of the city's transit system. An efficient and competent engineer, his extensive transit analyses and planning benefitted Chicago's harried transit riders for over four decades.

In 1911 RFK Jr. married Georgia Moore of Chicago and the union lasted until Mr. Kelker's death in 1957. On June 17, 1917, two months after the US declared war on Germany, Mr. Kelker left his Chicago transit duties to enlist in the military. He rose quickly through the ranks with promotions to captain and then to major, the rank he held at the war's end when he returned to Chicago and resumed his engineering duties. (*The Evening News*, Harrisburg, July 23, 1930, p. 1) That rank stayed with him in civilian life; he was often addressed and referred to as Major Kelker.

In 1939, RFK Jr. and his Chicago traffic-consulting firm, Harrington, Kelker and DeLeuw, prepared the comprehensive plan that was used to construct the city's first subway, which opened in 1943. His efforts extended beyond Chicago; he also established traffic plans to assist St. Louis and Los Angeles in their efforts to address overcrowded, inefficient public transport. Major Rudolph Frederick Kelker Jr. died at eighty-one, on April 19, 1957 in San Mateo, California. He is buried in the Golden Gate National Cemetery in San Bruno, California. His wife Georgia Moore Kelker lived on in California until her 1966 death.

Chicago and Its Transit System: A Concise History

I adore Chicago. This is the pulse of America.

—Sarah Bernhardt

The first resident where Chicago would rise was a mixed-race man from Saint-Domingue, the French colony that is now Haiti (https://www.britannica.com/place/Saint-Domingue), who arrived in 1780. Jean-Baptiste-Point-Du-Sable has the distinction of being the first nonindigenous settler of what is now a major commercial and industrial center boasting a population of 2.7 million. In 1803, the US Army built Fort Dearborn on the south bank of the Chicago River, and by 1830 the early stirrings of a growing community began when lots were sold to fund construction of the Illinois and Michigan Canal that would connect Lake Michigan with the Mississippi River. The Black Hawk War that ended in 1832 left the area free of any Native American resistance, and Chicago began to grow. It was incorporated as a town in 1833 and then as a city in 1837 when the population reached four thousand. From there, growth accelerated. In 1848, the first telegraph and railroad were established. Chicago's location in the grain-producing agricultural Midwest and its access to transport routes passing from the Mississippi through the Illinois Canal to shipping ports on Lake Michigan positioned it as an ideal agricultural trading center. In 1854, grain elevators were introduced, and the Board of Trade established wheat-trading standards that revolutionized the way crops were sold. Chicago, with a population of thirty thousand, became the world's largest grain shipping port.

In the second half of the nineteenth century, the city grew at a remarkable pace. Over this period the population expanded from thirty thousand to 1.7 million. (Chicago, Illinois Population History 1840–2018, https://www.biggestuscities.com/city/chicago-illinois) The city developed as a major commercial center due to the activities of its now-famous business tycoons. Philip Armour built a meatpacking industry, George Pullman built railway cars, Cyrus McCormick built farm machinery and Marshall Field built a retailing business. The world's first skyscraper, ten stories high, was built in 1885.

But this growth was not without major setbacks. A fire in October 1871 destroyed a third of the city but spared its factories and railroads. In 1877, a crippling national-rail strike resulted from labor protests against falling wages at the Pullman Palace Car Company, and in 1886, the Haymarket affair, a labor protest, became a national incident when Chicago police fired on protesting workers. Judicial misconduct that followed was exposed as a major scandal. The novelist Upton Sinclair's fictionalized exposé *The Jungle* shook the nation upon its publication in 1906 by revealing unsafe practices in Chicago's meat-packing industry, a vital component in the city's economy.

Note: Unless otherwise referenced, the above history is taken from History, https://history.com/topics/us-states/chicago.

Chicago's Early Transit History. RFK Jr. spent most of his professional career dealing with Chicago's vast, complex and ever-evolving transit system. Below is a brief history of that system to provide some perspective on challenges he and his fellow city officials faced throughout his four decades there. As in other cities during this time, Chicago's rapid growth placed great demands on city services. By 1880, the population had reached half a million, and business was booming. A need that was not being met was that of moving people from here to there and getting workers to their jobs on an antiquated transit network of horse-drawn vehicles. The Chicago City Railway (CCR), looking for more efficient alternatives, examined San Francisco's cable-car system that had been operating since 1873. The CCR bought into the technology and Chicago gained the distinction of being the first city after San Francisco to operate a cable-car line. The idea was revolutionary and while many eagerly anticipated the new system, others were apprehensive. Home and business owners worried that their properties would be devalued; businesses feared the new cars would be fast and dangerous and were concerned that shoppers would not travel to stores; and horse-car companies foresaw business losses.

But when cable cars began rolling on the Chicago Railway in 1882 (Cable Cars in Chicago, Wikipedia) they were an immediate success. The new system met the populace's transit needs, and some rode just for the joy of traveling at twelve miles per hour. The cable-car system was so successful, in fact, that the CCR extended track routes and built a rectangular "loop" around the city center alongside Lake Michigan. A passenger could board at any stop, proceed around the loop and return to the starting point. This original loop is the presumed origin of the today's Loop, Chicago's commercial center.

Chicago was not alone in adopting cable cars. Twenty-nine other cities ultimately implemented cable-car transit and collectively employed sixty-nine transit companies. From 1882 to 1906, three Chicago companies using three thousand cars provided a billion rides over 41.2 miles of cable track. But by the mid-1880s, as electric trolley cars were becoming the preferred means of getting around, cable-car use went into decline. The last cable car stopped running in 1906. [Cable Car Remnants, Forgotten Chicago, (https://forgottenchicago.com/features/cable-car-remnants/)]

Chicago cable cars images—Yahoo Image Search Results

Chicago's rail-transit system was a collection of privately owned companies, each operating its cars on its own track routes. The city collected a percentage from the fares, and it regulated operations. But with the aim of increasing profits, companies were not above colluding with and/or paying off city officials for various favors, including overlooking "burdensome" regulations or advancing legislation favorable to the companies. In 1881, Charles Tyson Yerkes (1837–1905), an aggressive financier from Philadelphia with a spotty business reputation and ample experience in navigating the minefields of big-city politics, arrived in Chicago and began investing in the city transit system. By 1886, Yerkes and his partners, not averse to employing bribery and blackmail, began investing in and gaining control of the city's streetcar companies.

He eventually controlled most of the companies and to secure firmer control and greater profits began lobbying to extend the city's franchise-license period. In 1895, Yerkes began a campaign for a ninety-nine-year franchise license to replace the city's twenty-year agreements. He lost his bid when Illinois Governor John Peter Altgeld vetoed all franchise bills, stating

"I love Chicago and am not willing to help forge a chain which would bind her people hand and foot for all time to the wheels of monopoly and leave them no escape."

But the transit wars did not end with the governor's veto. In 1897 state legislator John Humphrey introduced several bills that must have greatly pleased Yerkes and his associates. Humphrey proposed legislation granting fifty-year franchises and reducing the fare-percentage going to the city while increasing that going to the companies. The new mayor, Carter Henry Harrison IV, who succeeded his father as mayor, took a strong stand against Humphrey's bills and successfully lobbied legislators who voted to defeat them. But after those bills were rejected state legislator Charles Allen introduced a bill that the state legislature then passed that granted city councils the right to approve fifty-year franchises. The governor signed it, and the conflict shifted from the state legislature to Chicago's city council.

Five months after Allen's bill passed into law, a fifty-year franchise bill was put before the city council, setting the stage for a confrontation between Mayor Harrison and Yerkes, who had "friends" on the council, the Gray Wolves, a group of corrupt aldermen well known for their bribe-taking and a strong force in Chicago politics. (Gray Wolves, Chicago https:// en.wikipedia.org/ wiki/Gray_Wolves_[Chicago]) Mayor Harrison's response was, "If Yerkes can pass an ordinance over my veto, I'll eat my own fedora." Harrison, with votes from his council supporters, was able to get the bill buried in committee and it never reappeared. (Wikipedia, Chicago Traction Wars, https://en.wikipedia. org/wiki/Chicago_Traction_Wars) The mayor continued to work against the Allen law; it was ultimately repealed after he held out by refusing to allow any extension of city transit lines while the law was in effect.

Note: Traction as used herein refers to a railway vehicle that provides the power (traction) to move train cars.

Yerkes, soon after his defeat in the city council, sold most of his Chicago transit stock and in 1899 packed up and left for New York City. In 1900, he moved to London where he began investing in that city's subway system, the Tube. Yerkes used complex financial dealings and his usual suspect practices to gain significant control over the system, and as his control grew, he extended old lines and added new electric-powered ones. But he never got to see his new underground-rail services operate. He died in 1906 before the new lines opened. (Wikipedia, Charles Yerkes, https://wiki2.org/en/Charles_Yerkes)

Yerkes' loss in the Chicago city council and his departure from the scene did little to calm the raging transit war being waged over municipal ownership of the urban-transit lines. Two unsuccessful mayoral candidates, John Maynard Harlan in 1897 and former Illinois governor John Peter Altgeld in 1899, ran on platforms supporting city ownership. A referendum to approve municipal ownership was put before city voters in 1902, and it passed by a six-to-one margin.

With strong public support on the issue, the Illinois legislature in 1903 passed the Mueller Law that granted cities the right to operate transit companies through either acquisition or lease. To complete a purchase a city had to obtain three-fifths approval from voters. A twenty-year limit was placed on all franchise leases with cities holding the option of buying out a transit company at the end of the lease period.

Against the wishes of Chicago voters and many aldermen, Mayor Harrison in 1904 took a position against city takeover. He preferred to act through negotiation, believing it a more effective means to improve service. He faced bold opposition from Alderman William Emmett Dever, an influential and outspoken advocate for municipal ownership, who acted by sponsoring several transit-reform bills in support of acquisition. In the fall of 1904, Dever proposed a referendum seeking to approve the city's immediate takeover of the municipal-rail service. Mayor Harrison responded: "The Dever ordinance is a war measure and should be withheld until all other means of settling the traction issue have failed." In the city council, Harrison was able to get Dever's bill killed by again getting it sent to a committee from which it never emerged. But Harrison's handling of the acquisition issue ended his mayoral career. Facing disapproval from the public and from city labor unions, he withdrew his candidacy from the 1905 municipal election.

But before leaving office Harrison persuaded the city council to submit to the public a referendum concerning acquisition versus lease negotiation. Results showed strong rejection of negotiation and decisive support for municipal ownership. Democrat Edward Fitsimmons Dunne, who succeeded Harrison, ran his 1905 mayoral campaign on a platform calling for immediate ownership. In one of his first actions, Dunne submitted a plan to the city council that would grant a twenty-year lease to a group of investors acting on behalf of the city who would be granted authority to operate and build a new transit system. His proposal died in the city council.

In 1906, Dunne working with his colleague William Emmett Dever attempted to submit a plan for municipal ownership to a voter referendum. With support from influential newspaperman William Randolph Hearst and from the pro-ownership transit lobby, the city council chose to take up the matter. The council proposed, and most voters agreed by referendum, to issue $75 million in certificates to be used in purchasing the city's rail line companies. But here Mayor Dunne ran into problems. He struggled to meet the financial and legal requirements necessary to begin making acquisitions, and he was further frustrated when voter approval of the Mueller bonds did not reach the 60 percent required for them to be issued.

Amid Mayor Dunne's struggles and failures to establish city ownership, the city council rebuffed him and proceeded to negotiate franchise agreements without his participation. The Settlement Ordinances of 1907 set franchises for twenty years and gave the city the right to purchase the privately operated streetcar lines for $50 million. Streetcar fare was set at five cents with 55 percent of net profit going to the city. The ordinances established a Board of Supervising Engineers made up of accountants and engineers responsible for setting equipment and construction standards, and for monitoring and ensuring compliance.

Mayor Dunne, firmly opposed to these ordinances and still advocating municipal ownership, exerted his veto but the city council overrode him. He also lost with Chicago's voters, who in the 1907 municipal election approved the ordinances by a margin of forty thousand votes. And he lost his traction counsel, Walter L. Fisher, who had questioned the feasibility of municipal ownership and urged the mayor to accept the ordinances. Fisher resigned in protest. (Wikipedia, Chicago Traction Wars, https://en.wikipedia.org/wiki/Chicago_Traction_Wars)

Overcrowding. In the midst the ongoing battles over franchise-lease limits and municipal-versus-private ownership, the problem of extreme overcrowding on passenger-rail cars remained, a situation brought on by concentrations of population and of commercial activity in the Loop, Chicago's business center, and beyond. When rail connections were improved to allow trains to enter the Loop directly instead of having to stop outside, thereby requiring passengers to transfer, overcrowding increased further. The floodgates were now open, and the existing rail service could barely accommodate the mass of humanity now flowing into and out of the district. Rush-hour passengers faced extreme overcrowding, considerable discomfort and no small peril. In 1906, at least 130 passengers died using Chicago's transit system. (Barrett, P., 1983, *The Automobile and Urban Transit: The Formation of Public Policy in Chicago, 1900–1930*; Philadelphia: Temple University Press)

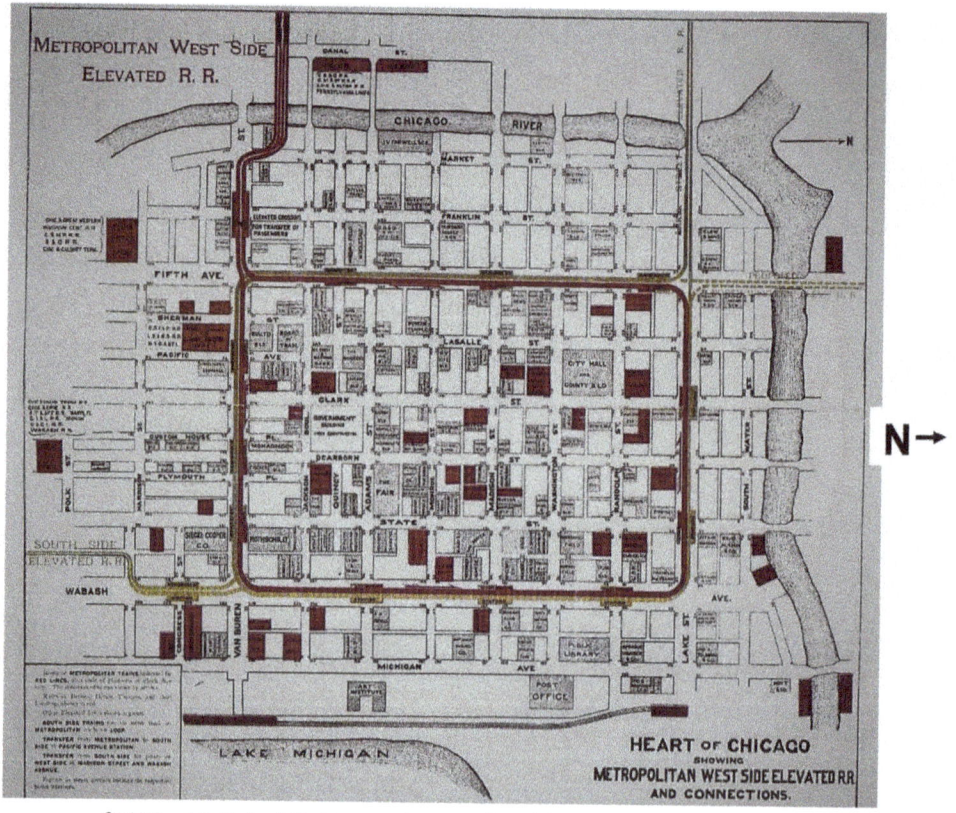

Loop map of 1898, with Lake Michigan at bottom (east) (1892—Chicago Elevated Railroad/ Rapid Transit, (https://chicagology.com/transportation/elevated/, p. 23). The Yerkes 1897 elevated railroad (red line), encircling the Loop, connects points south and west.

RFK Jr. in Chicago. In 1907, Rudolph Frederick Kelker Jr. arrived in Chicago and entered its bubbling cauldron of contentious transit battles. His Board of Supervising Engineer's duties included oversight of railway tracks reconstruction. (*Harrisburg Telegraph*, May 6, 1907, p. 6) He was surely aware of the city's transit situation and what he was getting himself into. He had dealt with big-city transit systems in Buffalo (pop. 423,715 in 1910) and in Brooklyn (1,634,351 in 1910) before his appointment in

Chicago (2,185,283 in 1910). (Population of the 100 Largest Cities and Other Urban Places in the United States: 1790 to 1990 *U.S. Census Bureau, 1998)* Now he was responsible for maintaining and restructuring the city's street-railway system, a vital component of life and well-being for the populace. He would spend most of his professional career dealing with the many and varied challenges of moving people about in the country's third-largest city. He would also apply his expertise in St. Louis and Los Angeles dealing with their transit situations.

In Chicago he sought to relieve congestion in the transit network's rail, bus, auto, taxi and pedestrian traffic. He dealt with severe overcrowding on railcars, construction of new track, re-routing for all transportation systems and the city's many other mass-transit problems. In 1923, RFK Jr. prepared a comprehensive mass-transit plan that outlined a more efficient and fluid traffic flow over all transit systems. His plan included the introduction of subway transit, although it would be another twenty years before underground service would begin in Chicago. Throughout his time in the Windy City, he dealt with city politicians and with rail-line owners pushing for more revenue. In 1939, as engineer for the Committee on Local Transportation and with the partners at his engineering-consulting firm, he prepared "A Comprehensive Plan for the Extension of the Subway System of the City of Chicago," the blueprint for the construction of the Chicago's first subway system.

A year after his arrival in Chicago, RFK Jr. received some unpleasant family news. The August 25, 1908, edition of the *Inter Ocean*, a Chicago newspaper, ran an article on page 5 with the headline "Father Refuses Son Aid," and the subheading "John P. Kelker, Arrested at Auditorium, Now Alone." The John P. Kelker the article referred to was RFK Jr.'s brother. After fleeing to Chicago from Lancaster, Pennsylvania, he had been arrested and detained at the request of the Lancaster police. RFK Jr. was well aware of his brother's criminal activities, and in the past had endeavored to help him. So, he most likely reacted to the news more in anger and disgust than surprise. "Now Alone" in the subtitle referred to RFK Jr.'s statement that he would not provide aid to his brother having already extended him $25,000. Their father, Luther Reily Kelker, also refused to help.

FATHER REFUSES SON AID

JOHN P. KELKER, ARRESTED AT AUDITORIUM, NOW ALONE.

Prisoner Wanted in Lancaster, Pa., on Forgery Charge, Has Brother Here —"I'm Black Sheep," He Says.

Accused of three forgeries, John P. Kelker, alias Bright, who was arrested Sunday at the request of the Lancaster (Pa.) police, was found yesterday to be the brother of R. F. Kelker, division engineer of the board of supervising engineers of the Chicago street railways. R. F. Kelker admitted that the man under arrest is his brother and that he would not again extend him his aid to get him out of trouble with the police.

Mr. Kelker said he had already expended $25,000 in the last ten years in the hope that the younger man would mend his ways.

Says Reform Is Impossible.

John P. Kelker was arrested on information furnished by the Lancaster police, who say he is wanted for forging three checks on banks of that city. He is alleged to have used the name of his father, who, it is said, has helped the young man on many occasions.

"Oh, I'm the black sheep of the family, all right," said the man when he had been brought to the police station. "I have tried to reform several times, but every attempt to live better has ended in more serious trouble than before. Now I have given up trying to keep out of trouble."

Father Refuses Further Aid.

The father, it is said, will not extend his son further aid, but let the law take its course. He thinks the son has been a "black sheep" long enough and it is time to curb him with something more effective than money and the exaction of promises.

The police are awaiting the arrival of the Lancaster authorities.

John Pearsol Kelker, then twenty nine, had a long history of forgery; he had cheated several family members and had already served three years in the state prison in Auburn, New York, and five years in the Huntingdon Reformatory, from which he was released in June 1908. Following release, he passed forged checks, then escaped to Chicago to avoid arrest. He was then transported in custody to Lancaster, where he stood trial, was fined $600 and sentenced to "solitary confinement and Labor" at the Eastern State Penitentiary in Philadelphia. (*The News-Journal*, Lancaster, Pa., Sept. 15, 1908, p. 2)

In 1911 at thirty-five, Rudoph Frederick Kelker Jr. ended his bachelor existence with his marriage to Miss I. Georgia Moore of Chicago. The wedding took place on May 18 in Roswell, New Mexico. After a honeymoon tour through Texas, the newlyweds returned to Chicago. (*Harrisburg Daily*

Independent, May 29, 1911, p. 3) Their union lasted forty-five years until Mr. Kelker's death, in 1957.

Cruelly overcrowded Chigago transit Cars

A political cartoon by Winsor McCay. (c. 1866/71–1934), the popular, widely published cartoonist. From the Chicago Examiner, Jan. 31, 1914, p. 3)

In 1914, RFK Jr. was named to the Board of Supervising Engineers as a "traction expert." He had previously served on the board but was discharged in 1912, probably for his loudly expressed criticism of the board's supervision of the city's rail system. After his dismissal he had offered to provide evidence of inadequate oversight of the traction companies but was not given the opportunity. Now he was replacing the board's traction expert, Michael Buckley who was being discharged "after three years consistent failure to do anything toward improving the traction service." (*Chicago Tribune,* June 27, 1914, p. 7)

Mr. Kelker, the committee and the rest of Chicago were facing the issue of railcar overcrowding and the intransigence of the rail companies—and their paid-off city officials—who refused to do anything that might hurt profits. The need was not in question: riders suffered discomfort and peril and needed relief. Cars ran during rush hours with all seats occupied and straphangers packed tightly throughout the standing-room area with others perilously clinging to the rear platforms. Attempts on the part of the transit commission to implement safety equipment, re-routing or other "burdensome" regulations were most often met with an evasive response or by simply ignoring any order. The usual excuse was that the order was unrealistic and that the company was helpless to do anything. Implementing changes cost money, and that reduced profits—the public would just have to bear the existing situation.

By December 1914, the Department of Public Service had filed 1,650 suits against rail companies. Mr. Kelker, acting as assistant to Montague Ferry, Commissioner of Public Works, calculated that if the city collected maximum penalties for those outstanding violations, it would receive $197,500. The suits were for "failure to post signs giving the train's destination, violations of rules affecting the use of transfers, failure to stop in the middle of certain blocks designated by the council and refusal to take on passengers at regular transfer points." (*Chicago Tribune*, Dec. 23, 1914, p. 10)

Alderman Eugene H. Block, an outspoken advocate for transit reform, was demanding answers, (*Chicago Tribune*, Dec. 27, 1914, p. 5) and he was acting in preparation for an investigation of the transit service. In a meeting of the local-transportation committee, Block aimed his frustration and ire at Bion J. Arnold, an accomplished and respected traffic engineer serving on the Board of Supervising Engineers, and at Leonard A. Busby of the transit lines. The *Tribune* headlined its reporting on the meeting with "Arnold for City or for Busby? Asks Ald. Block." The first four paragraphs quote Alderman Block and provide an idea of the session's atmosphere:

> For whom is Bion J. Arnold working?
>
> Has the huge salary that has been paid him out of the nickels of Chicago straphangers in recent years rendered him contemptuous of his duty to these same straphangers?
>
> Is he really an umpire on the board of supervising engineers or is he, in effect, the bulwark of the traction company in resisting the just demands of the city council for seats for car users instead of straps?
>
> Have we come to such a pass that the city is helpless in the face of autocratic one man power operating against it to nullify its traction needs and demands?

In his response, Arnold replied that he worked for the public and that Block was "playing to the galleries." Block replied, "Well, I'm going to keep right on playing to the galleries, for that is where the straphangers sit. They certainly don't have any place to sit in the street cars." He then went on:

> Anybody but a blind man can see what the trouble is by a fifteen minute excursion in the loop. To say that fancy investigations must be made to determine whether the public needs relief is just another extension of the comical line of bunk that these polished gentlemen hand out and which they intend to keep handing out up to the last minute that they can do so without having it effectively hurled back into their faces by a justly infuriated public.

Block then referred to a report prepared by RFK Jr., conducting "a careful checking of the shortcomings of the lines." Based on information provided in that report the city council had prepared and passed twelve orders by November 30 directed at ridership relief that had been delivered to Busby's committee. None of the orders had been acted on, with Busby declaring that they were "unreasonable."

After further discussion, Block ended the meeting in a statement not masking his despair:

> Circumlocution, evasion, "passing the buck," "ignorance of details" and convenient absence of the man "who could tell us all about it if he were only here" forms the regular grist of attempted negotiations with the street car people.

The following day, the *Chicago Tribune* (Dec. 28, 1914, pp. 1, 8), in its article "State Board to Investigate Straphanging," announced that it was organizing a "Straphangers' Dept." as part of a campaign "to aid in fighting your battle for better street service." Disgruntled rail passengers were asked to submit "specific, detailed complaints of inadequate car service" and were promised that "The Tribune's campaign for the relief of Chicago's straphangers will result in an early investigation of the city's traction evils by the state utilities commission."

The article also reported that the state legislator James E. Quan, the commission's chairman, had announced that he would arrange a "sitting of the commission in Chicago to hear testimony from users of the street car lines."

Quan outlined procedures to be followed and stated that he would press to begin hearing testimony as early in January as possible.

Meanwhile, Block announced that in a meeting that evening he would ask the finance committee for an appropriation for legal expenses:

> [...] to procure a court decision on the "reasonableness" of the demands of the council, as he believes any court will, that it will be up to Mr. Arnold to mend his ways or quit his job [...]
>
> [...] I say this without personal animosity to Mr. Arnold. Indeed I hope he will so conduct himself that he can continue to work in harmony with the council. But in the event of a decision by the court that the contentions are reasonable, the logical development would be steps to oust him from his job and put somebody in his place who will do the work properly.

At the meeting Block also presented "some things the company can actually do [...]" His list included adding more cars on routes both inside and outside the Loop, rerouting some lines to bypass the Loop, accommodating riders not stopping there and adding sufficient supervisors at important transport points, placing signs on cars showing the route taken and equipping all cars with "uniform heating devices."

He then gave his response to a letter addressed to his committee from Arnold, who in defending the status quo quoted a study of headway, i.e., the time interval between a train leaving a given point and the arrival of the next train at that point, and the number of cars in service. In the letter, Arnold said that the study showed that the number of cars "is equal to that furnished at rush hours throughout the city, and therefore does not seem to call for changes." Block responded: "If Mr. Arnold considers the 'service furnished in the rush hours throughout the city' does not seem to call for change, may heaven help us." In another letter, Arnold requested that due to the "abnormal conditions" of the holiday season, scheduled service checks be postponed to a later date. Block, probably smelling an excuse to delay or do nothing, replied:

> December is December, and December weather averages pretty much the same year after year [...] These conditions are only normal for the season and should be provided for as a matter of proper public service. In the light of these plainly discernible facts, Mr. Arnold's letter is sophistical [sic] and lame.

At the council meeting that evening (*Chicago Tribune*, Dec. 29, 1914, pp. 1, 4), the city council passed ordinances requiring that the transit companies act on the issues that straphangers and the council had demanded. The ordinances set requirements for stringent heating and ventilation, monthly reports on the number of cars in service, four more assistant corporation counsels to enforce court proceedings, posting of signs subject to fines of $1,000 and official checking of cars to be done by the board of supervising engineers, with RFK Jr. responsible.

Another provision that passed called for a seat for every passenger. A noble goal, but it is difficult to understand how it could have been implemented or enforced since there were not enough seats in the whole system to accommodate rush-hour riders.

The *Tribune* article responded to Block's success in passing the ordinance requiring monthly reports of the number of cars in service on the elevated lines: "[this] means a severe blow to the time honored tactics of evasion in telling the amount of service that is being given to the public." Two days later the *Tribune* greeted the new year with an article (Jan. 1, 1915, p. 7) announcing that the Cook County real estate board had allied itself with the newspaper's strap-hanging campaign and that the board had "celebrated New Year's Eve by dispatching to the public utilities commission at Springfield a formal petition charging the Chicago Railways company with endangering the lives of passengers by its conduct in overcrowding cars […]" The board was acting in its own interest since efficient and convenient transit service is a major consideration for property values and sales.

The article reported an attack on Bion J. Arnold of the Board of Supervising Engineers in a statement by the commissioner of public service, Montague Ferry, who said that Arnold was only posing as the straphanger's friend, "when as a matter of fact, he (Mr. Arnold) had blocked every move made by the department of public services, Transportation Supervisor Kelker, and the committee on local transportation, to get real street car service." Ferry went on to counter Arnold's justifications and arguments, then closed with:

> If Mr. Arnold were in good faith he would have passed favorably on the recommendations made by Transportation Supervisor Kelker of this department to the committee on local transportation and which were passed upon favorably

by the transportation committee and the city council, thus becoming ordinances. They are city ordinances, still Mr. Arnold refused to recognize them.

Two weeks later, the city's *Day Book* (Jan. 15, 1915, p. 4) reported that E. W. Bemis of the Board of Supervising Engineers was no longer supporting Arnold, the board's chairman, and that Bemis would submit a separate report responding to Arnold's service standards.

Discussions were dragging on among the streetcar companies, the city council, the real estate board and the Public Works Commission. Meanwhile, Local Transportation Supervisor Kelker, with a staff of eighteen field assistants, was busy analyzing transportation activity throughout the city. The field assistants were positioned at points inside and outside the Loop where they recorded the frequency of trains passing through those points, the number of cars in each train, the number of passengers standing and sitting in each car and variations in headway, the time interval between a train leaving a station and the arrival of the next train at that station, an important factor for service regularity and for maximizing the number of passengers transported. Some of the data were published in the January 15 issue of the *Chicago Tribune* (p. 13). The numbers illustrated in stark quantitative figures the conditions of extreme overcrowding that Chicago transit riders were being forced to endure. More data from Kelker's team, also published in the *Tribune* (Jan. 23, 1915, p. 16), give an idea of the extent of rush-hour crowding. Checking was done between 5 p.m. and 6 p.m. during a rush hour and the numbers of seated and standing passengers were recorded. The data were retyped here to provide a more clearly readable copy, and sites with highly packed cars were selected to show the extent of overcrowding.

Checking station	5 p.m. passengers/seats	5:30 p.m. passengers/seats	6 p.m. passengers/seats
State St. Bridge	1,500 / 1,200	2,000 / 1,200	1,400 / 1,000
LaSalle St. Bridge	3,100 / 1,600	4,200 / 2,100	2,400 / 1,100
Van Buren St. Bridge	1,300 / 800	2,100 / 1,000	1,300 / 700

Each data set was collected at a single stop and does not reflect that overcrowding increased at stops farther down the line. This was especially true for trains that left the Loop. This was confirmed by RFK Jr.'s data obtained on June 28 for the state public-utilities commission, as reported in the *Tribune* (Jan. 29, 1915, p. 12) in its article "Car Congestion Outside the Loop Shown Terrific":

> The state public utilities commission yesterday went deeply into the nature of Chicago's traction ills by procuring from City Transportation Supervisor R. F. Kelker, Jr. a comprehensive volume of information covering conditions not only in the loop but in successive zones extending as far southward as Fullerton Avenue. Mr. Kelker's figures, based on checks made last August, showed that overcrowding in the loop, terrific as it is, is surpassed when the cars reach a radius of approximately one mile from the loop [...]

At the city council's January 20 meeting, the local-transportation committee was informed of a curiously interesting letter the contents of which, if true, cast doubt on data collected by Mr. Kelker and his team. Alderman John Toman read the letter signed by an "Employe [sic] of Chicago Surface Lines" purporting to reveal an informer on Mr. Kelker's team who was notifying transit companies when and where inspections would take place. Alderman Toman claimed that when inspectors were sent to inspect runs where fewer than the scheduled number of trains were running, the rail company was able to rush more trains through the site to provide the appearance of a full schedule. He quoted from the letter:

> The city was checking up 12th st. on Friday, Jan. 15, 1915. This was known to the street car company, who instructed their supervisors to make the men do an extra trip. The orders were to switch at Campbell av. so the city employes [sic] would see and report the excellent service which was being given to the public. Of course, this was for the one day the city inspectors were on the job.

After reading the paragraph Toman pointedly asked RFK Jr. if he had notified streetcar companies when inspections were being made. The reply was emphatic "No." Toman's accusation was denied by two others present, John E. Wilkie, formerly of the US Secret Service, and Alderman Henry D. Capitain. In any case, the matter did not come up again. (*Day Book*, Jan. 20, 1915, p. 32)

But transit-overcrowding woes continued in the Loop and at points beyond. In January 1917 Mr. Kelker reported that the most congested area in the city was not the Loop but at the junction of Halstead Street and Milwaukee and Grand Avenues. His team observed and recorded that during a three-hour rush period 1,076 cars passed through the area (*Chicago Tribune*, Jan. 26, 1917, p. 9), and he devised a rerouting plan aimed at alleviating this too-common congestion problem.

On April 6, 1917, Chicago and the rest of America woke up to the news that the United States had declared war on Germany. American men of military-service age began enlisting for duty and the country became consumed with war preparations. RFK Jr. answered the call to duty by stepping away from his Chicago transit responsibilities and enlisting in the US Army. He entered service as a captain at Fort Sheridan in Lake County, Illinois on May 14, 1917. (*Harrisburg Telegraph*, May 14, 1917, p. 13) He served with the 311th Engineers Regiment, 86th Division, and was promoted to major on June 31, 1918, then to camp adjutant at Camp Grant, Illinois. (*Chicago Tribune*, July 31, 1918, p. 7) He served on staff duty in France, returned to Chicago after the armistice and resumed his duties with the city's transit struggles. His rank (title) of major remained with him after his return to civilian life, and he was thereafter often referred to or addressed as Major Kelker.

RFK Jr. and the Long Road to a Subway System. As Chicago grew, so did its transit problems. The 1910 population of 2,185,000 increased to 2,700,000 by 1920. (Wikipedia, https://en.wikipedia.org/wiki/Demographics_of_Chicago#Population) During that decade, people moved about the crowded city in taxis, trucks, fully packed surface- and elevated-rail systems and in a growing number of automobiles. More centrally located business areas, especially the Loop, were snarled messes of automobiles, trucks, railcars and pedestrians.

So, it is in no way surprising that city planners, and probably all Chicagoans, were thinking about getting people off the streets. That meant doing something that cities including Boston, Philadelphia and New York had already accomplished, operating efficient underground-transit systems.

Subway travel was not a novel idea in the early twentieth century. London had opened the world's first underground system in 1863 with a 3.7-mile steam-powered line. Charles Yerkes, noted above for his Chicago transit dealings, developed a major expansion of the London subways (or tubes) that was completed in 1899. Boston, in 1897, became the first American city to begin an underground system, followed by New York in 1904 and by Philadelphia in 1908. (Cudahy, B. J., 1982, *Destination Loop*, Brattleboro: Stephen Greene

Press) Chicago, with its ever-present transportation problems, only began earnest consideration of subway service after other major US cities were already successfully operating underground lines and planning expansions. Plans for subway construction were included in eight city-commissioned studies from 1902 to 1939. None were acted on until the 1937 and 1939 plans put forth by Harrington, Kelker and DeLeuw, Mr. Kelker's transportation-consulting firm.

Not everyone bought into the idea of subway service. As city planners explored the idea of subway travel some expressed opposition. Surface- and elevated-rail companies alike were fearful of competition. Charles Yerkes, during his time in Chicago, justified his opposition to subways, saying: "Chicago wants the crowds on its streets. It wants the bustle and the excitement which they bring." (Cudahy, p. 45) The city's *Day Book* (Jan. 22, 1914, pp. 6, 7) published its reasons for opposing subway transit:

> That the "comprehensive" Hearst-Tribune subway and the "initial" Tribune-News subway are both wrong and either one of them will end in just as many straphangers hanging desperately to straps as now is the view of members of the Cook County Real Estate Board Committee on Subways, officers of the Chicago Federation of Labor and officers of the Greater Chicago Federation and the Northwest Side Commercial Association.
>
> They are against subways mainly for two reasons. One is that Chicago is not an island city like New York, and while there are broad Illinois prairies for the city to spread out on it is foolish to haul people in the dark, bad-smelling tunnels away from fresh air. The other reason is that either of both the subway plans now proposed would only pour more people than ever into the loop, and in the course of twenty years there would have to be subways under subways in order to carry the hundreds of thousands of shoppers down to the narrow seven blocks of State street department stores which are the dumping ground of all urban transportation lines now.

The first of the many transit plans (Martin, T. C., "Bion Joseph Arnold," *Scientific American*, Sept. 9, 1911, p. 223) on the long road to subway travel was prepared by the transit engineer Bion J. Arnold, who had been engaged by the city to make recommendations for improved service. The plan was lauded as an important appraisal, and it served as a source and an example for many proposals that followed, but it had little impact. (Cudahy, p. 46)

In 1916, the Traction and Subway Committee put forth an ambitious plan for fifty-three miles of subway tunnel and five miles of trolley tunnel. The cost of the proposed system was put at $270 million, a frightening amount at that time. By comparison, the Panama Canal, completed in 1914, cost $325 million. (Cudahy, pp. 54, 55) Despite strong support from Mayor William Hale Thompson, the plan was rejected by the City Council. (*Chicago Examiner*, April 24, 1917, p. 1)

Acting in his role as traction expert on the Committee on Local Transportation, RFK Jr. prepared and submitted the 1923 Kelker Plan. His report was responsive to pressures of the current population and to projections of its growth, and to the fact that little had been accomplished in public transportation in the five years following the First World War. His plan was similar in many respects to that delivered by the 1916 Traction and Subway Commission while providing more extensive detail. Although RFK Jr. incorporated the use of subways, the report dealt mainly with improving efficiency and extending coverage of surface- and elevated-rail services. The report was unique in that it was the first Chicago plan to consider incorporation of bus service. The introduction of pneumatic tires and other technological improvements in the early 1920s made self-powered, trackfree bus transportation a viable alternative to railcars, and cities quickly adopted bus transit into their transportation systems. (Public transport bus service— Wikipedia)

RFK Jr.'s plan was prepared with extensive analysis and considerations from previous plans. Kelker included "a physical plan with explanatory maps, construction costs, capacity estimates and an outline of benefits to be derived." (1923 Kelker Plan, www.Chicago-L.org) His plan was praised as a helpful design for Chicago's transit service; however, it did little to move the city toward subway service.

A 1927 plan by Henry A. Blair, president of the Chicago Surface Lines that gave little attention to the prospect of subway service was largely ignored. But after 1927, the idea of realizing a subway system gained greater attention. The renewed interest was brought about by Chicago's continued population growth. Between 1900 and 1930, the population doubled to 3.4 million, adding increased stress to the transit system and other city services. (Cudahy, p. 54) This was reflected in the city council's 1930 plan and passage of an ordinance to set that plan in motion. The ordinance utilized proposals from previous commissioned studies to lay out specific plans for improved transit services. The plan was revolutionary in that it revived interest in improving transit service that included a subway system, and it spurred action. RFK Jr. was elected chief engineer in charge of planning and supervision of the proposed $300 million project. He was compensated at $100 per day, an outrageous salary for that time. (*The Evening News*, Harrisburg, Pa., July 22, 1930, p. 1)

But the early 1930s was no time for urban centers to begin large-scale development requiring major investment. The country was struggling through the crushing economic depression, and Chicago, like every major city, was unable to support such a costly public-works project. It would be 1938 before workers began digging tunnels under the city streets. (www. Chicago-L.org, 1930 Plan) In 1937, after years of plans that were commissioned and not executed, endless discussions and thwarted hopes, the stars finally began to align when financial help became available from the Roosevelt administration's Public Works Administration (PWA). Chicago's application for funding, based on the plan prepared that year by the Harrington, Kelker and DeLeuw traffic consulting firm, was well received by the PWA, and the city was awarded a grant and loan that provided the necessary funds for work to begin. The firm's plan took into consideration changing patterns in Chicago's traffic web with respect to cars, buses and both surface and elevated trains. One major consideration was the burgeoning number of cars, which had climbed from 35,000 in 1915 to 335,000 in 1927 and then to 501,000 in 1937. Automobile use was reducing ridership on surface- and elevated-rail lines, and the new plan addressed that issue.

The plan laid out a north-south subway service with intended routes and stations. But Secretary of the Interior Harold Ickes, a Chicago native and the overseer of PWA funding disagreed with some of the plan's aspects. Ickes did not approve of streetcar subways—that is, surface- or elevated-rail cars that could also run on underground tracks—and wanted these replaced by two north-south subway lines. Mayor Edward J. Kelly and his engineers had carefully calculated that streetcar subways would move more people than subway lines, and they rejected Secretary Icke's demands. But Ickes was the one sitting on the money and after a standoff Mayor Kelly decided that it was better to get the subways built with reduced passenger capacity than to risk that the underground system would slip away. (www.Chicago-L.org, 1937 Plan)

With PWA financing in hand, city engineers continued planning and soon made sufficient progress for construction work to begin, with ground broken in 1938. The design called for a northbound tunnel running through the Loop under State Street and ending at Chicago Avenue, just north of the Loop, with a parallel southbound tunnel under Dearborn Street, the next street to the west of State Street. Work on the northbound tunnel began on December 17, 1938, and on the southbound tunnel in March 1939. (www.Chicago-L.org)

When additional PWA funding became available, Mayor Kelly and his planners considered expanding the system already under construction. The Harrington, Kelker and DeLeuw firm was commissioned to prepare another study that called for an expanded subway system along with other strategies to optimize traffic flow. The firm produced "A Comprehensive Plan for the Extension of the Subway System of the City of Chicago" and delivered it on October 30, 1939.

A COMPREHENSIVE PLAN

FOR THE

EXTENSION OF THE SUBWAY SYSTEM

OF THE

CITY OF CHICAGO

INCLUDING PROVISION FOR THE
WIDENING OF E. AND W. CONGRESS STREET

CHARLES DE LEUW AND COMPANY, Consulting Engineers

R. F. KELKER, JR., Engineer; Committee on Local Transportation

DEPARTMENT OF SUBWAYS AND TRACTION
RALPH H. BURKE, Chief Engineer
PHILIP HARRINGTON, Commissioner

Submitted to the Mayor and the City Council of
the City of Chicago, October 30, 1939

Harrington, Kelker and De Leuw's 1939 plan for the first Chicago subway system. RFK Jr. is recognized as the engineer for the Committee on Local Transportation.

The expanded plan was grand: fifty miles of subway and other improvements at a cost of $267 million. (www.Chicago-L.org, 1939, A Comprehensive Plan for the Extension of the Subway System of the City of Chicago) The new plan included the subways already under construction and reinstated the north-south streetcar subways that had been eliminated at Secretary Ickes' insistence. It was the first of many Chicago plans combining rapid transit with automobile-expressway traffic in a common right-of-way. It also increased transit service to previously underserved areas.

Subway-tunnel spaces were excavated utilizing the deep-bore method, in which digging takes place below street level with waste removed through the shaft opening. This method was necessary for tunneling under the Chicago River. Some sections such as station mezzanines and crossovers between tunnels were prepared by the more disruptive cut-and-cover method, where tunnel space is dug out from street level. (www.Chicago-L.org, Blue Line: Milwaukee-Dearborn Subway) Construction proceeded but delays ensued, brought about in large part by the Second World War. The northbound State Street Line was registered as essential for wartime transportation, so its construction proceeded uninterrupted until its grand opening in 1943. However, the southbound Dearborn Street line was 80 percent complete in 1942 when construction was halted due to rationing of wartime materials. Work on that line did not resume until 1945 and was not completed until February 25, 1951. (www.Chicago-L.org, 1939, Comprehensive Plan for the Extension of the Subway System of the City of Chicago)

The northbound State Street subway, 4.9 miles from end to end, opened for fare-collecting service at midnight on Sunday, October 17, 1943, to great fanfare. The day before the official opening ten rapid-transit trains left from terminals around the city and converged on the new tunnel. The first train to reach North and Clyburn Station was greeted by ceremonies with a high school band blasting an ear-shattering rendition of "El Capitan." When the ten trains had all arrived at the State and Madison stop and unloaded their passengers, a red, white and blue ribbon was suspended across the tracks. Mayor Kelly in his ceremonial role let out a "There we go!" as he cut the ribbon. At the midnight grand opening, Kelly proclaimed: "This is the most significant event in Chicago history to date." One newspaper writer declared in the next day's Sunday supplement that the new system was "the most glorified hole in the ground that has ever been designed." (Cudahy, p. 61)

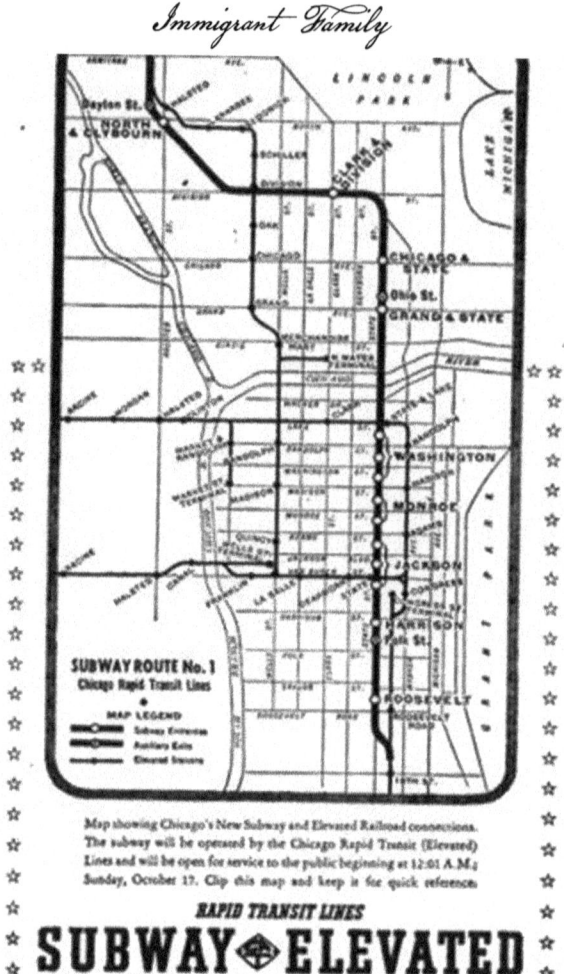

Map showing Chicago's New Subway and Elevated Railroad connections. The subway will be operated by the Chicago Rapid Transit (Elevated) Lines and will be open for service to the public beginning at 12:01 A.M.; Sunday, October 17. Clip this map and keep it for quick reference.

Chicago finally had its long-awaited underground public-transportation system, which was extended eight years later with completion of the southbound Dearborn Street subway. After the decades of planning and all the frustrations and political maneuvering, though, subway transportation did not become the city's significant people mover as it did in New York City, Philadelphia, Washington, D.C., and other cities.

Today, Chicago's vast, efficient metropolitan-transit service operates with only a small stretch running underground. It can even be argued whether a subway system as such even exists there, especially in comparison to major underground systems in other cities. Trains run underground, but only on the Red and Blue lines (the tunnels completed in 1943 and 1951), before continuing onto elevated tracks. Today twenty-two Chicago rail lines run 11.4 miles underground, only a fraction of the city's 224 miles of rail lines. (https://www.quora.com/Does-Chicago-have-underground-subways; Chicago Transit Authority, Facts at a Glance, https://www.transitchicago.com/facts/) The metropolitan-transit system of surface and elevated rail lines serves the city well. The many subway plans, from Bion J. Arnold's 1903 proposal through others drawn up before the Harrington, Kelker and DeLeuw plans of 1937 and 1939 represent much time, effort and expense. That mass of paper now occupies storage space among city archives where it gathers dust and is rarely visited except perhaps by a few interested historians. Maybe Charles Yerkes was right when he said "The underground arrangement would not be practical at all in Chicago." (Cudahy, p. 45)

Major Rudolph Frederick Kelker Jr. died on April 19, 1957, in San Mateo, California. His legacy was his contribution to the straphangers and transit passengers of Chicago and other cities who benefitted from his unrelenting efforts to make transportation more efficient and more comfortable. His distinguishing accomplishment was introducing subway service to Chicago, though the city would not develop its underground travel farther.

Chapter 7 will explore the life of Alexander Ramsey, politician and US Senator.

Addendum

Rudolph Frederick Kelker Jr. and a Friend's Suicide. RFK Jr.'s time in Chicago was intensely focused on moving people and goods efficiently around the city. Below is a brief story of an incident that must have surely shaken him and taken his mind away from buses and trolley cars. (*Chicago Tribune*, June 23, 1936, p. 7)

WINS 10 STORY RACE TO ROOF; DIES IN PLUNGE

Leaps as Wife Seeks to Stop Him.

On the evening of June 22, 1936, Mr. Kelker paid a visit to a friend and walked right into his successful suicide attempt. The friend, Thomas Baxter, was overcome with depression from financial losses and burdened by a strong sense of failure as shown by his suicide note left to his wife (included in the *Chicago Tribune* article).

In his note Baxter addressed his wife as "My Dear Harriet," saying: "We have no money and I am going to do the only thing I know by which you can get some and get enough so that you will have a chance to get on your feet. It is a pretty stiff price to pay, in a way, but not such a stiff one after all the disappointments of one sort or another of the last few years.

"You will be better off without me, anyway, because I am no good any more.

"You will receive between $5,000 and $6,000 insurance, and Dora and Beatrice [Baxter's sisters in London] will receive $4,000 between them. Don't spend a penny more than you have to. I am not worth it.

Mentions Helpful Friends.

"The insurance money should be paid promptly and Georgia and Pete [Maj. and Mrs. Kelker] will probably see you through for the few days you will have to wait."

The letter mentioned Edgar Cook and Jack Cook as other friends who would help Mrs. Baxter collect the insurance, recalled the kindnesses of Dr. D. M. Gallie, 1027 Greenwood avenue, Wilmette, loop dentist, and continued:

"It is not easy to write and say what I want to. My head is buzzing around. Some may say I was a coward and perhaps I am but I have known for a long time that there was practically no chance for making a decent living for both of us as I got too tired of standing on my feet for long at a time. You can't sell when you can hardly stand, and some kind of a field job was the only thing I was likely to get.

"Give Pete all my stuff on traction, as he may find some of it useful.

"I am sorry you haven't been happier these last 21 years.

RFK Jr., who came upon the note as he approached the building while Mr. Baxter was preparing to leap from the roof, notified Mrs. Baxter and they began a frantic search together with the building's janitor. The janitor searched outside and spotted Baxter climbing the fire-escape steps at about the eighth floor. He yelled, "Don't jump. Don't do anything. Your wife wants to talk with you." Baxter made no reply and kept climbing with the janitor in pursuit pleading with him to stop. When Baxter reached the roof he sat on the edge with his back to the alley below, paused and pushed off. His falling body blew past the janitor standing on the fire escape below.

> **" Think Kindly of Me."**
>
> "Try and think kindly of me once in a while. Mother thought I was a good son, my sisters thought me a good brother, and I wanted to be a good husband.
>
> "I am sorry for all the trouble I have caused you. I tried for years to do the best I could and although some may criticize what I am doing now I am doing what I think is the best for you.
>
> "Good-by, with love. TOM."

CHAPTER 7

Alexander Ramsey
Congressman, Governor, Mayor, US Senator, Secretary of War

(Getty Images)

Alexander Ramsey was born in Hummelston, Pennsylvania on September 18, 1815, to Anthony Kelker's granddaughter Elizabeth Kelker and her husband, Thomas Ramsey. Ramsey led a rather unexceptional life supporting Elizabeth and their five children with his Hummelston blacksmith business. He did, however, have the distinction of having served in the 1814 Battle of Baltimore where Francis Scott Key was inspired to write the poem that became the words of the national anthem. His life ended abruptly in 1826 when he committed suicide over the bankruptcy of his business. Elizabeth, left on her own, sent their children to live with relatives.

Ramsey Family Pedigree

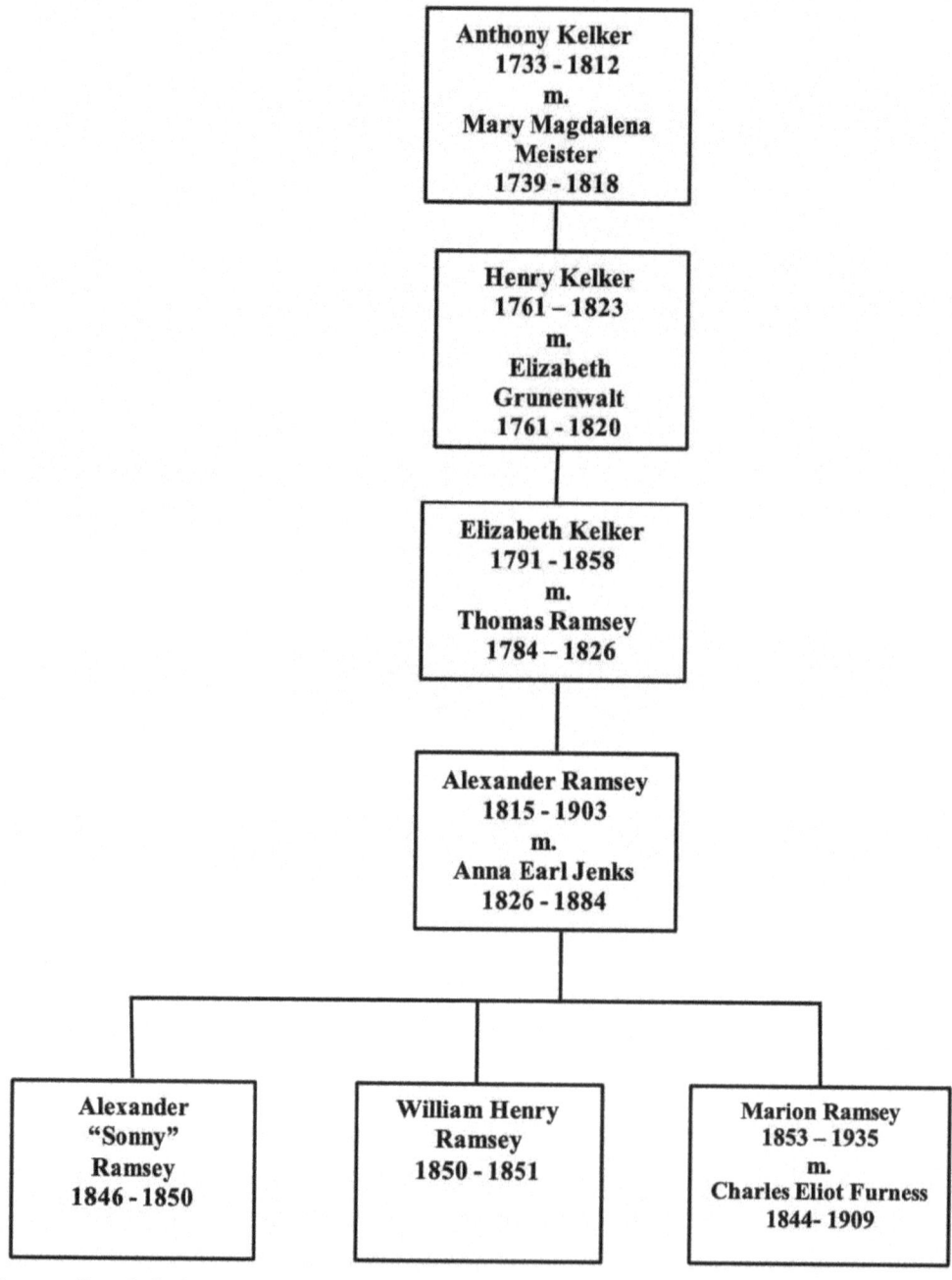

Ramsey Family Pedigree (Kelker Family Record; The Ramsey Family, Alexander Ramsey House, https://www.mnhs.org/ramseyhouse/learn/ramsey-family)

Eleven-year-old Alex was taken in by his granduncle and grandaunt, Frederick and Catherine Fager Kelker, in Harrisburg, where he joined their children Rudolph Frederick, then six, four-year-old Immanuel Meister and infant Henry Anthony. From 1826 to 1834, Alex attended school in Harrisburg, worked in Frederick's hardware store, was employed as a clerk in the Register of Deeds of Dauphin County and learned the carpentry trade. In 1835, he attended Lafayette College in Easton, Pennsylvania, and taught in Kutztown at what would become the Franklin Academy. In 1837, he returned to Harrisburg where he studied law, was admitted to the Pennsylvania bar and began to practice.

Alex. Ramsey,
ATTORNEY AT LAW.
NEXT DOOR TO THE REGISTERS OFFICE.

From the Harrisburg Business Directory, 1842

At this point in his young life Alex Ramsey began to feel the lure of political life, and in 1840 he became a Whig and supported William Henry Harrison for president. He took a step toward elective office in 1841 with a foot-in-the-door appointment as chief clerk in the Pennsylvania House of Representatives. The same year, with his political ambitions now bubbling forth, he ran as a Whig and was elected to the US House of Representatives. The victory, though, was short-lived. He lost his seat when his voting district was declared to be illegally constituted. Undeterred, he ran again and was elected in 1843 and 1845. He was on his way to a distinguished career.

In 1845, Alex took some time away from his political activities to marry Anna Earl Jenks, the daughter of Michael Earl Jenks, a judge and congressman from Bucks County, Pennsylvania. Of their three children only the third-born, daughter Marion, survived beyond infancy. Marion married Charles E. Furness in 1874 and they had four children, Anita, Alexander, Laura and their last child, Charles, who died in infancy. Alexander and Anna Ramsey's grandchildren were childless, thus ending the family line.

In 1849, Ramsey's career took a sharp upward trajectory with his appointment as first governor of the Minnesota Territory. His responsibility was to prepare the newly established territory for settlement as part of the nation's westward expansion. He then spent most of his career in service to Minnesota: territorial governor (1849–1853), mayor of St. Paul (1855–1856) and the new state's second governor (1860–1863). He spent twelve years in

Washington, D.C., as a Minnesota senator (1863–1877). In his last government office, Ramsey served from 1879 to 1881 as secretary of war in Rutherford B. Hayes administration. He died at the age of eighty-seven on April 22, 1903, in St. Paul, where he is buried. (Kelker Family Record, 1983; Chronology, A selected list of events in the life of Alexander Ramsey, from microfiche archives of the Minnesota Historical Society, M203, reel 28)

Westward movement and Manifest Destiny: a grand concept turned bloody. Manifest Destiny was the utopian, imperialist concept that settling the West to develop an agrarian society was an essential duty. It also came to be seen as a genocidal mission aimed at removing Native Americans from their land. In the mid-nineteenth century, Manifest Destiny was a guiding principle for many and an unacceptable mission to others—for example, both Abraham Lincoln and Ulysses S. Grant rejected it. The Whig Party also rejected it and saw "America's moral mission as one of democratic example rather than one of conquest." But the grand concept was realized in the western movement of settlers onto tribal lands in treaties that forced open land for white settlement and herded Native Americans onto reservations that led to bloody battles and widespread deaths among their nations, white settlers and US Army soldiers. (Wikipedia, Manifest Destiny)

Alex Ramsey played an important role in furthering this grand ideal through his success in wresting Minnesota land from its indigenous peoples. His Indian land-concession treaties were followed by broken promises that left those populations struggling to survive. Desperation and anger brought on the 1862 Dakota War, with many casualties on both sides. After their defeat, most Native Americans were removed from Minnesota and resettled to the west on reservations in what are now North and South Dakota. The remaining northern groups of the Ojibwe (Chippewa) were removed by treaty in 1863.

Minnesota and American expansion. America's westward expansion got an official start a year after the Declaration of Independence was signed when the Northwest Ordinance was passed by the Congress of the Confederation of the United States, that is, the third Continental Congress. The act created the Northwest Territory (Ordinance), the area now occupied by Ohio, Michigan, Indiana, Illinois, Wisconsin and the northeast corner of Minnesota. Then, in 1803 the land area of the young United States was nearly doubled during

Thomas Jefferson's administration with the Louisiana Purchase, that added vast areas west of the Mississippi River. The Florida Territory was ceded to the States by Spain in 1819, Texas was forcibly annexed from Mexico in 1845, the Oregon Territory was established in 1846 and the area now occupied by California, Nevada, Utah, Arizona and parts of Colorado and New Mexico was ceded by Mexico in 1848. The accumulation of lands into what is now the continental United States also included the 1818 British Cession that added a wedge of territory between northern Minnesota and the northern Dakota land, along with the 1853 Gadsden Purchase extending the southern border of what is now Arizona. The nation's land area was further expanded with the 1867 purchase of Alaska. (Wikipedia, Territorial Evolution of the United States)

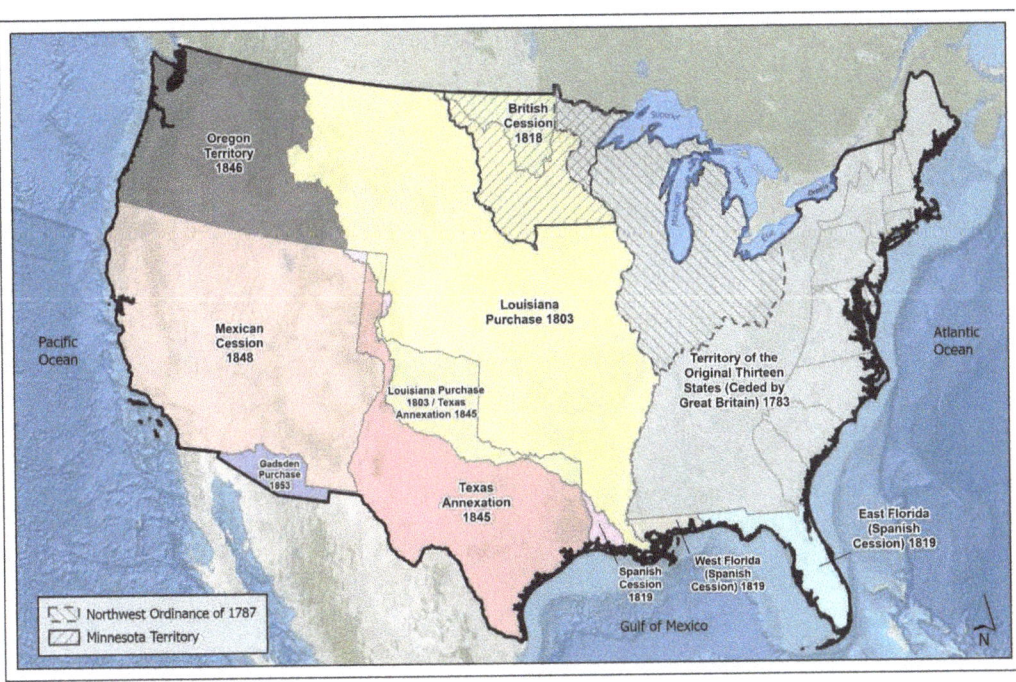

The Westward Movement. The assembly of lands to form the United States came about from lands purchased, conquered and ceded. The Minnesota Territory (bold black outline, forward leaning parallel lines) was formed in 1849 from lands derived from the Louisiana Purchase, the British Cession and the northwest corner of the Northwest Ordinance (shown within a dashed line with back leaning parallel lines). Map prepared by Adam Kelker.

The Minnesota Territory and the State of Minnesota. The Minnesota Territory and subsequently the state of Minnesota were assembled from sections of the Northwest Territory, the Louisiana Purchase and the British Cession of 1818, along with a small area from Iowa in the south. Minnesota became the thirty-second state on May 11, 1858.

Appointed governor, the Ramseys move west. The Minnesota Territory was established in the last hours of James K. Polk's presidency. He signed the bill after it was passed by Congress. Had Polk, a Democrat, been successful in getting the territory approved earlier in his administration, he would have appointed Henry Hastings Sibley (1811–1891) as its governor. But his successor, Whig Zachary Taylor, appointed Whig Alex Ramsey. (Alex Ramsey, Military History of the Upper Great Lakes, http://ss.sites.mtu.edu/mhugl/2019/10/30/alexander-ramsey/)

The new territory was a stage in the government's plan to develop the vast areas of the West, and Ramsey was appointed to further that process. He arrived in an area where local Native American nations coexisted with small numbers of American and European fur traders. But the huge, largely undisturbed territory was about to explode. Its population vaulted from five thousand counted in 1849 (according to the first ever Minnesota Territory census taken the year that Ramsey arrived) to a hundred thousand in 1858 when the territory became a state. Small settlements like St. Paul, St. Anthony and Stillwater swelled into towns as settlers continued moving in. (Minnesota Territory 1849–1858—Minnesota Historical Markers on Waymarking.com; www.waymarking.com/waymarks/WM6KPC_Minnesota_Territory_1849_1858)

When Alex informed Anna that they would be leaving for the new territory he recorded her response in a note in his personal journal, "Appointed Governor of Minnesota." She exclaimed "Minnesota! Where upon earth is it? Denmark?" Neither had seen the Mississippi River or ever given it much thought, but off they went with three-year-old Sonny, a nursemaid, a servant, Alex's brother Justus, and his secretary, Dr. Thomas Foster. (The Ramsey Family, http://www.mnhs.org/ramseyhouse/learn/ramsey-family: White, Helen McCann, 1974, Guide to a Microfilm Edition of The Alexander Ramsey Papers and Records, Minnesota Historical Society, St. Paul, p. 17) They first journeyed by rail and steamboat to the east side of the new state of Wisconsin. From there the party continued west by stagecoach to the

Mississippi's east bank at Prairie du Chien, Wisconsin. From there they traveled north by steamboat for nearly two hundred miles to St. Paul.

Their St. Paul home was not ready when the family arrived, so while waiting they moved in with Henry H. Sibley in Medanton, a little to the south. Sibley was then a representative to the US House from the Wisconsin Territories' at-large district; he would become state governor by defeating Alex Ramsey in 1858 in Minnesota's first gubernatorial election (Henry Hastings Sibley, Wikipedia). Although Democrat Sibley and Whig Ramsey disagreed on many political issues and would compete for the governorship, they shared similar goals and worked together amicably and productively to build the territory and the new state.

In June 1849, the Ramseys moved into their small, newly completed frame house, and Alex went to work in the territory's new capitol building. The transplanted Pennsylvanians endured their first frigid northern winter, shut in with little food and with supplies arriving on the frozen Mississippi, the only delivery route. Anna soberly noted that there was "nothing in the house to eat but strong butter and coffee without cream every potato and vegetable is frozen up [...] The sleigh in the river is splendid [...] Sonny enjoys it amazingly if mama will hold him and not let him get cold [...]" In March 1850, Alex noted: "All out of patience at not seeing a boat arrive [...] Ice out of the river as far as the eye can see." But in April, he added that "On Sunday the ice had disappeared from the river [...] Ten days back people were sleighing on the ice [...] this for nearly four months we had on the ice of the Mississippi a magnificent winter road." And later that day his journal entry stated that "Great noise in town— great tumult, and presently discovered that a boat was approaching, the first of the season [...]" (The Ramsey Family and the River, 1849–1900; http://egee. hamline.edu/GE04Guide/Files/Section3/Ramsey/Ramsey.htm)

Both 1850 and 1851 proved tragic. Sonny, the Ramseys' first-born, died in 1851 at four years, just five months before the birth of their second son, William Henry. Then William died the next year. (Chronology, A Selected List of Events in the Life of Alexander Ramsey, Minnesota Historical Society)

Settling the territory. When Ramsey took up his office in St. Paul, the territory had a white-settler population of six thousand, mainly fur traders. Its expanse was undeveloped except for a few small settlements. Fort Snelling and Fort Gaines were occupied by 317 US Army soldiers, there to keep the peace between Native American nations, largely Sioux and Ojibwe (Chippewa), and white settlers. The territory was calm, with the traders engaging with the native population in mutually beneficial fur trading. Ramsey's arrival and the government's desire to settle the West put in motion an era of fast-paced change that opened Minnesota to settlement and brought on bloody confrontations with the Indian nations.

Ramsey, in his mission to prepare for settlement fully recognized that more settlers would be enticed once basic services for transportation, communication and other necessary systems were established. With support from Henry Sibley he began efforts to expand transportation, clearing passages throughout the heavily forested region. In 1850, he set forth a plan to create a telegraph network along the Mississippi from Prairie du Chien to St. Paul. But despite conditions in the poorly serviced area, settlers continued arriving. And as they built homes in increasing numbers on land with native populations, tensions mounted. (Military History of the Upper Great Lakes, cited above). In 1851, Ramsey was appointed US Commissioner for Indian Treaties for the Traverse de Sioux, Mendota and Pembina nations and charged with negotiating land-cession treaties (Chronology, A Selected List of events in the life of Alexander Ramsey, cited above)

The federal government's territorial expansion plans were on a collision course with Native American communities over lands those nations had occupied for generations and over centuries. Ramsey spent much time in communication and negotiation with their representatives. His negotiations with the Dakota Sioux gained vast areas for the government—but those treaties would prove controversial for how terms had been presented to the Sioux and for how the tribes were never fully compensated as the treaties' terms stated. The resulting anger and resentment against government actions and the evident corruption set the parties on course for the bloody confrontation of the US–Dakota War of 1862.

The 1850 Sioux and Sisseton/Wahpeton land treaties. In 1850, the Dakota of the Wahpeton and Sisseton nations faced difficulties as animal populations they relied on for food and for their fur trade were being depleted. Needing money and productive land, with their survival at risk and with nowhere to turn but the government, they were forced into land-cession negotiations. The Wahpeton and Sisseton were not in a good bargaining position. Already struggling, they recognized that white settlers would soon outnumber them. So, with no options and only their land to offer, they agreed to negotiate.

Ramsey, Sibley and Luke Lea, the Commissioner of Indian Affairs in Washington, scheduled two land-cession meetings with four Dakota groups. They met for two sessions, first with Sisseton and Wahpeton representatives and the second with those of the Bdewakantunwan (Mdewakanton) and Wahpekute. Ramsey and Lea pursued separate sessions because they felt they could more effectively contend with any resistance they might encounter by dealing with smaller groups.

In July 1851, the tribe's negotiators traveled to Traverse des Sioux, the site chosen by Ramsey for the meeting. Negotiations went on for a week and a half. The negotiated treaty promised the Wahpeton and Sisseton of the Upper Dakota a payment of $1,655,000 for twenty-four million acres in the territory's south and west. Their communities would be removed to stretches of land ten miles wide along both sides of the Minnesota River (see map). Payment was to be made in ways intended to help them survive and to convert them to the European agrarian culture brought by the settlers. The largest amount was to go into a federal-government account from which annual payments would be made. Other funds were set aside for constructing schools, agriculture facilities and other services.

On July 23, the Dakota representatives signed two copies of the treaty. They were then presented with a third document by an appointee of the territory's fur traders. Two of the Dakota leaders abstained but the remainder signed, apparently assuming it was another copy of the treaty they had negotiated. It was not: it was a so-called traders' paper, directing the government to pay debts the traders claimed were owed them by local Indian communities. The money was to come from funds received for the land sale. The traders' paper was neither read aloud nor translated for the Dakota leaders. This deception was among a mounting number of such incidents that brought on the Indians' distrust in and resentment of the government. Broken promises and corruption led to bloody incidents.

After signing the Traverse des Sioux treaty, Ramsey, Sibley and Lea traveled to Mendota to meet with Mdewakanton and the Wahpekute representatives to negotiate for more land in the lower territorial areas. The parties met at a Mendota warehouse Sibley owned (he had business interests in the fur trade), then moved to nearby Pilot Knob where negotiations took place. An agreement was signed on August 5 giving $1,410,000 for a large part of the southern Minnesota Territory extending slightly into the Iowa Territory. The Mdewakanton and the Wahpekute agreed to relocate to a site by the Minnesota River near the small village of Morton. As in the Traverse des Sioux treaty, most of the money ($1,160,000) was placed in a federal account on which they would receive 5 percent interest. And again, treaty agreements were directed at conversion from their culture by funding education and agriculture. In consideration of overconsumption of alcohol, Article 6 prohibited the introduction and sale of "spiritous liquors" throughout the territory. (The Treaty of Mendota, Wikipedia)

The treaties of Traverse des Sioux and Mendota cost the federal government $3.75 million and opened an immense area of the Minnesota Territory for settlement. The Dakota peoples were removed to a twenty-mile strip of ten miles on each side the Minnesota River, where they would face even greater struggles to survive. (Relations: Dakota and Ojibwe Treaties, treatiesmatter.org/treaties/land/1851-Dakota)

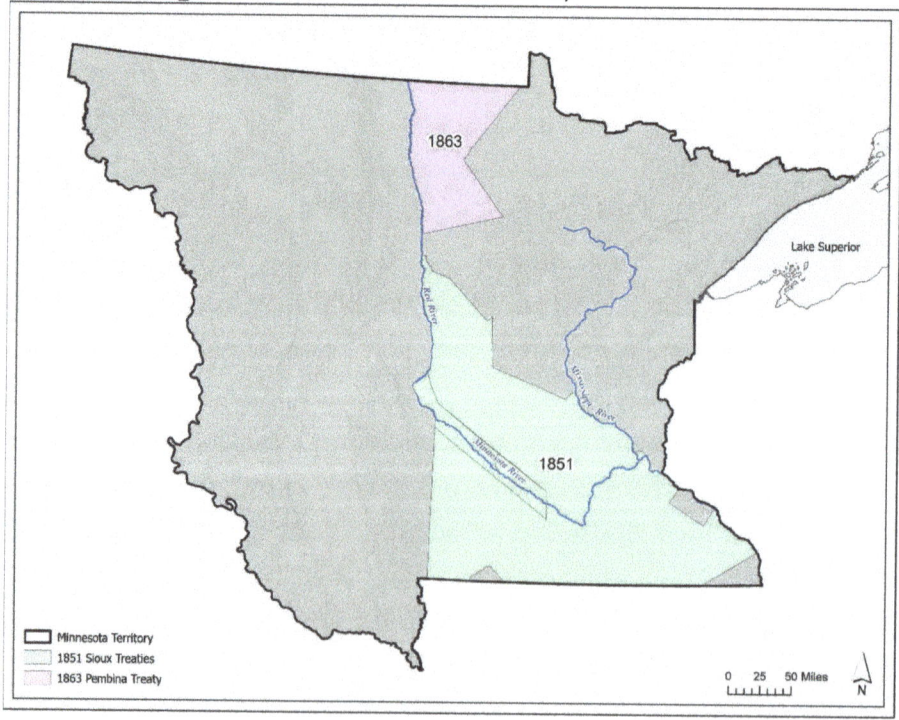

Lands ceded by the 1851 Traverse des Sioux and Mendota treaties (shown in pale green) and the 1863 Ojibwe Pembina treaty (shown in lavender). The map shows the Minnesota Territory in bold outline and the state of Minnesota bound on the west by the Red River to the point where the border continues south to Iowa and river turns southeast and becomes the Minnesota River. The strips on both sides of the Minnesota River are the lands to which the Wahpeton and Sisseton tribes were confined by the treaty. The territory in the north was negotiated from the Ojibwe (Chippewa) Pembina by Alexander Ramsey in 1863 after his 1851 Pembina treaty was rejected by congress. Map prepared by Adam Kelker.

Shortly after completing the Dakota cession agreements Ramsey traveled to the Red River Valley in the territory's north-central part to meet with the Ojibwe (Chippewa) and negotiate another land-cession treaty. The treaty set a land area bounded on the north by the international border, today's Canadian border. Together with the two recently completed Dakota purchases, this agreement would have meant enormous settlement areas opened in both the north and the south of the territory. But here regional politics and the slavery issue came into play. The question of permitting or banning slavery in newly formed territories and states was a contentious issue. Southern congressmen feared that adding settlement territory in the North destined to become slave-free states would reduce their influence in national politics. This Southern bloc was able to block the full set of treaties, but Ramsey was able to save the two Dakota treaties by abandoning the Ojibwe treaty. (William E. Lass, 1998, *Minnesota: A History*, second edition, W.W. Norton and Company, New York, p. 116)

Ramsey's success with the Dakota land-cession treaties was cheered by officials, both Whig and Democrat, whose interests included westward expansion. But the Dakota and others without interests in expanding settlement lands viewed his dealings more harshly. The Dakota had clearly been taken in. They signed away their land for money meant to assure their survival, then never received most of it. A large part was diverted by sleight of hand when they signed the traders' paper, and other payments that were never made. As more information on Ramsey's role in this deceit came to light, an investigative commission in St. Paul began an inquiry. Fifty-seven witnesses, including sixteen who were Dakota, gave testimony to a two-man committee. The commission found no evidence of fraud, but questions arose about Ramsey's role as treaty negotiator in the signing of the traders' paper. These findings were forwarded to the US Senate where, after review, his actions were declared "not only free of blame, but highly commendable and meritorious." Ramsey's Senate supporters did not deal with the evidence provided; they based their arguments on claims that the Dakota were dishonest, likely unable to honor their debts, couldn't handle large amounts of money and didn't tell the truth.

Ramsey was fully acquitted. (Mary L. Wingerd, 2010, *North Country: The Making of Minnesota*, University of Minnesota Press, Minneapolis, p. 204)

Ramsey's duties as territorial governor and supervisor of Indian treaties ended in May 1853. Although out of government, he was occupied with fallout from his actions in the Dakota treaties until well into 1854. Except for his term as St. Paul mayor from 1855 to 1856, he would hold no government position until elected Minnesota's second governor in 1860. He spent those interim years involved in land acquisition, railroad ventures and staying attuned to political developments.

Ramsey and his brother Justus actively acquired a large real estate portfolio that included lands in the Minnesota Territory and in Wisconsin. In addition to his own land purchases, he also bought land for Eastern investors. His business agent in Harrisburg was his first cousin once removed, Rudolph Frederick Kelker. The land acquisitions were aimed to profit from railroad expansion, and Ramsey was particularly interested in the Minnesota and Northwestern Railroad, incorporated by the territorial legislature in 1854 for the purpose of constructing a line from the Illinois border to Lake Superior. Ramsey and Edmund Rice were the directors for two railroads. Rice's brother Henry was in Washington working with two congressmen, Elihu B. Washington from Illinois and a James P. Doty from Wisconsin, to secure financing for the railroad through a congressional land grant. Ramsey made a trip east to lobby for passage of that land grant. The grant was not approved, and the project did not go forward. Ramsey was involved with other railroad companies—the Puget Sound and Pacific, the Lake Superior and the Minnesota and Pacific—and their efforts to get financing. But those ventures were doomed by unsuccessful attempts to get approval for issuing state-railroad bonds and the failure of a mission to New York seeking to negotiate any bond sales. No track was laid, and the companies went bankrupt.

The Whig Party's collapse in 1856 left Ramsey a politician without a party. After some careful consideration he joined the newly formed Republican Party, and soon thereafter was appointed to the party's executive committee by national chairman Edwin D. Morgan. He immediately began a flurry of travel, fundraising and campaign activity. He was active in the 1856 campaign supporting the first Republican presidential candidate, John C. Fremont, in his run against the eventual winner, Democrat James Buchanan. He traveled east seeking party support for campaign efforts in Minnesota. He campaigned in Wisconsin and Pennsylvania. He was in communication with Republican Party leaders Salmon P. Chase, Thaddeus Stevens, Thurlow Weed, Simon Cameron, Theodore Adams and Horace Greeley. He was successful in bringing funds to support Minnesota's Republican election campaigns and to draw nationally recognized speakers to support local Republican candidates. (White, pp. 18–23)

Having arrived in Minnesota in 1849 as territorial governor and US Commissioner for Indian Treaties through 1853 and having served as St. Paul's mayor from 1855 to 1856, Ramsey suddenly held no office, but he kept his nose in political activities. When Minnesota received statehood on May 11, 1858, he saw the opportunity to reassert himself as a major player in its politics and entered the first race for governor. His Democratic opponent in the election was Henry Sibley, his friend, colleague, rival and Ramsey's equal in political ambition and political savvy. Sibley won by 240 votes. When Ramsey ran again in the 1859 election, he won by a large margin. He served from 1860 to 1863 then resigned to become Minnesota's US senator. (Jayne Becker, 2018, "The Controversial Career of Minnesota's First Territorial Governor, Alexander Ramsey," MINNPOST, p. 3)

Republican politics and prewar Minnesota. In his first year as governor, Ramsey devoted great effort to working for the Republican Party in Abraham Lincoln's nomination, election and leadership in the Union war effort. He traveled to Chicago in May for the Republican National Convention where the Minnesota delegation first backed William H. Seward then shifted allegiance to Lincoln when it became clear that Seward would not get enough support. (Alexander Ramsey, Military History of the Upper Great Lakes, MHUGL, https://ss.sites.mtu.edu/mhugl/2019/10/30/alexander-ramsey/) Following the election Ramsey led a committee to Springfield, Illinois, to inform Lincoln that he had won the presidency. (White, p. 24) When South Carolina became the first state to secede from the United States, Ramsey and other northern governors signed a joint resolution of loyalty to the Union.

Perhaps it was fate that Ramsey happened to be in Washington on April 13, 1861 when the first shots of the Civil War were fired on Fort Sumter in Charleston harbor, South Carolina. Always keenly attuned to political opportunity, especially when it involved patriotic service, he rushed the next day to meet Secretary of War Simon Cameron (Some references say he spoke directly with Lincoln.) There he pledged a thousand Minnesota volunteers for the Union Army. He was fully prepared to make this commitment, the first by any state, for both Democratic and Republican Minnesotans had strongly backed his support for the war effort. In just two weeks the First Minnesota Regiment was formed and stationed at Fort Snelling just south of St. Paul.

After being reelected governor in 1861, Ramsey presented the Governor's Message to the state legislature to start 1862. In it he gave news and updates from the war and commended Minnesotans for aiding the war effort. "It is scarcely less indicative of the elastic energy of our people, than it is honorable to their loyalty, that, having made the first tender of armed aid to the General Government, upon the fall of Fort Sumter, in April last, our State was among the first which furnished their full quota of the half a million men called by the General Government to the National Defense." (Alexander Ramsey, MHUGL)

The US-Dakota War of 1862. The year 1862 was the most fraught and demanding of Ramsey's long career. Along with his support for the Union's war effort his term as governor is notable for the Dakota War and events that had led up to it. Ramsey is particularly remembered for his inflammatory September 9 speech to the Minnesota legislature in which he proclaimed that "the Sioux Indians of Minnesota must be exterminated or driven forever beyond the borders of the state." (Becker, p. 1)

Minnesota sites involved in the 1862 Sioux war. The surrounding states and provinces are shown as they exist today. Map prepared by Adam Kelker

The US-Dakota War was the culmination of years of mistreatment, mismanagement and treaty violations by the federal government. The Traverse des Sioux and Mendota treaties of 1851 promised money and supplies in exchange for immense land areas. Payments specified in the treaties were late or not made; most never reached the Dakota and were lost or stolen due to corruption at the Bureau of Indian Affairs and with traders demanding payment for goods alleged to have been supplied on credit. Removed to a twenty-mile-wide stretch of riverbank land, their populations struggled on a reservation that did not provide enough food. And further, during the Senate treaty-ratification process, Article 3 was deleted from both treaties, thereby removing the Indian land on the north bank. Declining wildlife, essential to their survival, was further reduced as settlers logged and cleared while new settlers continued arriving in increasing numbers.

In desperate need, the two northern Dakota groups were able to negotiate for food with the Upper Sioux Agency. However, when the Mdewakanton and Wahpekute Dakotas applied to the Lower Sioux Agency, they were refused credit. Driven by desperation and anger the Indians began attacking settlers. On August 17, four Dakotas on a hunting expedition killed five settlers. In a council meeting that night the Dakota, under their leader Little Crow, set out a plan to drive settlers from the Minnesota River Valley.

The next day Little Crow led an attack on the Lower Sioux Agency at Redwood. Attackers burned agency buildings. Settlers seeking refuge were able to escape across the river. Minnesota militia and a company of volunteers sent to fight off Dakota warriors were badly beaten. The militia commander was killed along with twenty-three men. Dakota warriors then swept along the river valley, killing settlers and burning villages.

Emboldened by their success the Dakota began an attack on the settlement at New Ulm. They did not attack nearby Fort Ridgely immediately as it was heavily fortified, so they headed toward New Ulm killing settlers along the way. By the time they reached the town, residents had set up defenses and were able to hold off the war parties although some Dakota skirted the defenses and set fires that destroyed most of the town. A thunderstorm that evening slowed the fighting and prevented more attacks and allowed time for residents to erect new barricades. The town was further protected with the arrival from nearby towns of regular soldiers, militia and two companies of the Fifth Minnesota Voluntary Infantry.

On August 20 and 22, the Dakota assaulted Fort Ridgely. Soldiers defending the fort successfully repelled the attack, but they were left unable to defend nearby farms and settlements. On September 2, a detachment was sent on a mission to find survivors, bury the dead and carry out reconnaissance on the locations of Dakota warriors. At Birch Coulee, some sixteen miles from Fort Ridgely, the formation was attacked by the Dakota. The three-hour battle left thirteen soldiers dead and forty-seven wounded and only two Dakota dead. That afternoon 240 soldiers marched from Fort Ridgely to relieve the embattled unit.

Meanwhile Indian attacks on stagecoach stops and river crossings in the Red River Valley brought steamboats and other river traffic to a halt. Stagecoach drivers, mail carriers and military couriers were killed while seeking refuge at settlements. Many settlers and employees of the Hudson Bay Company and other ventures were forced to shelter at Fort Abercrombie on the Red River.

While the Dakota were ravaging the settler population the state's regional representatives made repeated appeals for aid to Washington. Lincoln, preoccupied with the Civil War, eventually acted by forming the Department of the Northwest, and sending Gen. John Pope, commander during the Union defeat at the Second Battle of Manassas (Bull Run), to lead the operation against the Dakota. Pope assembled a force from three volunteer Minnesota regiments, and Governor Ramsey called upon Sibley, his friend and former rival, to take a leadership role in the defense.

On September 23 a military force under Sibley, who had just received promotion from colonel to brigadier general, engaged Dakota parties at Wood Lake in a battle that decisively ended the Indian rebellion and any chance to reclaim their land. After minor engagements along the skirmish line, over the course of the two-hour battle the militia attacked and overpowered the Dakota. Most warriors surrendered on September 26, and 269 of their captured men, women and children were released.

The six-week US-Dakota War was ended after more than six hundred white and mixed-race citizens and US soldiers had been killed. Up to a hundred Dakota died. The misfortunes of the Dakota groups would not end. They faced further suffering and hardship before being removed from Minnesota. (Dakota War of 1862, Wikipedia)

At the end of the war many Sioux fled west to the Dakota Territory and others to Canada. However, many who had been involved remained with their families. A large group of these Dakota and others met with Sibley's force at Camp Release, so named for the release of the Dakota's captives that took place there. Sibley took all the warriors into army custody. The 392 captured Indian men were tried for their roles in the war. The trials were hasty and unfair, some lasting only five minutes. All the Dakota were found guilty and sentenced to hang. The convicted Dakota warriors were taken to Mankato, and on November 7, 1,658 Indian noncombatants were made to journey for six days to Fort Snelling where they would be held the through the winter. (US-Dakota War of 1862 | Lower Sioux Agency | MNHS)

The sentence of hanging for so many men elicited controversy. Minnesota's Episcopal bishop published an open letter and traveled to Washington to urge Lincoln to act with leniency. On the other side, Governor Ramsey warned the president that unless all were executed "private revenge would on all this border take the place of official judgement on these Indians." Sen. Morton S. Wilkinson of Minnesota warned Lincoln that the white population opposed leniency. After Lincoln and his staff reviewed the convictions, the sentences of all but thirty-nine were commuted, and one more was later granted a reprieve.

The hanging ceremony, the largest mass execution in US history, took place at Mankato on December 26, 1862. A large single-scaffold platform was built in an open area to accommodate the simultaneous killing of the thirty-eight Indian men. The military in full dress uniform stood in formation along with a crowd of onlookers. The execution proceeded with the dropping of the single platform support, leaving the Dakota hanging by their necks. (Wikipedia, The Dakota War of 1862)

The 1862 mass execution of 38 Sioux warriors in Mankato, Minnesota. (Getty Images)

The noncombatants reached Fort Snelling on November 13 and were settled in a camp on a bluff about a mile west of the fort. Col. William R. Marshall, placed in charge of the Indian captives by General Sibley, then moved the captives to the river bottom just below the fort. In December, Marshall's men built a wooden stockade twelve feet high that enclosed about two to three acres as a concentration camp to house the Dakota. A warehouse near the stockade served as an infirmary and mission station. The military closely guarded the stockade and strictly controlled exit and entry. The captives endured a harsh existence during the freezing winter weather of 1862 to 1863. Measles and other diseases accounted for most of the estimated 130 to 300 who died.

On February 16, 1863, Congress put the finishing touches on the process of ridding Minnesota of its native Dakota. An act passed that day "abrogated and annulled" all treaties with the Dakota nations. Another act was passed on March 3 that authorized removing the Dakota from the land of their ancestors. In May, the noncombatant Dakota held at Fort Snelling were put on steamboats and transported to a reservation at Crow Creek in the Dakota Territory. (US-Dakota War of 1862 | Historic Fort Snelling | MNHS; https://www.mnhs.org/fortsnelling/learn/us-dakota-war)

Except for some minor skirmishes, the removal of the Dakota was essentially accomplished. Ramsey completed his Indian-removal mission in 1863 with a land-cession agreement with the Ojibwe tribes of the north that he had failed to accomplish in 1851 during his tenure as territorial governor and Indian commissioner. The guiding principle of Manifest Destiny had been realized in Minnesota.

To the U.S. Senate. In January 1863, the Minnesota legislature elected Ramsey to the US Senate. (Note: The Constitution in 1789 provided for senators to be selected by their state legislatures. The Seventeenth Amendment, ratified in 1913, established direct popular election of each state's senators.) At the end of Minnesota's legislative session Ramsey traveled to Washington where he was sworn in on March 4. He did not resign from his governorship immediately but remained in office until June while dealing with cession treaties with the Ojibwe, Red Lake and Pembina groups in the north.

The Ramsey family was now off to Washington. With their St. Paul home sold, new quarters were found at the National Hotel in Washington. Daughter Marion, then ten, was enrolled in a school in Philadelphia. (White, p. 28)

Ramsey's career in the Senate spanned two terms. He was sworn in on March 4, 1863, some two years into the Civil War, and served until March 3, 1875, at the end of the Grant administration and the start of the Hayes administration. Documents from the Ramsey archive collection at the Minnesota Historical Society (White, The Alexander Ramsey Papers and Records) show that his time in the Senate was busy and productive. He was occupied with military affairs throughout the war. After its conclusion, he represented Minnesota on commissions to plan military cemeteries at Gettysburg and Antietam and served on committees for naval affairs, patents and territories.

With an eye to the needs of his home state Ramsey spent significant time devoted to railroad expansion. The growing state of Minnesota needed broader rail service and Ramsey, now an influential senator, was able to deliver on something he had failed to do in 1854 as a citizen entrepreneur. In 1863, he introduced a bill to aid construction of the Lake Superior and Mississippi Railroad from Duluth to Prairie du Chien, Wisconsin. The bill passed in 1864 and the link between Duluth and St. Paul was completed in 1871. Ramsey was also involved in other railroad matters by helping to bring about bridge construction over the Mississippi at Fort Snelling and La Crosse, Wisconsin.

The Ramseys evidently settled into Washington life nicely and were active in the city's social life, at least judging by the following event. In December 1863, their first year in Washington, the Ramseys and other Senate and congressional dignitaries attended an event aboard a Russian fleet anchored off Alexandria, Virginia. According to the *St. Cloud Democrat* (Dec. 31, 1863, p. 2): "The ladies smiled, the states men [sic] bowed, the politicians watched, the reporters took notes." The language problem was solved by the presence of interpreters. But Ramsey set off a buzz among the American guests when he began speaking with some from the Russian contingent without an interpreter. The guests were taken aback that Senator Ramsey was speaking Russian. But, as it turned out, he was communicating not in Russian but in German, spoken by many of the Russian sailors. He had learned it in Pennsylvania's Dutch country, where the German language was common, while growing up in Harrisburg in Frederick and Catherine Fager Kelker's home. The American guests were pleasantly amused.

Ramsey's first Senate term came to an end on March 4, 1869, and he had little difficulty getting elected to a second term. The Republican-dominated

Minnesota legislature voted him to office again on January 20, 1869. (Wheeling Daily Intelligencer, West Virginia, Jan. 20, 1869, p. 1)

A significant part of Ramsey's time in office was concerned with the postal service. In 1866, he was appointed chairman of the Senate committee on post offices and postal roads, and in 1869 to a special postal-service commission to reach an agreement with France, and he traveled to Paris to negotiate a treaty. The trip turned into a family excursion with Anna and Marion along. Ramsey remained in Paris until November; Anna and Marion went on to Dresden where they spent the winter and where Marion studied German and music.

The Paris trip was not without controversy. Ramsey was roundly criticized for a "junket" at the expense of the U.S. treasury. The Lancaster Intelligencer (Aug. 4, 1869, p. 3) commented that "paying Mr. Ramsey ten thousand dollars [...] to negotiate a simple treaty about postage, is carrying the joke altogether too far [...]" The San Francisco Examiner (Sept. 14, 1869, p. 1) referred to the trip as misappropriating the people's money, the aim of which "is to swindle the treasury." Similar criticisms were published twice in the Detroit Free Press, in Danville, Vermont's North Star and in the Cambrian Freeman, Ebensburg, Pennsylvania.

The Fort Snelling Scandal. Ramsey's family visit to Europe was not the only questionable act of his Senate tenure. He was remotely but significantly involved in the Fort Snelling Sale Scandal. The affair involved the illegal purchase of Fort Snelling by manipulator and schemer Frank Steele. With inside help from the War Department, Steele parlayed his purchase into hundreds of thousands of dollars for himself and his collaborators, all paid by the federal government. Ramsey's participation helped Steele walk away from the affair with his dishonest gains. The details of the fraud were published in the Chicago Tribune (July 23, 1873, p. 2), the source for the story provided here.

Steele was quite familiar with Fort Snelling and its location on the Mississippi River. He operated a very successful ferry business delivering passengers across the river, to and from the fort. And as a savvy, conniving and devious business operator Steele saw the possibility to acquire Fort Snelling and increase his wealth. The acquisition scheme began on April 15, 1856, when Steele wrote a letter to Secretary of War Jefferson Davis seeking to purchase the fort. Davis refused, as the fort was in military use. But around that time an act was passed by Congress authorizing the secretary of war to sell any decommissioned military facility. Under that act the fort was sold to Steele in 1857 when new Secretary of War John B. Floyd signed off on the transaction. A suspicious congressional committee investigated, concluding about the slick deal that:

> The sale took place just six weeks after the new Secretary of War, Mr. Floyd, took office.
>
> The sale took place without consultation with General Winfield Scott, the army's Lieutenant General.
>
> The sale took place without any investigation into whether the fort was still in use [it was in use and continued to be into the twentieth century].

The fort's property value was estimated at $50,000 by the army, while Steele estimated it at $18,000 though the government had spent $50,000 in construction costs and $10,000 the previous year for improvements to the 7,300-acre reservation. Selling the property at $50,000 would be a per-acre price of $9.21 when land around the fort was selling for $50 per acre. On June 6, 1857, the sale was made for $90,000. Steele paid $30,000 up front with the remaining $60,000 due in two years at no interest, though loans in nearby St. Paul then had monthly interest rates of three percent.

But there's more. Before the sale Steele and a Kenneth McKenzie had each constructed a building on the Fort Snelling reservation. Their location on government property meant that Steele and McKenzie could not claim title to the buildings. But just before the sale Steele bought McKenzie's building for $15,000. So, consider what Steele was actually paying and what he was getting. The Steele and McKenzie buildings were valued at $25,000 and the on-site government building was valued at $30,000. Subtract the $55,000 value of those buildings from the $90,000 selling price and what Steele was actually paying for Fort Snelling was $35,000, a mere $4.79 an acre.

The sale was carried out with no regard to transparency. It was so secret that after the sale a potential buyer from St. Louis wrote to the secretary of war asking when the fort would be sold. The fraudulent purchase was in direct violation of the rights of Minnesota citizens, as state regulations required that the land be divided into forty-acre lots and sold at auction or by sealed bids. But here Steele and his collaborators were able to purchase the entire 7,300 acres intact.

On June 4, 1859, the US House of Representatives studied the affair and adopted the following resolutions:

> The management of the sale by the agents authorized by the Secretary of War [...] was injudicious and improper. Exclusion of competition should not have been permitted.
>
> The terms of sale adopted by the agents appointed by the Secretary of War are disapproved of, a credit unauthorized by law was given to the purchasers, the right of possession after the sale, reserved to the government was calculated to prevent a fair sale at a fair price.
>
> That the terms of sale adopted by the agents appointed by the Secretary of War to make said sale are disapproved of.
>
> That the evidence obtained by this committee be transferred to the Secretary of War.

But on July 9, just a little more than a month after the congressional resolutions were passed, Secretary of War Floyd placed Steele in possession of Fort Snelling. The secretary did this even though:

> The law required that title was not to be given until the consideration money had been paid. But despite the law, the congressional resolutions and still owing $60,000 for which he was paying no interest Steele took possession. And the fort was not abandoned. It was in active use by the military.

Steele was clearly annoyed by the congressional investigation and resolutions, and he responded with a brazen, blustery and audacious response designed to secure himself an even better deal. He wrote to Secretary Floyd:

> It is quite probable that you have heard that I intended in consequence of the actions of Congress and its influence upon the property, to decline further payment until some allowance was made by the Government for the damages that I have sustained consequent upon the actions of Congress in the investigation of the subject.

And he made this proposal:

If you will withdraw the contract from the hands of the attorney to whom it was sent [to commence suit to cancel it], I will waive all claim for damages, and make a payment of $10,000 within four months, and the balance due ($50,000) as soon as possible.

The matter was referred to Gen. William T. Sherman and on May 26, 1860. He replied that:

Mr. Steele is not anxious to fulfill the terms of the agreement [...] A fair compromise should be made with him [Steele], and none would be more fair than to credit him with the money paid—$30,000 with interest, and charge him with all monies received by him. He has had the use of the valuable ferry privileges, and has had the benefit of other rents and profits, and should make a declarative statement of the amount and receive the balance due him.

When the Civil War began in 1861, St. Paul was designated a rendezvous location for U.S. Army and Minnesota troops with Fort Snelling selected as the rendezvous point. Fort Snelling was chosen despite there being large areas of available land in the St. Paul area that could have been arranged to accommodate troops at lower cost. But its designation was thanks to the influence of parties with an interest in Frank Steele's ownership. Things were moving along very nicely for Steele. Fort Snelling was serving a critical need in the war effort, and he was situated exactly where he had schemed to be, in position to extract rent for governmental use of "his" property.

But here his scheme ran into the higher principles and integrity of new Secretary of War Edwin McMasters Stanton, who refused to make any rent payments. Secretary Stanton's rejection imposed no economic hardship on Steele. His ferry business was booming as military personnel in large numbers crossed the Mississippi to and from Fort Snelling. He could afford to wait until Stanton was no longer secretary of war to collect his rent, sell the fort back to the government and reap his riches, and that's what he did.

On January 24, 1868, Steele presented a bill to the government for $102,000. He asked for back rent at $2,000 per month for eighty-one months (April 1861 to January 1868) totaling $162,000. But there was still the $60,000 he pledged to pay in the original sale of which he had paid nothing. So, he deducted that from the rent bill for an invoice total of $102,000.

The war department acknowledged the rent payment, reclaimed a thousand acres, and paid back the $30,000 Steele had originally paid. Steele, no longer in possession of the fort, walked away with 6,300 acres. He split the land half-and-half with his collaborators, and within a few days sold his portion for $200,000. In summary, the government, as rightful owner of the land, paid rent to the party that had no legal right to the land. And the party with no right to any revenue payment collected $102,000 in rent and $200,000 from his illegally acquired property.

Steele's sale and Fort Snelling land grab were aided and abetted by a good word from US Senator Alexander Ramsey, then one year away from facing reelection and, of course, happy to receive support. Steele & Co. offered to help him win support from Minnesota Democratic legislators. All they asked was that he advise the secretary of war to settle the issue "upon an equitable basis," which Ramsey did. We don't know if the quid pro quo had any effect on Ramsey's successful campaign, but he was easily reelected by the Minnesota legislature.

The *Chicago Tribune* article from which this history was taken added this comment on the affair:

> We don't blame Frank Steele so much as the War Department. He is a respectable adventurer, and his idea of a government is something to be preyed upon. There is, however, no limit to the blame deserved by a department which, either from folly or corruption, would consummate such rascality. And, more than all, we blame Alex Ramsey, who, when conferred with the war department, and knowing the whole history of the fraud, should from either cowardly or corrupt motives, have permitted such villainy to triumph, not only without a word of protocol, but with his assent and connivance.
>
> Steele may be out of reach of the law. He has pocketed his plunder and is laughing at the people; but Ramsey seeks re-election, hoping for further assistance from Steele in the way of mutual favors, to again guard their interests with the stern and watchful integrity he has shown in the case we have related. With him the people can settle. They commenced to do so last Wednesday.

At the end of Ramsey's second term on February 19, 1875, the Minnesota legislature ended his Senate career, passing him over in favor of another Republican, Judge Samuel J. R. McMillen, the chief justice of the state's supreme court. Ramsey clearly desired a third term, but unlike his assured

1869 election victory he now faced strong opposition from the Republican governor, Cushman K. Davis, and a long-time political rival, Ignatius Donnelly. With seventy-one votes required to win, Ramsey led the January 21 first ballot with forty-two votes to Donnelly's forty-one and Governor Davis' sixteen. (*Worthington Advance*, Minnesota, Jan. 22, 1875, p. 1) But over the month of voting days that followed Ramsey saw his lead slip away, as did both Donnelly and Davis. On February 2 he was nine votes behind a rapidly rising Judge William Lochren. (*Grange Advance*, Red Wing, Minn., Feb. 9, 1875, p. 2) But on February 12 he regained his lead with fifty-two votes to Lochren's forty-five. (*Worthington Advance*, Feb. 19, 1875, p. 1) But Ramsey then began to lose ground again, and on February 26 the Minnesota legislature chose Judge McMillen, whose support rose quickly during the last days of the election process. (*Worthington Advance*, Feb. 26, 1875, p. 1) Alex Ramsey's time in the US Senate had ended.

The interim. Following the Senate defeat the Ramseys moved back to their spacious, well-furnished St. Paul mansion. Away from the clamor of Washington they enjoyed life's simpler pleasures. Alex read Dickens aloud and enjoyed life in his magnificent home. On the first of each month he went about collecting rent from his many properties. Anna tended her flower garden, sewed clothes for Marion's children and took pleasure visiting with her neighbors. In 1876, the Ramseys traveled to Philadelphia where they visited Marion's family and attended the Centennial Exposition. Alex was present at the 1876 Republican national convention that nominated Rutherford B. Hayes. In 1878, a former Republican colleague serving in the Hayes administration arranged for the president and his wife to visit St. Paul where they were entertained by the Ramseys. (White, pp. 34, 35) These post-Senate years out of office were a pleasant interval for Alex and Anna. They lived at a slower pace, spent more time together and were happily settled in St. Paul, which they'd made their home.

But the politics bug never left Alex. He remained in touch with his former colleagues and kept a close eye on national events, and when the opportunity to get back into political life presented itself, he grabbed it. In January 1879, President Hayes appointed him the thirty-fourth Secretary of War, (White, pp. 34, 35) For the Ramseys it was back to Washington where Alex would serve for the last two years of the Hayes administration.

Secretary of war. Once back in office, much time was spent dealing with patronage requests from around the country, with many arriving from Minnesota. Ramsey dealt with requests for civilian assignments, West Point appointments and posts in the western territories. Most could not be approved as few positions stood open and available.

Although Ramsey's time was largely spent on routine matters, one exception stands out: the Johnson Chestnut Whittaker incident at West Point. On April 5, 1880, Whittaker, one of the first black cadets to attend the military academy, was found tied to his bed, bleeding and unconscious with razor cuts to his hands and face. He claimed that he had been attacked by fellow cadets, but West Point administrators refused to believe him and accused him of fabricating the incident to win sympathy. A full year of widely publicized hearings led to Whittaker being found guilty in an 1881 court martial and expelled from the academy. His case was prosecuted by Major Asa Bird Gardiner, who would become both a major figure in Tammany Hall, the New York City political organization, and a disgraced attorney quoted as having stated that "Negroes are noted for their ability to sham and feign" and that blacks were "inferior." President Hayes was clearly unhappy with the verdict, and he overturned it in 1883, but West Point restored the expulsion, citing an exam that Whittaker had failed. (Wikipedia, Johnson Chestnut Whittaker) Although Ramsey sided with Whittaker he refrained from any public comments or opinions during the court martial. But in his annual departmental report in 1880 he indicated his dissatisfaction, declaring that West Point should strive "to keep the Academy open to boys from all conditions of life." His views were quoted in a June 1880 news story, that it was "ignoble to be governed by an imagined superiority" and "thrice ignoble to make active exhibition of so unworthy a sentiment by oppressing those we may deem beneath us. A true manhood dictates the extending of a helping hand." (White, p. 36)

Ramsey and President Hayes, dissatisfied with the West Point administration's handling of the case and seeking to reform court-martial procedures, removed the academy's superintendent, General Schofield, and replaced him with Maj. Gen. Oliver Otis Howard, probably best known for having Howard University named after him. (White, p. 37) Howard was a strong supporter of postwar Reconstruction and a leading figure in promoting higher education for people of color, including those freed from slavery. (Wikipedia, Oliver Otis Howard)

Whittaker moved on; he became a teacher, lawyer and high school principal in Oklahoma City and a psychology professor in South Carolina. He died in 1931. His two sons served as army officers in the First World War, his grandson was a member of the Tuskegee Airmen in the Second World War and his great-grandson served in the Vietnam War as a first lieutenant. In 1995, President Clinton restored Whittaker's commission, awarding it to his heirs and adding: "We cannot undo history. But, today, finally, we can pay tribute to a great American and we can acknowledge a great injustice." (Wikipedia, Johnson Chestnut Whittaker)

Ramsey, Sherman and President Hayes' US treasury-supported western junket. Ramsey's term as secretary of war ended on March 4, 1881, after Hayes chose not to seek reelection. Before leaving office, however, Hayes, along with Ramsey, set out on a grand tour of the western states that lasted seventy-one days and made eighty-one stops. (The 1880 Great Western Presidential Tour, http://www.usgennet.org/usa/topic/preservation/stories/presid.htm) The President left Washington by train on August 26, 1880, accompanied by his wife, Lucy, sons Birchard and Rutherford, Gen. William T. Sherman and his daughter Rachel, and Gen. John G. Mitchell. The party stopped in Rutherford's home in Fremont, Ohio and rested for several days before heading off to Chicago, Burlington (Iowa) and Omaha where Ramsey joined the party. (Baur, J. E. 1955, "A President Visits Los Angeles: Rutherford B. Hayes' Tour of 1880," *The Historical Society of Southern California Quarterly*, https://www.jstor.org/stable/41168522; and from information provided by the Rutherford B. Hayes Library and Museums)

The trip, although billed as non-political provided a platform for the president to ingratiate himself (and his party) to many potential voters. Much time was taken for pleasure. Hayes gave thirty-seven speeches, delivered in nine of the seventeen states he visited while never addressing any controversial issues. (Hayes, R. B., Chronological List of Speeches, Rutherford B. Hayes Collections, Collection ID: Hayes-1; Location, Hayes-1; Description ID: 594041) The arrival of the president and his entourage was everywhere eagerly anticipated, with huge crowds appearing at most stops with Hayes along with Sherman and Ramsey regularly holding forth from their train's rear platform. At many places the party would leave the train to be greeted by enthusiastic crowds and feted by local officials. At the stop in Virginia City, Nevada, for example, Hayes, Sherman and Ramsey spoke to a crowd estimated to be as large as seventy thousand. (*Baltimore Sun*, Sept. 8, 1880, p. 4) The traveling party was well taken care of onboard and at stops during which they occupied fine hotels and were royally treated. Scheduled events included receptions, speeches, visits to local sites, parades and women's events for Mrs. Hayes, Rachel Sherman and others.

Using mostly trains but also ferryboats, steamers and stagecoaches the party traveled from Omaha on to Utah, Nevada and San Francisco. From there it was north through Oregon, Washington and back to San Francisco where they were entertained by Leland Stanford, former California governor (1861–1863), US senator (1885–1893) and founder of Stanford University. The event at Stanford's Menlo Park mansion was captured in the photograph shown below.

The Hayes entourage at Leland Stanford's home, Menlo Park, Calif., Sept. 1880. (Rutherford B. Hayes Presidential Library & Museums)

From left: Rachel Sherman, General William T. Sherman, Ramsey, Lucy Hayes, President Hayes, Leland Stanford. (Cropped from the above photo, Rutherford B. Hayes Presidential Library & Museums)

The itinerary was mostly adhered to but on some occasions the president, unable to resist the temptation to explore, took side trips that shortened the time available to greet local populations. The party left San Francisco for Los Angeles where the city had made extensive plans for the President's visit. But as the group approached Los Angeles Hayes' made a last-minute decision to visit Yosemite Park. (see photograph below)

The Hayes entourage at Yosemite, 1880. (Rutherford B. Hayes Presidential Library & Museums)

The Hayes party's Yosemite side trip forced Los Angeles (population 11,200) to significantly alter its program to accommodate a shorter visit. But the citizenry, while disappointed, showed no lack of enthusiasm with large cheering crowds greeting the visitors. Hayes and his entourage arrived on October 23 at seven in the morning and were greeted at nine by the reception committee in a parade of carriages. Hayes, his wife and sons were situated in the first carriage, with Ramsey in the last carriage. They rumbled off for a whirlwind visit that included a short tour of surrounding orchards and ranches, a visit to the town's Agricultural Park with horses and livestock on display and then on to a splendid meal at the Cosmopolitan Hotel. The visitors were then moved on to the Baker Block, an ornate structure (no longer extant) where the president, Sherman and Ramsey spoke to a crowd of five thousand enthusiastic citizens. Then it was off to the Horticultural Pavilion where another grand meal was served, and then to the railroad station where they boarded their train and pulled out for their next stop, at San Gabriel. (Baur, "A President Visits Los Angeles," pp. 36–42)

The Los Angeles visit, although curtailed, was typical of how the president's party was greeted at the dozens of stops made during over two months of touring. The travelers were enthusiastically welcomed, cheered, wined, dined, and greeted with parades, flowers, gifts and crowds. The Los Angeles visit is also notable, however, for a gaffe Ramsey made at his Baker Block speech. In what was probably an off-the-cuff remark he said that what California needed was "more water and better society." From the crowd, someone yelled out, "So does Hell." The usually calm and amiable Ramsey was taken aback and couldn't cobble together an explanation to qualify his words. For him, it was a rare moment of public embarrassment. (*Los Angeles Herald*, Oct. 24, 1880, p. 2)

From San Gabriel the president's party moved north to Monterey and Sacramento, then to stops in Chicago and Ohio before starting the ride back to Washington, D.C. The tour ended with their November 1 arrival in the capital, just in time for everyone to vote in the presidential contest between James A. Garfield and Winfield Scott Hancock. The trip was remarkable for the fact that it was the first visit to the Pacific coast by a sitting president, though it's difficult to understand what else was achieved. It is reasonable that a president of the United States would want to reach out to the people and become more familiar with the country's social diversity and landscapes. But Hayes and Ramsey were away from Washington and their official duties for seventy-one days in a time when travel was slow, and communication was dependent on surface mail or telegraph. How could they have responded to a national crisis three thousand miles from Washington? The tour was indeed a chance for the president to become familiar with the West and to gain insight into the ways of those living beyond the Mississippi. Yet he was nearing the end of his term and had little time to realize benefits from any knowledge gained. It's hard to avoid the conclusion that the tour was a U.S. treasury-funded grand junket. Ramsey and the Shermans were happily along for a comfortable and enjoyable ride. Ramsey served out his remaining months as secretary of war until Hayes' term ended on March 4, 1881. His career in government was over. In 1881, he ran for another Senate term, but Minnesota Republican legislators failed to support him. Samuel McMillen, who had defeated Ramsey in the 1875 election, was chosen for a second term. So, it was back to St. Paul where he would spend the rest of his life active in business and community affairs.

Retirement years, 1881–1903. Now out of office, Ramsey and Anna settled nicely into life in St. Paul where he prospered for another twenty-three years until his 1903 death at age eighty-eight. But the early 1880s were not kind to the Ramseys as the family endured a series of tragedies. In 1880, while Alex and Anna were still in Washington, the infant son of daughter Marion and son-in-law Charles, Charles Eliot Furness Jr. died of whooping cough. Then on January 24, 1881, Ramsey's brother and business partner Justus committed suicide.

While Alex and Anna were settling into life in St. Paul, Marion's husband, Charles Furness, accepted a position with a Minnesota railroad company, and the Furness family moved to Minnesota and took up residence with the Ramseys. But in 1882, Charles developed mental illness, went east for medical treatment and never returned to his family. (White, p. 38)

The final blow landed on November 29, 1884, when Anna, at fifty-eight and after thirty-nine years of marriage, died after a long illness. Alex entered into his journal, "Wife—my dear wife—Oh how I loved her—Died at 41/2 this PM—58th year of her age." (Anna Earl Jenks Ramsey [1826–1884], WikiTree FREE family Tree, https://wikitree.com/wiki/Jenks-907) General Sherman wrote his condolences, "Will you permit our sad family to mourn with you in this sacred grief and think on what great occasion for all sympathies you so highly loved and admired Mrs. Ramsey that this time the loss is personal." Rudolph Frederick Kelker wrote from Harrisburg, "Oh, I thought, if only I could be with you, as you faced your hell, or sought seclusion in your mansion, to dwell upon the memory of the loved one, with whom you had so many years trodden the path of life, who had so nobly helped you bear its trials, and shared with you the joys […]" Former colleague and political rival Henry Sibley wrote: "You have my most profound sympathy in your distressing bereavement." (Ramsey Papers, Minnesota Historical Society, Microfiche Roll 28) Marion, now with three young children and apart from her husband, assumed her mother's role as mistress of the house. (Timeline | Alexander Ramsey House | MNHS, htpps://www.mnhs.org/ramseyhouse/timeline; White, p. 38)

For Alex, being away from the political scene that had so consumed his life must have been a challenge to his inner-driven political instincts. But he did get two appointments from Washington to serve on government commissions. The first came in May 1881 from William Windom, President Garfield's secretary of the treasury, who asked Alex to serve as special examiner on a commission to investigate charges against the superintendent of the US Mint in San Francisco. Ramsey traveled to San Francisco where he spent several months investigating before the commission produced a report clearing the superintendent of all charges. (White, p. 38; *New York Times*, Sept. 11, 1881, p. 2)

Ramsey's other government commission in retirement was from 1879 to 1881 as chairman of the Edmunds Commission that was investigating the practice of polygamy in the Utah Territory (Utah became a state in 1896). President Garfield denounced the practice in his inaugural address and in 1882 his successor, Chester A. Arthur, was able to get the Edmunds Act passed into law. It criminalized polygamy, disqualified polygamists from jury duty and barred them from holding public office. What followed was a tug-of-war between the Mormons and the federal government over the Edmunds Act. Most Mormons did not comply, assisted by court rulings from local Mormon-dominated courts. President Arthur pushed Congress to put the Utah Territory under its direct control, but he was unable to do so before he left office. But his unsuccessful struggle reinforced the Supreme Court's decision that polygamy was not protected by the First Amendment and that the amendment did not prevent the federal government from exercising broad authority over federal territories. (Biographies and Memoirs, https:/erenow. net/biographies/the-forgotten-presidents/8.php; White, p. 38; Alexander Ramsey (1879–1881) Miller Center, https://millercenter.org/president/hayes/ramsey-1879-secretary-of-war)

Ramsey's career, an assessment. Alexander Ramsey started life in difficult circumstances and rose to high office. Orphaned at eleven and sent off to live with his granduncle Frederick Kelker's family, he went on to a successful career in government, something seemingly preordained by his instincts for the rough and tumble of political life. He gained many distinctions. He was a member of the US House of Representatives, first governor of the Minnesota Territory, territorial US Commissioner of Indian Affairs, mayor of St. Paul, second governor of the state of Minnesota, a US Senator from Minnesota and Secretary of War. He thrived in the political arena driven by those qualities essential to a successful political career: intelligence, ambition, a glad hand, an ability to wheel and deal in the political arena, a nose for opportunities and an ability to cultivate friendships with those who could aid in his upward mobility.

He was a loyal Whig, and when that party collapsed he became a stalwart Republican. At the 1860 Republican convention he supported William H. Seward until Seward's candidacy collapsed. He then supported Abraham Lincoln. He was a member of the committee that went to Springfield to inform Lincoln that he had been elected president. During the first weeks of the war he was the first governor to commit state troops to the Union's war effort.

Ramsey surely counted among his successes the removal of the indigenous Dakota peoples from Minnesota, clearing the way for white settlement, the building of railroads across Minnesota, public-works projects delivered to state during his time in the Senate, reforms in the US Postal Service, construction of bridges and other improvements along the nation's rivers, the founding of the Minnesota Historical Society and many others. But we must acknowledge his more questionable actions. Removal of Minnesota's Native American nations allowed for the rapid development of Minnesota into a rich and flourishing state, but it was accomplished with deceit and bloody methods. Ramsey's role in the "traders' paper" deception during the signing of the Traverse des Sioux treaty was investigated by Minnesota and federal legislative committees. He will always be held to task for his resounding statement to the Minnesota legislature that "the Sioux Indians of Minnesota must be exterminated or driven forever beyond the borders of the state." And following the Sioux defeat in the US-Dakota War in 1862 Ramsey urged President Lincoln to hang hundreds of Sioux warriors before the president reviewed the convictions and reduced that number to thirty-nine. And then there was Ramsey's role in settling the Fort Snelling Scandal, when the high-stakes schemer Frank Steele promised to get support for the senator's upcoming election in exchange for a good word to the secretary of war to "settle" the affair. Ramsey was not averse to taking advantage of his position to secure some very nice perks. Two examples are his Paris trip with the whole family along for the alleged purpose of negotiating a postal treaty and the government-funded western excursion of seventy-one days with President Hayes and General Sherman.

But Ramsey cannot be faulted solely for his transgressions while serving as a public servant. He carried out his duties as an elected official with professionalism and a concern for his constituents. He could recognize a wrong, as he did in the Johnson Chestnut Whittaker incident at West Point. He was responsive to the country's needs as he sought to build its infrastructure through the construction of bridges, improvement of the waterways, addition of new rail lines and improvements to the postal service. He was forever mindful of Minnesota's needs, and as a US senator he used his influence to benefit the state he and his family made home.

Ramsey's warm and loving relationship with Anna and the strong support she gave him were of great benefit to his life and career. That close bond helped them to survive the tragedy of losing two infant sons, and it was surely a source of strength when their daughter Marion's infant son died, when Alex's brother Justus took his own life and when son-in-law Charles Furness became mentally ill and was placed in an institution away from Marion and their children. Alex, who possessed all the traits of an aggressive, firmly opinionated, sometimes bullying and sometimes hard-headed politician, was warm, caring and supportive of his family.

Prominent political figures are easy targets for praise and criticism. The praise can be fulsome, and the criticism can be harsh. Here are two different opinions on Alexander Ramsey published in 1883, shortly after his career in government had concluded.

Praise and Criticism

GOVERNOR RAMSEY.

Alexander Ramsey was elected United States Senator by the Legislature of Minnesota on Wednesday last. Without making any comparisons to the disparagement of the other candidates, it is simply just to Gov. Ramsey, to say that it will be a source of congratulation to the whole country that a gentleman so eminent for his patriotic devotion to principle, so able, so wise, and so good a man has been chosen to represent the noble young State of Minnesota in the council halls of the nation. He is one of the men on whom the country in her darkest hours can rely with the most unflinching confidence. He at least will never desert her.

Chicago Tribune, Jan. 16, 1863, p. 2

Governor Ramsey, U. S. S.

Our duplicated friend, Governor and Senator Alexander Ramsey, is one of the keenest financiers of our State. He knows which side his bread is buttered as soon as he gets it spread. He takes care of Minnesota, at the small charge of Five Dollars a day.— He attends to the United States, at Ten Dollars a day. He makes a trip to Washington, Senatorially, and furnishes his "advise and consent" to the President, for the trifling mileage of Eighteen Hundred Dollars As Governor, he journeys into Kentucky, Tennessee, and Arkansas, looks into the condition of our soldiers, incidentally, and into his cotton operations, particularly, and charges his expenses to the State.— The Governor is cute. The Senator is shrewd. The Governor and Senator, combined, are so duced smart that they come very near making Alexander Ramsey a public swindler.— *Pioneer.*

Goodhue Volunteer, Red Wing, Minn., March 6, 1863

Chapter 8 presents an appreciation of the unrecognized Kelker women and their crucial roles in the family history.

Addendum
Alexander Ramsey

An article from the *New York Times* (Aug. 8, 1880, p. 8) gives us a look at Ramsey's personality, his temperament and his interaction with his colleagues. It has been transcribed from the original archival copy to provide print clarity.

Alexander Ramsey

PERSONAL CHARACTERISTICS OF THE SECRETARY OF WAR

From the Washington Republic

As much as there is that is interesting in the man himself, there is very little in the daily life and habits of the present Secretary of War that calls for special notice. He lives in a manner becoming his position and fortune, but there is not a clerk in his department who is less ostentatious. He knows nothing of the latest quirks and turns of fashionable society; he has no taste for the vanities which go to make up fashionable accomplishments. He goes on his humdrum way, faithfully performing ever duty as an officer and a citizen, and nature made him this gentleman. He was early in life an orphan, and he has had his struggles in life, and no doubt the way has at times seemed hard and uneven; but he had a stout heart and a cheerful disposition, and these generally in the long run get the best of bad fortune and human errors.

Mr. Ramsey was born near Harrisburg, Penn., in 1815, and all the school education he ever obtained was before he was 14 years old, for in 1828 he was a clerk in Register's office in Dauphin County. In 1841 he was Clerk of the State House of Representatives. Running up rapidly in public favor, he became very popular, and the district elected him to Congress two terms, (Twenty-eighth and Twenty-ninth Congresses.) He was appointed Territorial Governor of Minnesota in 1849, holding the office until 1853. He settled in St. Paul where he has since resided, and he was at one time Mayor of the city. In 1859 he was elected Governor of the State of Minnesota, and was re-elected in 1861. He was elected to the United States Senate and took his seat in 1863, and was re-elected, his second term expiring in 1865. He was appointed Secretary of War last December, to take the place of Mr. McCrary, appointed United States Judge.

The personal habits of Mr. Ramsey are of the simplest character. He is always well-dressed, but his clothes are not likely to be of the latest cut. His general air is that of a prosperous farmer or manufacturer. He generally wears a shocking bad hat, and he never looks like a statesman of the Sumner type. He is always too happy with the world to think of his personal appearance. He goes to bed early unless he has something to keep him up, and he is an early riser. He breakfasts at 8 and 9 o'clock generally finds him at his office going through the mail. He takes no lunch, and dines at about 6:30, and dines right royally. The evening he gives up to his friends and social duties. The Secretary is very fond of jolly company, and is himself full of humor. He is also a capital story-teller and a most hearty laugher. A more genial, kindly, honest, manly face was never set above a pair of shoulders, a perpetual reminder of the Cheeryble Brothers. Mr. Ramsey is about 5 feet 10 inches tall, and weighs about 210 pounds. His hair is white and a trifle thin on top, and excepting a tuft of white beard beside each ear, his face in cleanly shaven and as round as an apple.

As a speaker, Mr. Ramsey is forcible, direct, and earnest. In his 12 years' service in the Senate he did little talking as compared with many other Senators, but nobody could state his views clearer and more effectively. He managed the bills of his committee with unusual skill, and if he was crossed in debate he roused all his latent strength and became a dangerous adversary. In the Senate he was the most popular of men. His gentleness and unvarying good nature were fully appreciated there. It must be a serious case that makes him lose his temper. Persons who have known him intimately for years say they have never seen him angry and never knew him from anybody who sought his charity of assistance. It is rather strange that he has preserved that serenity of disposition in all his rough Western experiences, for it should be known that Mr. Ramsey had a long and trying association with the Indians, and that it was he who negotiated and closed the famous treaty with the Sioux in 1851, by which 40,000,000 acres of rich land, now known as Southern Minnesota, were acquired and thrown open to settlement. The knowledge of Indian affairs acquired by Mr. Ramsey in a residence of over 30 years among the red men makes his qualifications for present office particularly strong, and there can be no doubt that he is a good Secretary of War.

Ramsey namings. Ramsey is little remembered beyond Minnesota today. But his life, the good, the bad and the rest, was significant and his actions helped both Minnesota and the United States grow and prosper. He is in part remembered by having his name attached to two counties, two cities, two parks and several schools. An extensive collection of his archives is kept at the Minnesota Historical Society in St. Paul, and another collection is stored at Dickinson College in Carlisle, Pennsylvania.

Ramsey named sites (Alexander Ramsey Legacy (Alexander Ramsey, Wikipedia)
—Ramsey County, Minnesota
—Ramsey County, North Dakota
—The city of Ramsey, Minnesota
—The city of Ramsey, Illinois

—Alexander Ramsey Park, Redwood Falls, Minnesota
—Ramsey Park, Stillwater, Minnesota
—Ramsey Junior High School, St. Paul, Minnesota
—Ramsey Elementary School, Montevideo, Minnesota
—Justice Page Middle School, Minneapolis, Minnesota, founded in 1932 as Ramsey International Fine Arts Center, then re-named Alexander Ramsey Junior High School, and in the 2016–17 school year again re-named for Justice Alan Page, the first African-American, Minnesota Supreme Court Justice and former professional football player.
—The Liberty Ship *SS Alexander Ramsey*, launched in 1942

The Ramsey mansion in St. Paul, listed on the National Register of Historic Places in the United States. From Wikipedia.

The Ramsey home, St. Paul. The Ramseys had long dreamed of living in a magnificent home, and they began to see their dream realized in 1868 when construction began on their St. Paul mansion. Their hopes for a splendid home had grown more intense while living among and admiring the magnificent Georgetown mansions during Alex's US Senate career from 1863 to 1875. In 1866, Anna wrote to their daughter Marion that "Papa and myself [sic] rode over to Georgetown. I was astonished to see so many beautiful fine grounds. Papa made the sensible remark: he wished he owned such a home; how he would enjoy it: I wonder if we all would not also." The Ramseys with Alex's wealth from his real estate holdings and money inherited from Anna's father had the means to proceed.

Construction was completed in 1872 while the Ramseys were still in Washington. The family moved in after Alex left the Senate in 1875. The home was a modern marvel, equipped with hot and cold running water, gas lighting, hot-water radiators and all the latest technology. It was lavishly furnished. In the days just before completion Anna traveled to New York where she went on a shopping spree at the A. T. Stewart department store and purchased furnishings that filled two boxcars. The home today contains Anna's original A. T. Stewart furnishings. Some furniture has been repaired and renewed, with 95 per cent of the original furnishings remaining there today.

Marion inherited the home from her father, and her daughters Laura and Anna inherited the home from her and lived out their lives there. They never married and, with no heirs and with a desire to preserve the mansion, willed it to the Minnesota Historical Society, which now owns and manages it. The mansion was placed on the National Register of Historic Places in 1969. (About the House | Alexander Ramsey House | MNHS)

Ramsey in retirement.

Alexander Ramsey and granddaughter Laura Furness on the porch of the Ramsey Mansion. Photo: Edward Augustus Bromley, 1901, courtesy of the Minnesota Historical Society.

CHAPTER 8

The Kelker Women

Giving, devoted yet lost in history. While women have played major roles in the Kelker family history, they are not well recognized in this book. This is an unavoidable consequence of women's status through most of the eras covered in these pages, not a bias on the author's part. The Kelkers and other women of the eighteenth and nineteenth centuries, and even beyond, were subject to laws and rigid social norms that confined them to the home and prevented their participation in any professional or political endeavors. Intelligence and capability hardly mattered. Women of that time had no voice in any pursuit outside the home, and even in the home they were subordinate to their husbands. They had little means for airing their proposals and grievances since social norms prevented them from speaking in any public forum. The unfortunate result of such suppression is that, except for their family status and occasional instances of recognition, most are not adequately represented in our historical records.

The women of past times lived in a world run by and for men who held fast to their privileged status. For women the paths to accomplishment and professional success were locked, blocked and impenetrable. They were largely excluded from higher education and from gainful opportunity, and without the basic rights granted to men they were powerless to challenge that system. They could not vote, could not initiate any legal action and could not seek election to local, state or national offices. Social restrictions held them quietly in the background. When a woman brought her inherited wealth to a marriage the money came under her husband's control, and she had no say in how it was used. Society's standards did not tolerate women speaking in a public forum, leaving no opportunity for them to agitate against their repressed status. When a woman did appear with a man on a public-speaking platform, the presentation was referred to as "promiscuous." Those able to find work outside the home could teach schoolchildren or labor at menial jobs for very low wages. The most a woman could strive for was to be a loving servant to her spouse, raise the children and manage the household.

A few women who did succeed to get their works before the public hid their identity behind pseudonyms. Mary Ann Evans published her widely read novels as George Eliot, and the Brontë sisters published under masculine pseudonyms. Had they not acted in this way their works would likely have remained little known.

A growing number of women in the nineteenth century did speak out about their low standing in society. They challenged social boundaries, made public speeches and organized and campaigned for equal rights. The women's suffrage movement that began in 1848 was led by bright, capable and determined activists from Susan B. Anthony and Elizabeth Cady Stanton to Carrie Chapman Catt, Ernestine Rose and others. They did indeed speak out, campaign, organize and lead the national women's suffrage movement. They fought powerful resistance from political and religious leaders, from most men and even many women. Their seventy-two-year struggle succeeded with the 1920 signing of the Nineteenth Amendment that finally secured voting rights for women. The history of the women's suffrage movement shows what should have been obvious all along: women can do the job.

Ernestine Rose (1810–1892), the prominent Polish-born suffragist and abolitionist spent thirty-two years in the young United States fighting for equal rights. Rose expressed her hopes and resolve for women's rights in an 1851 address at the second American women's rights convention in Worcester, Massachussetts:

> How much more beneficial would be woman's influence, if, as the equal with man, she should take her stand by his side […] in the Legislative halls, in the Senate chamber, in the Judge's chair, in the jury box, in the Forum, in the Laboratory of arts and sciences, and whatever duty would call her for the benefit of herself, her country, her race. For at every step, she would carry with her a humanizing influence. (Doress-Worters, Paula (ed.), *Mistress of Herself*, Ernestine Rose, Speech, Worcester, 1851, pp. 94, 97–98; quoted in: Anderson, Bonnie S., *The Rabbi's Atheist Daughter*, Oxford University Press, 2017, p. 4.)

Women have faced another form of discrimination that continues to have unfortunate consequences today. Genealogical records favor men. In families, the man's last name is the one that gets passed on to the next generation. A family tree grows under that name, while that of the woman is not further recorded, except for maiden names, appearing as a sort of middle name. We examine genealogical records without acknowledging this inherent bias. Historical encyclopedias list brief to extensive biographies of men and their accomplishments but hardly mention women. To the detriment of researchers, historians and the author of this book the lack of knowledge that results from this practice leaves us with little information of all those who stood at their husbands' sides, labored to keep home and family intact and devoted their lives to the health and welfare of their children. This huge void in our record keeping deprives us of the history of their struggles, accomplishments and service.

From what we do know about the Kelker women it is clear they were in every way essential to the success and well-being of their husbands and children and that their lives should be equally recognized in proportion to that of their men.

In 1743, when Regula Braetscher Kölliker arrived in the colonies from her native Switzerland with her husband, Heinrich, and their two surviving children, the concept of a woman in the home with the husband the dominant figure was the norm, fully accepted, firmly entrenched and undisputed. To the best of our knowledge, Regula embraced her role and went about taking care of her home and family. We can only imagine what it was like for her to have seen three of her children die during the twenty-eight-week journey to America and wonder how she managed to nurture her family in a new land and to adjust to a new language and culture. She must have been an emotional bulwark for them in their new life as they struggled to build a house and establish a farm that would provide their livelihood. Regula's daughter-in-law Mary Magdalena Meister, Anthony's wife, lost an infant daughter and raised seven prosperous and accomplished children. We see her and Regula's strength in the Kelker women of succeeding generations.

Unlike Regula, wives in wealthier families of that time could afford servants, cooks and housemaids to relieve them of the daily burdens of cleaning, cooking and caring for children. But even with the free time their status afforded them they couldn't participate in any kind of career beyond their homes where they had to be satisfied with activities such as sewing, gardening and socializing. Beyond the home women could participate in church affairs, do charitable work and accompany their husbands at social gatherings and other events, but not much more. That reality was faced by three generations of Kelker women in Harrisburg, from Catherine Fager Kelker to Mary Anne Reily Kelker to Agnes Keyes Pearsol Kelker.

Anthony and Mary Magdalena's youngest son, Frederick, began his business career in Harrisburg and became a prominent contributing member of his community. Much of his success can be attributed to the presence and support of his wife, Catherine Fager Kelker. She raised three remarkable sons, Rudolph Frederick, Immanuel Meister and Henry Anthony, each of whom built successful business careers and were generous in service to their community. The Kelker Family Record (p. 89) notes that Catherine "was a woman of exemplary piety, humble, devoted, unostentatious, and remarkable for her meek and gentle spirit. In the Church, and in the sewing circle, Sunday school, mission society, and benevolent society, her labors were unremitting." That was Catherine's life, typical of women of that time. She possessed courage and an inner peace that would serve her through her long and painful terminal illness.

Frederick and Catherine's oldest son, Rudolph Frederick Kelker, married Mary Anne Reily, daughter of a prominent Myerstown, Pennsylvania family that had relocated to Harrisburg. Her father, William Reily, served in the Pennsylvania State Legislature and reached the rank of brigadier general in the army. (Kelker Family Record, p. 95) Historical records reveal little of Mary Anne's life. However, when we look at the successes of her husband and their sons Luther Reily and William Anthony we can conclude that she dutifully and faithfully brought out their best qualities.

We also know little about Agnes Keyes Pearsol Kelker, Luther Reily's wife. She supported her husband through his business successes and through his illness. She bore their three children. Most prominent was Rudolph Frederick Kelker Jr., who spent most of his professional life in Chicago developing the transportation system from the horse-transit and cable-car era into our period of automobiles, subways and buses. He married Georgia Moore about whom we unfortunately know little. From what we know of RFK Jr.'s sister Mary Reily Kelker Sturges, it appears that she lived a happily married life, performing her household duties according to the prevailing societal norms.

Anna Earl Jenks Ramsey shows us how a woman of her time with stature and privilege could make the most of her situation despite her gender-suppressed status. Anna married Alex Ramsey in 1845 and in 1849 the couple and their young son left Pennsylvania for the Minnesota Territory. Anna was privileged to be able to bring a nursemaid and a servant along on the journey. While Alex was performing his duties as territorial governor, mayor of St. Paul then state governor, Anna remained in the background supervising the household. Freed from many household duties because of her husband's status, she was able to live a productive life outside her home, an opportunity not available to most women. Here is an excerpt from her biography from WikiTree (https://www.wikitree. com/wiki/Jenks-907):

> As first lady [i.e., as the governor's wife] Anna was considered to be upper class, fashionable and intelligent. She was the proper Victorian woman, finding "her greatest happiness in the great duties of wife and mother." She also reigned as the center of social activity in the capital city, hosting parties and events, and having "that rare characteristic whose possessor every stranger recognizes as a friend." Charitable work occupied much of her time. She became an active volunteer in the House of Hope Presbyterian Church and taught Sunday School classes at the nearby Fort Road Mission. A favorite cause was the Home for the Friendless in St. Paul, an organization that offered shelter for destitute women and their children. Anna served as the organization's vice president and visited twice a week. Anna also mailed food and household goods anonymously to local families in need. During the Civil War Anna became a public figure, volunteering at hospitals full of Union soldiers and serving as the president of the Ladies Volunteer Aid Society for the 2nd Minnesota Regiment. She also presented the state regimental flag to Colonel Willis Gorman and the 1st Minnesota Regiment on the east steps of the State Capitol and spoke to the assembled soldiers, thanking them for their service on behalf of the ladies of St. Paul. Anna accompanied her husband to Washington, D.C. when he was elected senator in 1863. She became one of the belles of Washington society, attending operas and other events with Mrs. Lincoln and the wives of other senators, as well as President Lincoln's second inauguration. In 1868 the Ramseys began building a "mansion house" in St. Paul. Completed in 1872, the home held a prominent place in the city's society. Famous visitor to the residence included Mrs. Elizabeth Custer, who stopped on her way to the Dakota Territory in the spring of 1876, and President and Mrs. Rutherford B. Hayes.

Credit goes to Anna Earl Jenks Ramsey for finding a way to participate productively outside the confines of her home.

The life of Anna and Alex's daughter, Marion Ramsey Furness, shows that even an intelligent and educated woman had to be satisfied with a domestic existence. At age sixteen, Marion was one of the few American teenagers of that time to visit Europe where she spent time in Paris and studied music and language in Germany. Also at sixteen she was given a grand coming-out party in Washington, D.C., and was courted by eligible bachelors. But Marion's life beyond husband, family and home was limited to social contacts. She raised three children and when her husband suffered mental illness, he lived the remainder of his life apart from the family. With three children in her care and without her ill husband, she confidently stepped forward following her mother's 1886 death to assume management of the family's St. Paul mansion. Her daughters Laura and Anna, unmarried and childless, inherited the mansion and maintained and preserved it. Thanks to their care and concern the mansion is now a well-preserved historical landmark.

Women of today have emerged from the social restrictions of their forebears and become increasingly active and prominent in industry, public service, education and all aspects of society. Credit that to the passage of the Nineteenth Amendment in 1920, which finally gave women the right to vote and set off a revolution in a society too long accustomed to thinking of women in the limited frameworks of cooking and child rearing. Women today continue to assert that they face both mild and overt sexism, yet paths to success grow increasingly open to women who are qualified, dedicated, ambitious and who are provided opportunity.

A superb example is that of Dr. Ellen Stofan (see Chapter 9 and Addendum below), who through her scientific knowledge and career in the study of outer space, political and administrative savvy and hard work has made a career of advancing science and of spreading its message to the general public. Too many Kelker women who came before Ellen Stofan could not reach her level of success. It would have been unthinkable and unattainable. Perhaps some time in the future we will stop considering successful women unique, and their accomplishments will stand on their own, not as having been made by a woman.

We should acknowledge the Kelker women, rich and poor, who served their families through successes and failures. Details and records of their stories, which could tell us so much about them, barely exist. What does remain informs us that even under the laws and social norms that restricted their lives, they performed with dignity and devotion. In this, they earn our recognition as much as their husbands—perhaps even more, as we are compelled to respect the faint yet enduring outlines they have left in history. Let their importance to the world we live in continue to grow.

Chapter 9 presents the lives and careers of father and daughter NASA space scientists Andrew and Ellen Stofan.

Addendum
Ellen Renee Stofan at a Congressional Hearing

An Overlooked Congressional Witness. Women's public gains have continued since passage of the Nineteenth Amendment in 1920, but old attitudes and behaviors persist, and their accomplishments, successes and demonstrated competence are still too often ignored. A February 25, 2017, article in the *Atlantic* reminds us how some men still go about their business acknowledging men and ignoring women.

In 2017, the US House of Representatives Committee on Science, Space and Technology held a hearing with four former NASA officials to discuss the agency's future missions, a return to the moon, putting humans on Mars, commercialization of space and other items. Ellen Stofan, the only woman on the panel, was the best informed of the four since she was the most recently retired from NASA following her tenure as its chief scientist. The men were mostly a decade or more removed from the space agency. Her fellow invited witnesses before the committee were Harrison Schmidt, former Apollo astronaut and former US senator; former astronaut Thomas Stafford; and A. Thomas Young, former director of the Viking Mars program and former director of the Goddard Space Flight Center. Stofan spoke about NASA's Earth science mission, the agency's Mars trajectory, human space exploration and other ongoing NASA ventures, and she answered most of the committee's questions. She later commented that she was frustrated that "in some cases [the three men] weren't entirely up to date on what's going on. When you're talking about the future of NASA, you'd want to hear someone who was more recently involved."

When the official photo of the committee's hearing was released, it showed the three former NASA men along with the committee chairman, but no Stofan. And further, the committee's Twitter account posted ten tweets about the hearing with none mentioning her. When asked for a comment by Rebecca Boyle, the *Atlantic* writer, Stofan responded diplomatically, speaking highly of her three fellow witnesses but also expressing her frustration. "I understand that it's probably mostly because they are the Republican witnesses. I was invited by the minority party, the Democrats. But the optics of being the only woman […] You know, I understand, that's the way the system works. I hope we're turning away from that system."

Boyle then wrote, in characterizing the "system" that Stofan referred to, as "ossified gender roles, the prevalence and endurance of bias, and the underrepresentation of women (especially women of color)," which "demonstrate[s] the detrimental effect of these biases on Ph.D.'s salaries and careers and the importance of representatives and role models."

In the outcry that followed, one woman commented: "Don't ask questions about encouraging young people to get into STEM (Science, Technology, Engineering, Mathematics) and then make it look like that it's only for old white guys." Another wrote: "As a woman seeking a STEM career, for that matter who cares about science […] this bewilders me." Ellen added that "If we turn a blind eye, or don't show that women are there, what are we telling people how women are valued? What are we telling girls about their ability to go into different careers? The message it sends to women is not a great one."

The slight may have been omission rather than commission. But it tells us that old ways die hard, and that women who are striving to succeed and to contribute still face long-entrenched barriers.

Chapter 9 presents the lives and careers of father and daughter NASA space scientists, Andrew and Ellen Stofan.

CHAPTER 9

Andrew John Stofan and Ellen Renee Stofan
Father, Daughter, Space
Scientists, Administrators

Andrew John Stofan
(andy stofan nasa photos—
Yahoo Image Search) Results

Ellen Renee Stofan
(photo: Jim Preston,
 Smithsonian National
 Air and Space Museum)

The Stofans, Andy and Ellen, father and daughter, represent a pair of space scientists and top administrators whose careers extend from NASA's very beginnings in 1958 through the age of space stations and interplanetary exploration. Both have advanced our knowledge of space. They have provided organizational and administrative successes and leadership in space exploration. Andy, who trained in math, physics and engineering, developed more efficient and powerful rockets that have made it possible to send more men, women and advanced instrumentation on space missions. As a National Aeronautics and Space Administration (NASA) Deputy Associate Administrator he directed design and engineering for the Freedom space-station project, and as director of NASA's Lewis Space Center (now the John Glenn Research Center) he turned an institution on the brink of closure into a vibrant research facility and vital contributor to NASA's space program.

Ellen, with a lifelong interest in space and geology (PhD in geology, Brown University), has directed and participated in NASA missions to study Venus, Saturn, Mars, distant moons and comets. In 2016, she accepted the position of chief scientist at NASA, where she was responsible for overseeing all agency operations and advising its director. In 2018, she was chosen as the first woman to direct Smithsonian's National Air and Space Museum, the world's fifth most visited museum in pre-pandemic 2019. (The world's 10 most visited museums in 2019 | Vogue France) In 2021, she left the Air and Space Museum to become Smithsonian's Under Secretary for Science and Research. Along with her many responsibilities she promotes science education and works to open opportunities in science to young women of all races and ethnicities.

Andrew John Stofan. Andy Stofan was born on January 26, 1935, to Andrew and Ida Christine Kelker Stofan. His public-school education was in his family's hometown of Oberlin, Ohio, where his father, Andrew Sr., supported the family with his Stofan Studios photography business. Andy, like his parents, his older brother, Richard and his younger brother, Paul, attended Hiram College in Hiram, Ohio. He entered an undergraduate program sponsored by Hiram College and Carnegie Mellon University where he studied three years at Hiram in a liberal-arts program majoring in physics and mathematics and two years at Carnegis Mellon in a mechanical-engineering program. (Andrew J. Stofan '57—Hiram College Office of Alumni Relations; Andrew J. Stofan | NASA) Immediately after his 1958 graduation from Carnegie Mellon, Andy joined the Lewis Research Center in Cleveland, Ohio, at that time a unit of the National Advisory Committee for Aeronautics (NACA). Lewis was renowned for advances in aircraft technology, but in the 1950s it refocused its efforts toward high-energy rocket fuels and propulsion technology to advance development of military rockets. Andy began at Lewis as a research engineer and then spent the next thirty years as a NASA engineer and administrator. (Historical Biography—Andrew J. Stofan | NASA; Andrew J. Stofan | NASA) Andy is married to Barbara Bedell Stofan, his high school sweetheart, who, in step with the family's commitment to science was a science teacher.

Russia's Sputnik launch on October 4, 1957 caught the world and America's aeronautics industry off guard. In response to calls for action from Congress and from a stunned public NASA was established on October 4, 1958, and its first order of business was to get the US into space. Shortly after Andy's arrival, the Lewis Research Center was transferred from NACA to NASA, and he spent the next decades as an engineer and administrator closely involved in NASA's race to the moon, development of orbiting space stations and other major projects.

NASA's incredible success in putting men on the moon is among history's most magnificent achievements. But beyond being a grand international spectacle, significant scientific and technical achievements were gained. Astronomers and geologists got a greater understanding of the moon's composition, much of it from the 842 pounds of moon rocks delivered back to earth. (How many pounds of moon rocks were brought back to earth—Yahoo Search Results) The technology developed during the program provided for the development of orbiting space stations that can now host and support humans in orbit for years and where experiments can be conducted that cannot be performed on earth.

Early work at the NASA Lewis Research Center. Following his 1958 graduation, Andy joined Lewis' Flight Propulsion Laboratory as a research engineer in the Propulsion Dynamics Division just a few months before the center was transferred to NASA. Under NASA it directed its resources to space-related propulsion research while it continued development of jet engines and aeronautics. Andy's first project was to improve ejector nozzles that provided supersonic engines with added thrust. [19990110621. pdf (nasa.gov)]

In 1960, Andy joined the Chemical Rocket Systems Branch of the new Rocket and Aerodynamics Division at Lewis, where he studied the phenomenon of fuel sloshing in propellant tanks. His observations on the behavior of fluid in those tanks were critical to solving the sloshing problem in Centaur booster rockets in 1962.

The Centaur Booster Rocket. In 1957, the year Russia sent Sputnik 1 into space, General Dynamics/Astronautics Corporation proposed the development of a new second-stage booster rocket (see the Addendum below that describes the components of space-rockets.**) that** would provide the capability to maneuver heavier space vehicles once in space. That second-stage booster became Centaur, and when combined with the first-stage Atlas booster it became a powerful propulsion system that sent men, women and material into orbit, to the moon and on to planets over the next fifty years.

In 1958, the Air Force developed a more advanced proposal for the promising Centaur project. The Advanced Research Projects Agency (ARPA) accepted the Air Force proposal and assigned it back to the Air Force. But ten months after the establishment of NASA in July 1958, the Centaur project was assigned to the Lewis Center. (The Centaur Upper Stage Rocket | NASA)

In 1962, Andy was assigned to deal with the problem of fuel-tank sloshing. As fuel is burned during liftoff and flight the volume in the tank decreases. The remaining fuel becomes subject to sloshing and may not always be in position to be pumped from the tank into the engine. Sloshing is caused by the space vehicle's control system, vibrations during launch and coasting while in space. Andy's previous 1960 experience with sloshing was called on to deal with the problem in the Centaur fuel tanks. He and his group solved the problem by the strategic placement of baffles in the fuel tank. The team also improved Centaur's propellant (fuel) utilization system with new gauges to measure the boiling of cryogenic propellants and with a new system that regulated the simultaneous depletion of the liquid-hydrogen and liquid-oxygen fuels, thus ensuring minimal fuel waste. (Andrew J. Stofan | NASA)

About rocket fuels. Centaur was the first NASA rocket to use liquid-hydrogen propellant, and much of the work in adapting it as rocket fuel was done by Andy and his group at the Lewis Research Center. A variety of fuels (propellants) have been used to lift rockets into space. All must produce sufficient thrust, or push power, to move the payload off the launchpad through the planet's gravitational pull and into space, and once in space to move the capsule into orbit or deeper into space. The ideal fuel should burn with high efficiency, i.e., with maximum thrust from a unit volume of fuel. At NASA fuel efficiency is measured by specific impulse, or how many units of propellant produce a unit of thrust. In addition to having a high specific impulse the ideal propellant should be light to reduce the energy needed to lift the rocket off the launchpad and into space.

Nothing burns without oxygen, and rocket fuels are no exception. So, with little or no oxygen existing in the upper atmosphere and beyond, rockets must include an oxygen-supplying agent. For kerosene rocket fuels, oxidizing agents are used such as liquid oxygen and chemicals including hydrogen peroxide, nitrous oxide and others. Liquid hydrogen, now used in most space flights, uses liquid oxygen to produce the burn.

Adapting liquid hydrogen for use as a rocket fuel. Hydrogen is highly flammable and ideally suited as a rocket fuel because it produces a significant increase in thrust over other fuels. But adapting it for use as rocket fuel presented several challenges. It is an abundantly available gas in the atmosphere, but to be used as rocket fuel it must be converted to the liquid state by subjecting the gas to extreme pressure. To be maintained in the liquid state it must be stored at an extremely low temperature (-253° Centigrade or -423° Fahrenheit). Liquid hydrogen together with liquid oxygen (storage temperature: −218.79° Centigrade or −361.82° Fahrenheit) as oxidizer have been the fuels used by Centaur rockets.

In 1966, Andy became the head of the Propellant Systems Section at Lewis, charged with assessing the feasibility of using liquid hydrogen as the Centaur's propellant. With little known about the nature and behavior of liquid hydrogen in microgravity, he and his group set about characterizing the gas with respect to its suitability for space flight. He was instrumental in gaining understanding of the gas's properties and behavior under space conditions. (Andrew J. Stofan | NASA) In preparation for a manned moon landing, NASA sent seven missions with Centaur second-stage rockets to the moon between 1966 and 1968 to determine the feasibility of making a soft landing. Andy and his group were closely involved in monitoring performance and making improvements throughout these missions. (Surveyor 1— Moon Missions—NASA's Jet Propulsion Laboratory) Their study produced essential information and procedures for the Apollo manned moon missions.

Titan and Centaur. In 1969, Andy assumed the position of Assistant Project Manager for improving the Centaur. At that time NASA was searching for more powerful rocketry to send off the heavier payloads that would be required for planetary probes. For that purpose NASA was considering the possibility of mating the Centaur with the Titan III first-stage rocket. (Centaur Program—Glenn Research Center | NASA)

Titan rockets have a glorious history. In 1956, the Martin Company was awarded a contract to build the first Titans, the Titan I and Titan II ICBMs (intercontinental ballistic missiles). With the formation of NASA Titan rockets became the workhorses for space travel for the next decades. In the early space program they were used to power the orbital Mercury flights (suborbital flights were powered by Redstone rockets). In 1976, Titan launched the Viking Mars landers, and in 1977, it sent deep-space probes to Saturn, Jupiter and the edge of our solar system. In 1990, the Titan IV version was lifting payloads of 12,700 pounds (6.35 tons). After 368 missions and making the continued exploration of space possible, Titan was retired in 2002. (Remember the Titans | Lockheed Martin)

As Assistant Project Manager for the Improved Centaur Program Andy with his group set about upgrading Centaur's design and integrating it with the more powerful first-stage Titan rocket. In 1970, he moved on to become head of the Titan/Centaur Program Office. NASA was relying on Titan/Centaur for missions deeper into space, and deep-space missions require "can't fail" development. Every detail and every contingency must be anticipated and accounted for. The work that Andy and his Titan/Centaur group carried out was critical to the first landing of a space vehicle on Mars. Viking 1 was launched on August 20, 1975. It entered orbit around Mars on June 19, 1976 and landed on Mar's surface on July 20, 1976. Viking 2 left earth on September 9, 1975, entered Mars' orbit on August 7, 1976, and landed on September 3 at a site distinct from the Viking 1 landing site.

The search for life beyond earth is at the heart of every interplanetary mission. The Viking Mars missions revealed that life, at least as it exists on earth, is not possible on the Red Planet. Analysis showed that the planet's soil is extremely dry, and that its chemistry is oxidizing and not suitable for the existence of microorganisms or any forms of life. Further evidence against the presence of any kind of life on Mars, at least as we know it, is that the soil is sterilized by constant bombardment by strong rays of ultraviolet light. However this does not exclude the possibility that life did at one time exist on Mars.

One of the many obstacles that Andy and his group had to overcome was finding a way to provide energy to Mars landers once they settle on the planet's surface. Variations in sunlight falling on the planet made it impossible to utilize solar panels. So, both Viking landers were powered by electricity generated from heat emitted from the decay of radioactive plutonium (Pu^{239}).

The use of plutonium as an energy source prolonged the useful life of the Viking landers and allowed scientific testing and observation to continue over a long period. The last transmission from Mars was from Viking Lander 2, after sending signals for three years and seven months. (Viking 1 & 2 | Missions—NASA's Mars Exploration Program)

The Improved Centaur Program also sent two Voyager spacecraft on a forty-year interstellar mission. Voyagers 1 and 2 were launched in 1977. Voyager 1 entered interstellar space in August 2012 and Voyager 2 in November 2018. The mission's primary objective to study Jupiter and Saturn was accomplished with a series of important discoveries. Volcanoes were observed on Io, one of Jupiter's four moons, and greater details from Saturn's rings were revealed. The Voyagers then moved on to explore Uranus and Neptune. Voyagers 1 and 2 are the only spacecraft to have reached these outer planets of the solar system. [Voyager—Mission Overview (nasa.gov)]

Following Andy's success in the Improved Centaur Program he was made head of the Launch Vehicles Directorate in 1974 where he was responsible for the Titan-Centaur and Atlas-Centaur offices. There he assumed the tasks of directing the design and engineering of the launch vehicles. His administrative challenge was to coordinate the interactions of the mission planners, the Air Force and the aerospace-industry teams. (Stofan to Retire from NASA on April 1, NASA release 88-16, February 8, 1988) During his 1974 to 1978 tenure at the Launch Vehicles Directorate ten Atlas-Centaurs and six Titan-Centaurs were launched in the Viking and Voyager programs. According to a NASA biography of Andy's space career, "Much of the Titan-Centaur vehicle's success can be attributed to Stofan's leadership of NASA, the Air Force and aerospace industry teams." (NASA—Stofan's Management Skills Raise Glenn's Profile); (Andrew J. Stofan | NASA)

The NASA Lewis Research Center. In 1978, Andy moved to NASA headquarters where he served as Deputy Associate Administrator for the Office of Space Science. In that position he managed all NASA ground atmospheric and space programs. In 1982, he returned to Cleveland to become the Lewis Research Center's fifth director. When he assumed the directorship, he was fully aware of the challenge he faced. Budget cuts throughout the 1970s had forced facility closings and staff downsizing. The resulting lack of focus and the outside perception that the center was not productive had lowered morale among the staff. In fact, just before Andy's arrival Congress almost closed the center. Clearly a program of revitalization was needed, and Andy enthusiastically embraced the challenge. He later recalled his attitude upon taking over: "I needed a challenge and Lewis was a challenge. It was in trouble. It was in real trouble here. Morale was bad. So, when I came in this was the type of thing that I love."

He began by changing the center's management style from what had been a poorly functioning, top-down autocratic system to one in which management, engineers, scientists from all departments and the unionized workforce were included in decision-making processes. He was well aware that getting everyone to buy into the new approach would be a challenge in itself, and he initiated a comprehensive program throughout all levels to change old hard-set attitudes and assumptions and to establish a culture of trust and open lines of communication and to let everyone know just where he or she fit into the overall mission. To sell the new management system Andy set out educational programs based on a participative/consensus approach. (Andrew J. Stofan | NASA)

> We did this because we found that there was (and is) a lot of confusion in people's minds about what is participative management, what decisions do you participate in, and which ones do you not participate in. Is everything done in a participative manner or is this just another management style that one can use? The educational programs start out with styles with first-line supervision where they spend a week learning about management styles and interacting with our senior staff. I talk with every class about management philosophies, how you interact with people, and the future of Lewis. One of the things we are doing that is very valuable with this firstline supervision program is to have them work on a problem that directly affects the Lewis Space [or Research] Center. A list of six or seven problems is provided to them to choose from or they can select their own problem. However, the requirement is that the problem has to be real and they have to come up with recommendations to solve the problem.

The educational process was also carried out in informal settings.

> I meet with approximately 100 people at a time, every other week, in a relaxed, informal environment, at breakfast or after work at our picnic grounds with beer and pretzels. I talk to the group about my management philosophy, where the lab is going, and what the vision of the future is. After these discussions, they know

where the Center is headed and they know where they fit into the entire process. It takes a lot of time (about a year) and a lot of effort to communicate with that many people, but it has had an impact on the way people view their jobs. [Stofan's Human Element Speech (1986) (nasa.gov)]

Andy, through discussion and input from all levels, spent six months defining the center's objectives, all directed at remaking Lewis into a vital contributor to NASA again:

1. the space station's power system, a high NASA priority
2. the Advanced Turboprop Program
3. renovating the Altitude Wind Tunnel to perform advanced icing research
4. the Advanced Communications Technology Satellite Program
5. the Shuttle/Centaur Program, a high NASA priority

(NASA—Stofan's Management Skills Raise Glenn's Profile)

Andy's installation of participative management was a remarkable success that brought Lewis back from near closure to a vibrant, productive institution. Through his leadership all the objectives listed above were reached, new employees were hired for the first time in years, and a fresh spirit of accomplishment prevailed at all levels. But beyond science and technology people's lives were impacted. From top to bottom each employee now felt he or she was being acknowledged as a contributor and playing an essential role in the center's mission, not just working away isolated from management. As Andy put it: "We are creating an environment where people can really feel that they are part of the institution and that they belong." [Stofan's Human Element Speech (1986) (nasa.gov)]

Space Station Freedom. In 1986, Andy left his directorship of the Lewis Research Center to become Associate Administrator of the Space Station Office where he assumed control of the design of the Space Station Freedom. (Andrew J. Stofan | NASA) Freedom was to be a permanently orbiting space station developed in cooperation with Japan, Europe and Canada. The groundwork for a permanent orbiting space station had been established by the successful Skylab project. Skylab, NASA's first orbiting space station, was launched on May 14, 1973. It lifted off uncrewed, and the first of its successive three-man crews reached it by space shuttle on May 25. The three crews spent

171 days in orbit. Following the departure of the last crew in 1974 the Skylab space station was abandoned, and NASA ground controllers shut down its systems. It remained in free-flight orbit for five years until it finally fell to earth in 1979. [History's Highest Stage (nasa.gov)]

Skylab's many successes in prolonged operation of an orbiting space station, establishment of an operational scientific laboratory in a gravity-free environment and seamless replacement of crews established the feasibility of a permanent orbiting station. Ronald Reagan gave his presidential endorsement to space station development in his 1984 State of the Union address, and in that year NASA established the Space Station Freedom project in collaboration with its international partners. [Space Station Freedom (astronautix.com)]

Andy assumed control of Freedom's spacecraft design. But Freedom hit rough going as Congress withheld sufficient funding that necessitated changing the design. Continuing budget shortages forced redesigns, loss of capabilities and construction delays. Budget shortages led to seven major redesigns between 1984 and 1993. In the end the Freedom project was abandoned. But finally, after inadequate funding, political wrangling and administration changes, the Clinton Administration in 1993 announced that the *Freedom* project would merge into the International Space Station. [State of the Union Address: Ronald Reagan (January 25, 1984)]; (infoplease.com)

Andy's two years as associate administrator for the Space Station Office were challenging. But he reorganized the project, established a Space Station Program Office and negotiated design contracts essential to the program. (Andrew J. Stofan | Glenn Research Center | NASA) His accomplishments were lauded by the NASA administrator Dr. James C. Fletcher: "NASA and this country owe Andy a debt of gratitude for his years of dedicated work to the nation's civil space program." (Stofan to Retire from NASA on April 1, NASA Release 88—16, February 8, 1988)

Taking leave of NASA. In 1988, after thirty years as an engineer and administrator from the Mercury program to the *Freedom* project and through five presidential administrations, Andrew John Stofan retired from NASA. But leaving NASA didn't end his professional career. He joined Martin Marietta Astronautics as Vice President of Advanced Launch Systems and

Technical Operations. And in 1991, after three years at Martin Marietta, he joined the aerospace startup Analex Corporation in Cleveland, a company organized by retired NASA employees. Following his employment at Analex he served as director of Electro-Optical Systems at Lockheed Missiles and Space Company before concluding his professional career.

Andy Stofan's career in space engineering and administration and the successes he brought about were significant and substantial. A NASA 2016 biography published when he was inducted into the Glenn (formerly Lewis) Research Center's Hall of Fame summarizes his many significant accomplishments. (Andrew J. Stofan, Glenn Research Center Hall of Fame 2016 Inductee, Biography, NASA)

Stofan had a legendary career with many highlights. His cryogenic fluid management work was significant to the 1960s space program, his management of the launch vehicles efforts led to major successes in the 1970s, and his management of NASA's space science and space station efforts impacted the agency. Stofan, however, considers his four years as Lewis Research Center director his most important. In that role, he not only provided the hope that was needed to carry on, but empowered the staff with the confidence needed to create their own successful destiny. His generous mentoring, cooperative management approach, and leadership style empowered the staff to not only have a vision but to motivate everyone to contribute to the vision. Beyond his adept management skills, it was this "can-do" attitude, confidence, and ability to build relationships that really made him a leader. In addition, a generation of younger managers incorporated Stofan's managerial philosophy and skills into their work. The center is still feeling the effects of Stofan's legacy today.

Addenda
Andrew John Stofan

Awards and Participation. Andy's distinguished career has been recognized by numerous awards. In addition to his induction into the Glenn Research Center's Hall of Fame he has received:

–the NASA Exceptional Service Medal, 1975
–NASA Distinguished Service Award, 1981
–the Presidential Rank of Meritorious Executive, 1982
>   (Andrew J. Stofan | Glenn Research Center | NASA).

Throughout his career he used his talents to benefit numerous civic, educational, technological and cultural institutions. He has served:
–as member of the policy committee of the Cleveland Federal Executive Board
–on the Board of Trustees of the Cleveland National Air Show
–as member of the Cleveland Area Development Corporation Steering Committee
–as board member on the State of Ohio Technology Information Exchange
>   (Stofan Andy—biographical sketch (1984) (nasa.gov))

–as board member of the Cleveland Council of the Boy Scouts of America
–as board member on the State of Ohio Information Exchange and Innovation Network
–on the Board of Governors of the Aviation Hall of Fame (Historical Biography—Andrew J. Stofan | NASA)
–and on the Board of Trustees of Hiram College. (Andrew J. Stofan '57—Hiram College Office of Alumni Relations)

A Primer on Rockets and NASA Projects. A space mission begins with a launch vehicle mounted on a launchpad. The vehicle contains three basic components:

<u>First-stage rocket.</u> The powerful first-stage rocket powers the launch vehicle off the launchpad, through the atmosphere and into space. The rocket with its full load of fuel adds considerable weight to the launch vehicle, but after that fuel is exhausted the first-stage rocket is jettisoned and a second-stage rocket takes over. The first-stage rockets used by NASA were developed by the military's long-range missile program. Redstone, Atlas, Titan and Saturn rockets were utilized by NASA through early exploration of space and the moon mission, and for establishing the space station.

<u>Second-stage rocket.</u> The upper-stage rocket propels the space vehicle farther into space or into orbit after the first stage has been discarded. It remains with the space vehicle to provide maneuverability. Mercury, the first NASA space program, used the Agena as its second-stage rocket. This was replaced by the Centaur for the Gemini and Apollo missions. Andy Stofan played a major role in the development of the Centaur's propulsion system.

<u>Command module.</u> The flight is controlled from the command module where the flight instrumentation and the astronauts are located.

<u>Other components.</u> Each space vehicle is designed to meet that mission's needs. Apollo moon rockets, for example, carried a third-stage rocket, the lunar lander, modified for rendezvous and docking maneuvers. The prelaunch vehicle stood 363 feet high and weighed almost 6.4 million pounds, much of it first-stage rocket fuel. The lunar module, the third-stage rocket, is designated LM, the service module is SM, the command module is CM.

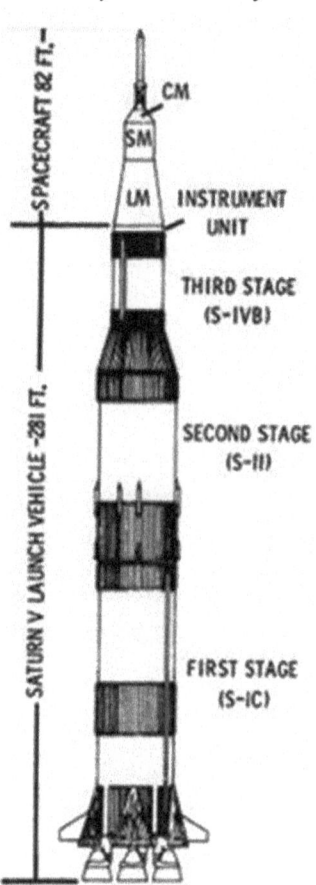

The Basic Components of a Saturn Apollo Lunar Rocket. [saturn_v_diagram.jpg (540×673) (si. edu)]

Ellen Renee Stofan,
Space Scientist

Biography. Ellen Stofan, like her father, spent her career as a space scientist and administrator. She was born in Oberlin, Ohio, on February 24, 1961, four years after Sputnik and one year before John Glenn became the first American to orbit the earth. She seems to have inherited her space genes from her space-engineer father and her devotion to science from her mother, Barbara Bedell Stofan, an elementary-school science teacher. Not all the Stofan family members pursued careers in science, however. Her sister Lynn broke the mold by becoming a lawyer.

Stofan, from the age of four when her father took her to see a NASA launch, has displayed a devotion to things celestial, and her intense interest in space and the planets has never slowed. (Profile | Ellen Stofan, NASA Chief

Scientist—SpaceNews) She graduated from William & Mary in 1983 with a major in geology. She then received her master's degree in geology, and in 1989 her PhD in geology, both from Brown University. Her NASA career began as a postdoctoral fellow at the Jet Propulsion Laboratory (JPL) in Pasadena, California. From there her professional career began a steep ascent. [Ellen Stofan | Smithsonian Institution (si.edu)] During twenty-five years as a space scientist she has held key administrative and scientific positions and significantly contributed to our understanding of the planets. She is married to Timothy P. Dunn, whom she met during her undergraduate years at William & Mary. They have three children.

Early career in space exploration. Stofan's career as a planetary geologist began in 1989 at NASA's Jet Propulsion Laboratory, thirty-one years after her father began his NASA career and a year after he retired. Like her father, she went on to a distinguished career as a NASA scientist. In 1994, she became the JPL's chief scientist for the New Millenium Program where she supervised a team of a hundred scientists. [(Ellen Stofan, Former Chief Scientist at NASA, Named to Head National Air and Space Museum | National Air and Space Museum (si.edu)] The program began in 1995 and focused on the development and validation of new technologies for space travel. Two of the program's missions, Deep Space 1 and Deep Space 2 (DS1 and DS2) were carried out during her tenure as JPL chief scientist. (NASA's New Millennium Program: Taking Risks to Reduce Future Danger | Space)

Deep Space 1. The mission was launched on October 24, 1998 to test twelve new technologies developed by NASA and its contractors. The most notable was a test of an ion engine that provides cheaper, faster, farther travel for space vehicles. An astounding fuel efficiency of 90 percent reduces the amount of fuel, and thus weight, that needs to be on board for deep-space missions.

Ion engines are incredibly powerful. They can propel spacecraft at speeds over 200,000 mph, compared to the space shuttle, for example, that can "only" reach speeds of 18,000 mph. Ion engines are not used to launch flights because they have extremely low acceleration rates. It takes three days for a space vehicle powered with an ion engine to reach full speed, not a problem once maximum speed is attained on long-term deep-space missions. The successful performance of ion propulsion on Deep Space 1 set the stage for the many similarly propelled deep-space missions that followed. (NASA—Ion Propulsion: Farther, Faster, Cheaper)

The Deep Space 1 mission was by any measure a smashing success. It spent three years, one month and twelve hours in deep space before its ion engine was turned off. Designed as an engineering test flight, it also added a flyby of Asteroid 9660 Braille in July 1999. When the primary mission ended in September 1999, NASA devised an "extended mission" plan that kept Deep Space 1 operating until December 18, 2001. A benefit from the extended mission was an approach to the coma of Comet Borrelly, sixteen miles from its nucleus (a coma is the luminous-particle cloud surrounding the frozen nucleus that forms as the comet warms in approaching the sun). (what is a comet's coma definition—Yahoo Search Results)

All twelve of the mission's new technologies performed well with no failures, including those devised by Ellen and her group of engineers, although Deep Space 1 did have problems along the way. In November 1999, the star-tracker attitude-control system that handles the spacecraft's orientation failed, resulting in its being unable to point its antenna toward earth. NASA engineers had to devise a ground-controlled system to keep the spacecraft correctly positioned. The new system functioned well enough to allow Deep Space 1 to visit the comet but plans to reach other targets had to be scrapped. (In Depth | Deep Space 1—NASA Solar System Exploration)

Deep Space 2. On January 3, 1999, two mini 5.3-pound space probes, named Scott and Amundsen for the famed Antarctic explorers, were launched on a test mission to study the Mars surface. They were launched from Cape Canaveral aboard a Delta II rocket and then were dropped to the Mars surface where they were to begin signaling to NASA. The mission's purpose was "to flight-test advanced technology concepts for space missions" and to characterize Martian soil. Its stated objectives were to explore the carbon-dioxide ice cap approximately 620 miles (a thousand kilometers) from the planet's south pole. Other objectives were to record meteorological conditions, analyze samples of polar deposits and take multispectral images.

When the spacecraft reached Mars in December 1999 Scott and Amundsen were successfully released and landed on the planet's surface. But once on the surface no signal could be detected from either probe.

The mission failed, but subsequent Mars missions carried out with the advantage of improved technology fulfilled the objectives set out for Deep Space 2. (In Depth | Mars Polar Lander / Deep Space 2—NASA Solar System Exploration)

Earth images from space, SIR-C radar imaging. In 1994, Ellen Stofan began participation as an experimental scientist on a NASA project to obtain high-definition images of earth taken from space. Useful and often spectacular images were obtained from a radar-imaging system, SIR-C/XSAR (SIR designates Spaceborne Imaging Radar, C/X designates the radar bands used and SAR designates Synthetic Aperture Radar). The imaging system was developed by the Jet Propulsion Laboratory together with Italian and German groups and was designed to make simultaneous observations in geology, hydrology, ecology and oceanography. The imaging systems were mounted aboard the Space Shuttle Endeavour and the earth images were transmitted from the shuttle to earthbound NASA scientists where they were analyzed for soil moisture, the state of the seas and

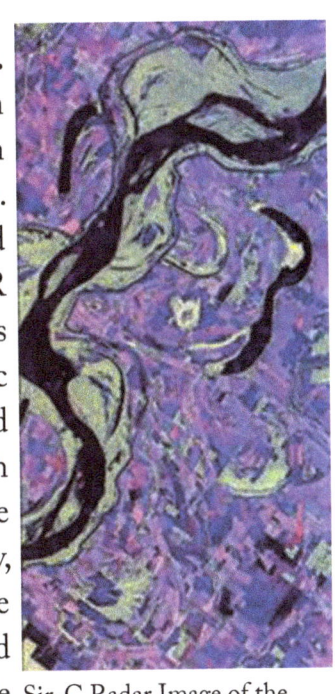

Sir-C Radar Image of the Mississippi River. (NASA Visible Earth—Home)

weather conditions, (all useful for weather prediction). [Spaceborne Imaging Radar-C Precision (nasa.gov)]

Two missions were launched in 1994: the first operated from April 9 to April 20 and the second from September 30 to October 11. Each mission scanned approximately 50-million square kilometers of the earth's surface of 510-million square kilometers. (SIR-C/X-SAR—Radartutorial)

1995–2013, London and Proxemy Research. In 1995, Ellen moved to England where she had accepted an honorary professorship at University College London. She took the new position while continuing her JPL work. She remained at University College until 2000 when she returned to the US to take up a vice-president position with Proxemy Research, a space-consulting firm in Laytonsville, Maryland. (ellen stofan university college london—Yahoo Search Results) At Proxemy she continued as an honorary professor at University College.

While at Proxemy, in addition to Ellen's Venus exploration work, she took up the chairmanship of the Inner Planets Panel as part of a National Research Council Planetary Sciences Decadal Survey. Its mission was to gain an overview of planetary science and the current state of knowledge and to make recommendations for the next decade. [1-Stoffan-InnerPlanets-Panel. ppt (usra.edu)] This panel was just one of many assignments, scientific and educational, that she has undertaken over her career.

2013–2016, NASA Chief Scientist. In 2013, Stofan returned to NASA as its chief scientist, a critical position in the agency. There she served as the chief in-house analyst tasked with overseeing and assessing progress on all ongoing projects and with developing recommendations for planning of future ventures. She reported directly to Charles Bolden, then NASA's director. Stofan advised Bolden on scientific matters, NASA's strategies for space-science programs and its coordination efforts with other government agencies, international space agencies and the scientific community. (nasa ucl—Yahoo Video Search Results)

Her vast experience in the many facets of space exploration and research served her well during her tenure as scientific director. In that role she coordinated the scientific program with the engineering and human-ecology programs. Exploring space is indeed a comprehensive scientific endeavor, a vast undertaking that involves physics, chemistry, biology, geology and other scientific disciplines. Yet space exploration can't be done with science alone. Spacecraft don't even get to the launchpad without engineering to invent, design, build, launch and propel space vehicles. And efforts to send astronauts into space to explore planets, moons and comets require a knowledge of human physiology to create conditions for space travelers to survive and function in the unforgiving environments of space. So, the challenge to NASA directors like Stofan is to keep these three components—science, engineering and human ecology—moving together in a carefully coordinated effort from concept through the mission, and that requires a comprehensive knowledge of all that is going on at NASA.

As chief scientist Ellen served as principal investigator for the Titan Mare Explorer (TiME) project to explore Saturn's largest moon, but, unfortunately, that mission never got off the launchpad. The mission was planned to explore the Ligeia Mare, a hydrocarbon sea on Titan. The funding application reached the final stage of the selection process, but it was not selected. (Profile | Ellen Stofan, NASA Chief Scientist—SpaceNews) The Titan Mare mission had originally been proposed to NASA by Proxemy Research with Ellen as principal investigator and was to launch in 2023 and continue for seven-and-a-half years with between three and six months spent on Titan. It would have yielded valuable information about the surface chemistry of that moon and would have served as a model for future missions. One important part of the mission was a floating probe that was to land on the Ligeia Mare, the moon's second-largest hydrocarbon sea, and begin transmitting data immediately after splashdown. For perspective, the Ligeia Mare has a surface area of about 130,000 square kilometers, larger than Lake Superior's 82,103 square kilometers. [Proposal Development and Production (nasa.gov)]; (Mystery Feature Evolves in Titan's Ligeia Mare | NASA)

Apart from her efforts to study the hydrocarbon mega-lakes of Titan, Ellen was closely engaged in long-range efforts to search Mars for evidence of life. She has long held that life in some form existed at one time on the planet Mars, and perhaps still does. She expressed her views in an interview published in *Space News* early during her tenure as NASA Chief Scientist: "We are exploring Mars, where it is very likely that life evolved, around the same time life evolved here on Earth. Conditions on Mars deteriorated after about a million years, so life either went underground, or became extinct. It will likely take future Mars astronauts to find the best evidence of Mars Life." (Debra Werner, *Space News*, Oct. 30, 2013)

Putting astronauts on Mars to search for signs of life is among NASA's high-priority, long-term projects, and during Ellen's tenure as chief scientific officer, she was closely involved in the ongoing planning process. The challenges that must be met to put humans on Mars are formidable. Traveling to and from the Red Planet is eight months of space flight each way, and throughout the long voyage astronauts must be maintained in a safe and comfortable environment with all needs provided for. Successful landings of relatively light spacecraft on the planet's surface have been made, but sending three astronauts, their living quarters, enough oxygen, a laboratory facility with instrumentation and packing everything into a Mars lander demands extensive and precise planning and an acute awareness of possible problems. Ellen, fully aware of the imposing complexities and intricacies involved, estimates a manned Mars mission could take place sometime in the mid-2030s and that NASA acting alone can't do it. It must be an international effort.

Among her many tasks as chief scientist was overseeing the many ongoing NASA missions and project developments. During her tenure seventeen earth-orbiting satellites were monitoring and recording changes across land surfaces, oceans and the atmosphere. The Hubble Space Telescope was launched in 1990, and throughout its long tenure in space it has yielded data on the universe's expansion, confirmed the prevalence of black holes in nearby galaxies and, together with other significant discoveries, has given us a more accurate estimation of the age of the universe (13.7 billion years). The telescope's images of dark space, i.e., space that would appear blank with standard telescopes, reveals its dense population of galaxies.

Hubble Space Telescope image showing galaxies not detected by conventional telescopes. Home (hubblesite.org)

The earth-orbiting Kepler telescope was launched in March 2009 to search for planets beyond our solar system (exoplanets) continued operating through Ellen's tenure, finding new planets and providing descriptions of their characteristics. At its retirement in 2018, Kepler had discovered more than 2,600 planets. In the search for signs of life the atmospheres of candidate planets were analyzed for indications of their suitability to support life, e.g., the presence of water, oxygen and other essential elements. [Home (hubblesite. org)]

During Ellen's chief-scientist period at NASA, the agency maintained satellite space stations that constantly monitor the earth's atmospheric and land conditions, from wind patterns to earth warming, glacial melting, draughts and other indicators of global warming, and it continues to observe. Specific "hot spots"—for example, the Arctic and Antarctica, India and California—are constantly monitored for significant changes. Camera systems aboard the space station also analyze the condition of crops and return data that farmers can use to improve quality and yields, from adding potassium to regulating irrigation and more.

Ellen resigned from NASA in 2016 following the presidential election. During her busy three years as chief scientist she was involved in committee and advisory activities within and beyond NASA. She supported the agency's programs in planetary science and astrophysics and supported commercial space activity. She worked on science policy with President Obama's science advisor and the National Science and Technology Council. (Ellen Stofan—Brooke Owens Fellowship) Always busy, always involved.

The Air and Space Museum. After departing NASA Ellen continued in her position as consulting senior scientist at Johns Hopkins Applied Physics Laboratory. Then in April 2018, she was named director of the Smithsonian's National Air and Space Museum in Washington, D.C. She brought her twenty-nine years of experience as a space scientist to a museum largely devoted to the exploration of space. The new position was also an ideal fit her long-held passion for spreading the wonders of science from the laboratory to the general population, with a special emphasis on getting the message to minorities and young people.

The National Air and Space Museum is the second most-visited museum in the United States and the fifth most-visited in the world. More than six million people visited the museum in 2018. Its massive collection of air and space exhibits are at two museum sites, the original 161,145-square foot facility on the National Mall and the 71,000-square-foot Steven F. Udvar-Hazy Center in Chantilly, Virginia. [Smithsonian Institution—National Air And Space Museum (tourofdc.org)] The Smithsonian also operates a restoration center in Suitland, Maryland, where donated objects are brought to museum standards. There, the *Enola Gay*, the World War II bomber that dropped the atom bomb on Hiroshima, underwent a long and extensive restoration. [Into the Attic Of the History Of Flight—The New York Times (nytimes.com)]

Directing the National Air and Space Museum is a multitasker's challenge or perhaps, nightmare. Managing the museum's many functions carried out at three different locations into a working, growing and smoothly running operation requires constant vigilance, patience and highly refined managerial skill. Day-to-day operations, integrating new exhibits, fundraising, dealing with Congress, keeping abreast of operations at all levels at all sites, planning programs, preparations for the future, dealing with public relations, developing publicity, planning and offering effective educational programs and simply coping with inevitable daily problems are but some of the things that require constant monitoring. It's a big, demanding job.

One of Ellen's major priorities at the Air and Space Museum was to raise money for and oversee a complete renovation of the museum. The billion-dollar project began in 2018, and it is funded by an appropriation of $750 million from Congress with the remainder from individual donors. Jeff Bezos of Amazon donated $70 million toward the renovation. The budget provides $130 million for a new education center, something dear to Ellen's heart. Significant donations have come from other individuals and organizations, with the renovation scheduled for completion in 2025. [Exhibitions Reimagined | National Air and Space Museum (si. edu); Smithsonian Names Ellen Stofan Under Secretary for Science and Research | Smithsonian Institution (si.edu)]

Spreading the word. Ellen's leadership role at the Smithsonian gave her a bully pulpit to preach the word of science to her favorite target audiences: young women and minorities. She has long been an outspoken advocate for science education, and the Air and Space Museum's new education center provides a splendid opportunity to showcase nature's wonders and to show how science works to understand them. One aim of her educational efforts is to encourage young people and minorities to get involved in scientific exploration. Upon taking over the directorship she expressed her disappointment that most girls are not attracted to science: "I think the message kids lose is that science, technology, engineering and math [STEM] are fun and a way to solve big challenges that the world has." She also pointed out that fields such as commercialization of space, artificial intelligence and robotics are going to take off and that it's critical to have a diverse workforce. Girls will "lose out economically" otherwise, and the progress of science will "lose out talent-wise, idea-wise and creativity-wise." She spoke of the challenges for minority students: "I can't tell you how many times I still hear stories from people of color who are made to feel unwelcome" at universities and laboratories. "I think we're still not there in treating each other as talented individuals." (Fauquier scientist aims to reimagine the National Air and Space Museum | News | fauquier.com)

Ellen working with young women in a science-education program. https_2F2Fblogs-images. forbes.com2Fjoanmichelson22Ffiles2F20182F112FEllen-tofan-w-girls-NASM2018-01706-1. jpg (960×553) (conceptschools.org)

Among Ellen's high-priority pursuits is the struggle for gender equality in scientific professions. As a woman in a space industry dominated by men, she has seen indifference to and lack of opportunity for bright, educated and dedicated women. In an interview with c/net (Ellen Stofan, new Air and Space Museum head, talks NASA, Star Trek—CNET) made shortly after her appointment as the Air and Space Museum's director she was asked if she ever felt that her gender was a challenge to her career path in science. "I did. You can't help but look around and realize you're one of the few women in the room, if there were any other women at all. I had a fellow student say to me, 'You don't need a job, you have a husband.' Up until that point, I hadn't thought of us as men and women, but it was clear to me he had. He clearly saw me as something lesser. To me, we're all just scientists."

In March 2021, Ellen left her position at the Air and Space Museum to become Under Secretary for Science at the Smithsonian. In that role she oversees the institute's science museums, science-research centers and

Smithsonian Libraries. Entities that fall under her oversight include the Air and Space Museum, the National Museum of Natural History, the National Zoo, the Smithsonian Conservation Biology Institute, the Museum Conservation Institute, the Smithsonian Astrophysical Observatory, the Smithsonian Environmental Research Center and the Smithsonian Tropical Research Institute. Her job description includes collective scientific initiatives and commitment to research across the institute. She addresses issues from biodiversity and global health to climate change, species conservation, astrophysics and the search for life outside our solar system.

What Ellen has experienced throughout her career is what most if not all women experience in male-dominated professions. But with her role of oversight of science at the Smithsonian, with the mission of promoting awareness and understanding of science, she stands in a unique position to reach out to young women and infect them with the excitement of scientific discovery and to open their minds to the rewards of a scientific career.

Hidden Figures. One of Ellen's partners in promoting science among minorities and young women is Margot Lee Shetterly. In her book, *Hidden Figures* (New York: HarperCollins, 2016), Shetterly recounts the experience of four talented Black women mathematicians who made major contributions to NASA's early space missions despite segregation and gender bias, only to then be essentially ignored or underrecognized for their achievements, that is until the book and the movie of the same title were released. Ellen and Margot have appeared in forums showcasing these Black NASA mathematicians as role models for young minority women.

From the age of four when she watched a NASA rocket lift off from its launchpad Ellen Stofan has been focused on space. That explosive prelude to her distinguished career set in motion a lifelong adventure devoted to space exploration that has revealed significant knowledge. At each step along the way, from Brown University to the Jet Propulsion Lab then to University College London and to Proxemy, NASA, the National Air and Space Museum and as Smithsonian's Under Secretary for Science and Research, she has established a record of accomplishment. Her career is further distinguished by her consuming interest in extending the idea that a career devoted to science can be fascinating, rewarding and fulfilling. She directs her message to women of all ages, underrepresented as they are in scientific professions, to encourage them to choose careers in science. She makes a special effort to reach out to young minority women to tap that potential rich source of expertise that will make significant contributions. Ellen Stofan's career continues. Surely many exciting adventures lie ahead.

Chapter 10 tells the story of Ellen's cousin Robert Kelker-Kelly, soap opera star and airlines pilot.

Addenda
Ellen Stofan

Beyond the laboratory, reaching out. Beyond her space career, Ellen spends time and energy reaching out to numerous groups. She lectures and participates in committees, boards, panels and organizations, giving frequent talks and lectures, all part of her mission to communicate the wonders of science.

Some positions Dr. Ellen Stofan has held:

—co-chair of the World Economic Forum's Council on the Future of Space Technology [Ellen Stofan, Former Chief Scientist at NASA, Named To Head National Air and Space Museum | National Air and Space Museum (si.edu)]

—public-speaking engagements at the World Science Festival, SciFest Africa and at numerous schools and universities around the world [Ellen Stofan, Former Chief Scientist at NASA, Named To Head National Air and Space Museum | National Air and Space Museum (si.edu)]

—chairing panels including the National Research Inner Planets Council and the Venus Exploration Group (Dr. Ellen Stofan, Chief Scientist | NASA)

—appointment as a member of president-elect Joe Biden's Agency Review Team to support NASA's transition (Ellen Stofan Age, Wikipedia, Family, Height, Net Worth & Biography—Wiki Project (projecttopics.org))

—Under Secretary for Science and Research at the Smithsonian [Ellen Stofan | Smithsonian Institution (si.edu)]

—together with *Hidden Figures* author Margot Lee Shetterly, served on the advisory board of Terra Alpha Investments (Hidden Figures Author Margot Lee Shetterly Joins Terra Alpha Investments Advisory Board—Terra Alpha).

Selected awards

—Presidential Early Career Award for Scientists and Engineers
—NASA Distinguished Service Medal
—one of CNN's extraordinary people of 2014 (Profile | Ellen Stofan, NASA Chief Scientist—SpaceNews).

Books

Tom Jones (former astronaut) and Ellen Stofan, 2008, *Planetology: Unlocking the Secrets of the Solar System,* published by *National Geographic*

Tom Jones and Ellen Stofan, 2017, *The Next Earth: What Our World Can Teach Us about Other Planets, National Geographic* special edition.

Peer Reviewed Publications

"Preliminary Analysis of an Expanded Corona Databased for Venus," Ellen R. Stofan, Suzanne E. Smrekar, Simon W. Tapper, John E. Guest, Peter M. Grindrod, (Geophysical Research Letters, 2001 Vol. 28, Iss. 22, pp. 4267–4270)

Exploring Venus as a Terrestrial Planet, Stofan, Ellen; Cravens, Thomas E.; Esposito, Larry W., eds. (2007. American Geophysical Union, Book Series: Geophysical Monograph Series.

Stofan, Ellen; Jones, Tom (2008). Planetology: Unlocking the Secrets of the Solar System. National Geographic. ISBN 978-1-4262-0121-9.

Venus as a Mantle Plume Laboratory, Suzanne E Smrekar 1, Ellen R Stofan, Nils Mueller, Allan Treiman, Linda Elkins-Tanton, Joern Helbert, Giuseppe Piccioni, Pierre Drossart, (Science, April 30, 2010, pp. 605–608)

Unlocking the Secrets of the Solar System, Stofan, Ellen; Jones, Tom (2008). Planetology:. National Geographic. ISBN 978-1-4262-0121-9.

CHAPTER 10

Robert Kelker-Kelly
TV Soaps and Aviation

[1579189331Robert Kelker-Kelly 2.jpg (303×180) (allcelebritywiki.com)]

Biography. Robert Kelker-Kelly is best known as a soap-opera actor. He spent nineteen years playing leading characters in *Another World*, *Days of Our Lives* and *General Hospital*. He left his acting career in 2014 to pursue his passion for aviation.

Robert was born on April 18, 1964 in Cleveland, Ohio, to Robert Kelly, a forensic pathologist, and Jonetta Kelker Kelly, a nurse. At the age of seven, his parents divorced, and he went to live with his father. At eleven, his father remarried, and Robert returned to live with his mother. Just three months later his father died from a heart attack. (Robert Kelker-Kelly wiki | TheReaderWiki)

He caught the acting bug during his time at Wichita Collegiate School in Wichita, Kansas that he attended from 1977 to 1980. There he played leading roles in *Guys and Dolls*, *Camelot* and *Oliver*. [Robert Kelker-Kelly Actors | Soaps.com (sheknows.com)] He attended the University of Kansas but left without graduating and went to Florida to pursue theater roles. There he performed in a movie (he claims he can't remember the title). His path to the soaps began when he left Florida for Los Angeles where he broke through with a major role in the long-running soap opera *Another World*.

Early career, He described his entry into the soap-opera world in an interview he gave to Welovesoaps.net, an entertainment website. [(9) We Love Soaps | Facebook] He left for California to "chase" (his word) a Playboy Playmate he had met in the Sunshine State. The relationship ended, and his early career in Los Angeles proceeded much like that of many struggling actors. He was homeless and sleeping in his Jeep or wherever he could find overnight accommodation, sometimes at a fellow actor's place. He got a job in a headhunter's office, but still couldn't stretch his budget enough to afford an apartment. Things changed when he had the good fortune to find an established agent who counted among his clients the successful actors Alec Baldwin and Bob Hoskins. The agent's formula for aspiring actors was first to get them into soap operas, a strategy that had worked for Baldwin and Hoskins. Acquiring that agent paid off when Robert landed a role in the long-running soap *Another World* (or *AW*), and he moved to New York City where the soap was produced.

Another World. AW premiered in 1964, the year Robert was born, and continued through 8,891 episodes to its finale in 1999. Robert joined the show in 1987 as Sam Fowler, a character who was an artist, an art director for a publishing company and a country singer. One story line had Sam arriving in the fictional town of Bay City to meet up with his half-brother. There he meets Amanda Cory, recently returned from Paris and the daughter of wealthy parents who operate a publishing company where Sam has been hired as artistic director. Amanda works at the company under an assumed name, they become friends and lovers and over time she reveals her identity. A crisis occurs when Amanda becomes pregnant. Great plans for a wedding fall apart when Sam goes to Chicago to return a wedding gift stolen by Amanda's kleptomaniac grandmother and gets arrested in the process. He is not able to get back to Bay City by the start of the wedding. The guests leave, Sam finally arrives later in the day, explains his absence to an upset Amanda, and they return to the church for a late-night wedding. Their child is born shortly after the wedding. The marriage eventually falls apart when Amanda begins sleeping with another man though they get back together until Sam leaves to pursue a career as a country singer. Robert left *AW* in 1990. His character was played in succession by two replacement actors until 1993 when Sam Fowler was written out of the script. (Sam and Amanda Fowler—Wikipedia)

While performing in *Another World* Robert met production assistant Linda Rattner. They married in 1988. (Robert Kelker-Kelly wiki | TheReaderWiki) He declared Linda to be the best thing he got out of his time on the show. After his time at *AW* ended the couple left for California where they experienced "a dry period," in Robert's words. He had to take on non-acting jobs. But fortune struck in 1992 when he landed a role on *Days of Our Lives* (aka *Days* or *DOOL*), one of the longest-running soap operas. But his professional good fortune did not follow through to his marriage; He and Linda divorced that year.

Days of Our Lives. Since its beginning in November 1965, *Days* has continued for more than 14,000 episodes. (Days of Our Lives—Wikipedia) The original story focused on two families of doctors in the fictional town of Salem. Through the years *Days* in its many story lines has followed the usual soap-opera arc of conflict, love, sex, love triangles, marriage, divorce, adultery, abortion, pregnancies (wanted and unwanted), mental illness and, of course, prolonged suspense to keep its viewers tuning in. In 1992, Robert replaced Peter Reckell who originated the major character Beauregard Aurelius "Bo" Brady in 1982. (Note: In soap operas that run for years it is not uncommon for an actor to leave a role while the story line continues uninterrupted with a replacement actor taking over that role.)

By any assessment Bo Brady was a colorful character with just the reckless personality to keep the audience tuning in. Bo was the result of a torrid affair between crime boss Victor Kiriakis and Bo's mother, Caroline Brady. During the Bo character's long spell on Days he was a Salem Police Department detective, commissioner and captain, a bounty hunter, a private detective and a merchant marine. He was married to and divorced from Hope Williams; their second marriage was declared invalid because she was still married to another man. Bo married and divorced Billie Reed twice and had a child with her during their second marriage. His marriages produced five children, and apart from those marriages he had flings with five other women.

Peter Reckell and Kristian Alfonso originated the roles of Bo and Hope, and Robert took over in March 1992 with a new love interest, Billie, played by Lisa Rinna. (*Daily Press*, Victorville, Calif., July 16, 1995, p. 70) Robert gave his take on Bo in an interview given after his first six months in the role: "He's fun to play because he's no hero at all. He rushes in there whenever his emotions tell him to, and he doesn't put up with a lot of crap from others. He's also waking up to reality regardless of what he feels [...] I hope the writers keep Bo in the direction he is in now because it brings a sense of excitement to the whole thing." (These Are the Days of Kelker-Kelly's Life | Archive | tulsaworld.com)

Robert received *Soap Opera Digest*'s award for outstanding lead after two years, but the next year he was replaced by the returning Peter Reckell. The soap-opera press was abuzz about the sudden change. The *Days* producer, Corday Productions, issued a matter-of-fact statement: "The show chose not to pick up Kelker-Kelly's contract option." Rumors swirled, including one about Robert and the executive producer not getting along and having a run-in. Another suggested trouble between RKK and his romantic costars, but in their interviews neither Lisa Rinna nor Kristian Alfonso had negative things to say, and Alfonso vehemently denied that she had threatened to leave if Robert remained. (*Daily Press*, Victorville, Calif., TV Update, July 23, 1995, p. 4) Although years later costar Lisa Rinna, who left the show two months after Robert's departure, said in a December 3, 2015, interview (RHOBH's Lisa Rinna on DAYS Leading Man: "I Hated Robert Kelker-Kelly"—Daytime Confidential) that "I hated Robert Kelker-Kelly; hated him with a passion! He hated me with a passion."

Soap Opera Digest's "bombshell" on *Days*, showing Robert and Peter Reckell, his predecessor and replacement. (SOAP OPERA WEEKLY 7/11/95 ROBERT KELKER—KELLY RUTH WARRICK SHARON CASE | eBay)

As Robert stated to *Soap Opera Weekly*: "I went as far as I could with Days of Our Lives […] I learned a lot as a person; I grew a lot as an actor […] I want to go do something that has a little more meat to it, something that has a little more variety to it." Regarding any tense relations with Rinna and Alfonso, he remarked: "We've had our good times and bad times. That's just the way this business works." And about being replaced by Peter Reckell: "Well, good for him. That's great. I wish him all the luck." (*Soap Opera Weekly*, July 11, 1995, p. 3)

The termination seems to have had little effect on Robert's career. He soon landed roles in two TV series, *Touched by an Angel* and *Hart to Hart*. And in 1996 he returned to *Another World* but did not resume his Sam Fowler role. His new character, Bobby Reno, is described as having "a colorful past and a yearning for love." He had undergone transplant surgery receiving the corneas of Ryan Harrison who was killed by his, i.e., Ryan's, own brother, then moved to Bay City where Ryan's love, Vicky Hudson, lived. He and another character competed for Vicky's affections, but she claimed she could never love another man as much as she had loved Ryan, setting the stage for the ongoing story line. (*Austin American-Statesman*, July 21, 1996, p. 225)

In 1997 Robert married his longtime squeeze, actress Miriam Parrish. They met while working on *Days*; she was twenty and he was thirty-three. He left *AW* in 1998 and did not appear in another soap until he joined *General Hospital* in 2001. In the interim he landed a role in *Rescue 77*, a TV series. When he returned to soaps, he joined *General Hospital* (or *GH*) where he played the evil conniving Stavros Cassadine, probably his most recognized soap role, although his Bo role on *Days* and his much-reported dismissal both gained significant attention.

General Hospital. *GH* has been in production since April 1, 1963. As of February 23, 2018, fifty-five years from its premiere, some 14,000 episodes had been presented. It is the oldest of all TV soaps. Action takes place in the fictional town of Port Charles, New York, although the town's name was not mentioned until the late 1970s. Like all soaps, story lines usually center around a core family, families or individuals in some fictional location, although through the years the writing may stray from the original setting. Since the late 1970s, the Quartermaine and Spencer families have been central characters around which *GH* story lines revolve. (General Hospital, Wikipedia)

Robert's character, Stavros Cassadine, was first played by John Martinuzzi for a month in late 1983. Robert then reprised the role from June 1, 2001, until the second of Stavros's deaths, on November 9. He then reappeared as Stavros in hallucination episodes from February 2002 until December 2003, and appeared again as Stavros in 2013 and 2014. [Stavros Cassadine (Robert Kelker-Kelly) | General Hospital Wiki | Fandom]

Stavros (then played by John Martinuzzi) had "died" to end his 1983 appearance, having become obsessed with Laura Spencer, who was devoted to her husband, Luke Spencer. He then kidnapped her and lied that Luke had died. Believing Luke was gone, Laura married Stavros, they had a child, then upon learning that Luke was not dead, she returned to Port Charles. Stavros intended to kill Luke but he died pursuing him and falling down the General Hospital stairs.

With Robert's appearance in the role in 2001, the script revealed that Stavros had in fact been placed in cryogenic suspension and hidden in a room somewhere underneath General Hospital. In his second coming he went after Laura and his brother, Stefan. He murdered Stefan's girlfriend, Chloe, and framed Stefan for the crime. He then died a second time when his sister Helena, equally evil and conniving, trapped Luke, Laura, Nikolas (Laura's child with Stavros), his girlfriend and others beneath Wyndemere Castle, a Cassadine family inheritance near Port Charles. While trying to free Nikolas, Stavros "died" by falling into a bottomless pit.

Robert appeared as visions of Stavros, then it was discovered that he was still alive. Luke and Laura, trying to locate their lost daughter, Lulu, were kidnapped by Helena and Stavros, who were holding Lulu, with whom Stavros was now obsessed. Laura offered to be with him if he would release her. Lulu was rescued by Dante Falconeri, son of a mob boss and a longtime *GW* character, who locked Stavros in a cryogenic chamber, dead again for the third time.

Stavros appeared a fourth time in 2013 and 2014, carrying on more mischief and dying for the fourth and perhaps last time. After being unfrozen, he again kidnaped Lulu and told her he's fertilized one of her frozen eggs so they will have a child together. Dante, now Lulu's husband, comes to his wife's rescue and kills Stavros. (Stavros on General Hospital—Everything You Need to Know—Soaps In Depth)

Out of the spotlight, into the air. 2014 marked the last year Robert appeared in soap opera roles. He left acting to pursue his lifelong passion for flying airplanes. His transition began in 1999 and 2000 when he studied aviation maintenance at the Northrop/Rice School of Aviation Technology. (Robert Kelker Kelly—Pilot—Air Methods | LinkedIn) Since departing the limelight he has accumulated extensive experience in many aspects of aviation.

He was employed by DB Aviation from 2006 to 2008 as assistant-chief pilot "responsible for the professional standards of the flight crews under his authority and operations and training safety management goals." Among his other duties he oversaw "day-to-day operations of the flight department, including but not limited to scheduling of flight crews, review of flight-risk assessment tools, administering performance reviews, assisting with the hiring of new flight crew, management of pilot staff." [Assistant Chief Pilot (apertureaviation.com)]

He flew Lear 60XR jets for Fielding Aviation from 2009 to 2013, and from 2013 to 2015 he was responsible for domestic and international preflight planning and security for Spirit Jets, along with obtaining weather reports, choosing routes, assessing aircraft performance and accounting for aircraft-maintenance status. From January 2016 to January 2018, Robert taught pilot ground school and flight-simulator use to new and retraining pilots. From 2018 to 2021, he was Gama Aviation's charter captain, responsible for flight safety in accordance with Federal Aviation Administration (FAA) regulations. In this same period, he was an air-med pilot for St. Louis Children's Hospital. (Robert Kelker Kelly—Pilot—Air Methods | LinkedIn)

Life has changed for Robert Kelker-Kelly. He seems to have settled into his new life as a fully trained professional pilot and family man. He is happily settled with his wife and child. His has been an interesting journey, from Kansas City to the soap-opera world to piloting passenger jets, and he has attained success in two seemingly unrelated professions. He should write about his unique life.

Miscellaneous Addenda

Note: While digging through old newspapers and other records I came across items of interest that don't necessarily fit with the narrative but are in some way relevant if not interesting.

Kelker Siblings Separated as Children and Reunited as Students at Hiram College. The running theme of this story is Hiram College in Hiram, Ohio. The school claims as alumni several members of the Kelker family who somehow found their way to the small out-of-the-way undergraduate liberal arts institution. The college was founded in 1850 by the Disciples of Christ, a protestant denomination. It exists in the village of Hiram in the historic Western Reserve that occupies the northeast corner of the state. Both the college and the village are small. The college now enrolls about 1,100 students, the largest in its history. The village population is approximately the same.

Dr. Henry Creath Kelker (1875–1943) of Cleveland (see the Chapter 3 section on Jacob Kelker) somehow discovered Hiram College and sent five of his six children there. John, the oldest and the first to attend, graduated in 1924. He was followed by Stephen, 1926; Ida, 1928, Amelia, 1933; and James, 1935; Dr. Kelker's four nephews also attended and graduated from Hiram College. They were the children of his brother Challen (my grandfather) Marius Cook Kelker (1866–1914) and my grandmother Faith Hills Kelker (1872–1914) of Morrow County, Ohio.

Challen and Faith farmed in rural Mt. Gilead, Ohio. From family photos it appears they lived a rather meager life. They were, however, blessed with four children in what must have been a happy and loving family. But family life was shattered on October 14, 1914, when Challen died, and then again nine days later when Faith passed away. Challen suffered a scratch while filling a silo. The scratch developed into what was diagnosed as blood poisoning that led to his death at age 48. Faith died of tuberculosis at age 42. The children, ages 7, 6, 5 and 3 could have been moved to orphanages, but by great good fortune they found homes with relatives. Challen had four married sisters, three of whom were childless, and they took in the children. The two older boys, George Hills, age 7, and Rudolph Frederick, age 6, were taken in by their aunt Bertha Kelker and her husband Herbert George in Garrettsville, Ohio, about three miles from Hiram. Aaron, my father, at age 5 went to live with his aunt Catherine Kelker and her husband Ernest Galleher in Alameda, California. Katherine, the youngest at age 3, was adopted by Hannah Lua Kelker and her husband Fred Livingston in Westerville near Columbus, Ohio. The three aunts must have been thrilled to all-of-a-sudden have children in their home. Almost miraculously the suddenly orphaned children found happy, secure homes with aunts and uncles.

The Kelker siblings re-united at Hiram College. From left, Rudolph, Aaron, Katherine and George. The photograph is from a family album. It was most likely taken in 1927 or 1928 when they were together as students.

The children grew up apart from each other, but they reunited as students at Hiram College. George, Rudolph and Aaron were joined by Katherine who enrolled in 1928 to complete the reunion.

George completed his studies in 1928, Rudolph in 1929, Aaron in 1931 and Katherine in 1932. George earned a Ph.D. from the University of Michigan and spent his career as Professor of Forestry and Wildlife at Utah State University. He and his wife Dorothy Mills Kelker raised three boys. Rudolph completed a master's degree from Ohio State University and spent his life as a farmer and schoolteacher in Garrettsville, Ohio. He married

Amelia Katherine Kelker (1910–2002) and they had four daughters and a son. Upon graduation Aaron taught high school science in the Cleveland area. While there he received a master's degree from Western Reserve University. He then taught high school science in Chillicothe, Ohio before moving on to Hiram College where he taught science before becoming an administrator. He married Martha Taylor (1905–1969), and they had two boys, my brother John and me. Katherine married Ralph Rhodes, her high school sweetheart. The couple settled in Norristown, Pennsylvania and raised three daughters and a son. Katherine was active in community affairs..

The Hiram College connection and the next generation. Many of the children of the four Kelker siblings attended Hiram College. George and Dorothy sent two of their three boys, Rudolph and Amelia sent their son and three of their daughters and Aaron and Martha sent their two sons. Katherine and Ralph's four children did not attend Hiram College. In somewhat of a mini-reunion two of my cousins were together with me in the class of 1961 and we all graduated together. Below is a photograph of the three of us taken on our graduation day.

Photo from Hiram College graduation day, June 4, 1961. From left to right, George and son Douglas, Rudolph and daughter Amelia and Aaron and son Norman (me). (*The Evening Record Courier*, Portage County, Ohio, June 5, 1961)

So, the Kelkers and Hiram College share a long relationship. And that relationship has been of great benefit to the family, and even a bit to the college. I am pleased that my father Aaron spent twenty-five years at Hiram as a teacher and administrator. And none of this would have happened without the family unity displayed by the aunts and uncles who took in the suddenly orphaned Kelker children and Dr. Henry Creath Kelker who discovered Hiram College.

Hiram College and Families of the Brothers
Challen Marius Cook Kelker and Henry Creath Kelker

Children of Rudolph Frederick (1841–1908) and
Ida A. Cook Kelker (1836–1909)

Sibling	Life	Birthplace	Attended Hiram College
Albion Jacob	1864–1865	Morrow County, Ohio	
Challen Marius Cook	1866–1914	Morrow County, Ohio	
Mary Catherine	1868–1941	Morrow County, Ohio	
Hannah Lua	1871–1943	Morrow County, Ohio	
Henry Creath	1875–1943	Morrow County, Ohio	
Ida Lois	1881–1941	Morrow County, Ohio	
Bertha Alice	1884–1969	Morrow County, Ohio	

Children of Challen Marius Cook Kelker and
Faith Hills Kelker (1872–1914)

Sibling	Life	Birthplace	Attended Hiram College
George Hills	1907–1972	Morrow County, Ohio	yes
Rudolph Frederick	1908–1984	Morrow County, Ohio	yes
Aaron Hubbell	1909–1972	Morrow County, Ohio	yes
Katherine Elizabeth	1911–1996	Morrow County, Ohio	yes

Children of Henry Creath Kelker and
Elizabeth Scheerer (1874–1949)

Sibling	Life	Birthplace	Attended Hiram College
John Rudolph	1901–1981	Cleveland, Ohio	yes
Henry Frederick	1903–1922	Cleveland, Ohio	
Stephen Marcellus	1904–1975	Cleveland, Ohio	yes
Ida Christine	1906–1976	Cleveland, Ohio	yes
Amelia Katherine	1909–2002	Cleveland, Ohio	yes
James Marius	1912–1975	Cleveland, Ohio	yes

The Kelker's Harrisburg Hardware Businesses from 1805. For nearly 100 years three generations of Kelkers provided the Harrisburg community with turpentine and tar, shovels and saddles, paints and pipes and all manner of hardware goods and building supplies. It all started with Frederick, Anthony and Mary Magdalena's youngest, who in 1805 opened the first store in Harrisburg that dealt exclusively in hardware. That business served a population of approximately 2000. As Harrisburg grew to 64,000 over the next century Kelker hardware stores supplied tools and materials for the homes and buildings constructed over that period. Only from the years 1823, when Frederick sold out due to ill health, to 1842, when his son Rudolph Frederick bought back in, was a Harrisburg hardware business out of Kelker ownership.

F. Kelker & Co., (1805–1823): On April 1, 1805 Frederick Kelker (1780–1857) with two partners, Abraham Oves and William Moore, established the first store in Harrisburg that dealt exclusively in hardware. On April 1, 1811 Frederick purchased the interests of Messrs. Oves and Moore and became the sole owner of the business. He continued operating F. Kelker & Co. until July, 1823 when, with his health failing, he sold his entire interest to George Oglesby and Jacob Pool.

Oglesby & Poole, (1823–1832): The new partners operated the business until March of 1832, when Jacob Pool left the partnership and Joel Hinckley took over his interest.

Oglesby & Hinckley, (1832–1842):. The business continued under this partnership until 1842. Rudolph Frederick Kelker entered the business in March, 1835 and remained with the firm for three years learning how to manage and operate a hardware business. Due to declining health he was forced to leave the firm in May, 1838. But he returned in November, 1842 when he purchased Mr. Hinckley's interest and continued the business under the name R.F. Kelker & Co.

58   HARRISBURG BUSINESS DIRECTORY.

CHEAP HARDWARE STORE

Oglesby & Hinckley,

Respectfully inform their friends and the public generally, that they continue at the Old Established Stand, *No. 5, South Front street,* where they offer at Wholesale and Retail, a large and general assortment of Hardware and Fancy Goods, Paints, Oils, &c., among which may be found the following articles.

Locks, Bolts, Hinges and Screws, together with building materials generally.
Planes, Saws, Chisels, Braces, &c.
Iron, Steel, Anvils, Vices,
Screw Plates and Smith Bellows,
Saddlery and Coach Trimmings,
Mill, Crosscut and Circular Saws,
Nails, Brads and Spikes,

Shovels, Spades and Forks,
Gilt, Mahogany and Pine fram'd Looking Glasses, and Looking Glass Plates,
Astral, Hall and Mantle Lamps,
Britannia Tea Ware,
Fine Waiters, Brass and Plated Candlesticks,
Plated and Britannia Castors,

Wetherill & Brothers warranted pure White Lead, Venetian Red, Red Lead, Litherage, Chrome Green and Yellow, Flaxseed Oil, Spirits Turpentine and Varnishes, Window Glass, &c.

Together with almost every article generally found in Hardware Stores. They are determined to sell at as low prices and on as reasonable terms as any other establishment. By strict personal attention and constant efforts to please, they hope to merit a continuance of public patronage.

From the 1842 *Harrisburg Business Directory*

R.F. Kelker & Co., (1842–1846): RFK and Mr. Oglesby operated the business until Mr. Oglesby's death in March, 1846. Two months later, in May, he took on his brothers Immanuel Meister (1822–1880) and Henry Anthony (1825–1915) as partners and renamed the business Kelker & Brother.

WHOLESALE AND RETAIL
HARDWARE AND FANCY STORE.

R. F. KELKER & Co.

(Being R. F. Kelker & George Oglesby.)

No. 5 SOUTH FRONT-ST.

Have constantly on hand, and offer for sale, on reasonable terms, Iron, Steel, and Nails of all kinds, Elliptic Springs, Anvils, Vices, Smith's Bellows, Building Materials, PAINTS, Oils, Turpentine, TAR, Pitch, Varnishes, Looking Glasses and Looking Glass Plates, Window Glass from 7 by 9 to 23 by 36, Machine Cards, Saddlery, Coach and Venetian Blind Trimmings, Silver and Steel Framed Spectacles, Common, Patent and Lunette Watch Glasses.

WATCH GLASSES, CLOCK AND WATCH MATERIALS, TWINE AND CORDAGE, POWDER AND SHOT.

ALSO—A large lot of MAHOGANY BOARDS, PLANKS, VENEERS and Carvings.

Kelker & Brother, (1846–1851): This fraternal triumvirate operated R.F. Kelker & Co. until 1851 when Rudolph Frederick was forced to leave because of failing health. Immanuel Meister and Henry Anthony carried on under the name Kelker & Brother. The partnership lasted until 1878.

KELKER & BROTHER,
NO. 5, FRONT STREET, NEAR MARKET, HARRISBURG.
WHOLESALE AND RETAIL DEALERS
IN
AMERICAN AND FOREIGN
HARDWARE AND CUTLERY,
PAINTS, OIL and GLASS, VARNISH, MECHANICS' TOOLS, BUILDERS' HARDWARE, WIRE, ZINC, SOLDER. SADDLERY and COACH TRIMMINGS. LEAD PIPE, ELLIPTIC SPRINGS, BAR and SHEET IRON. WAGON BOXES, &c., &c., &c.,
Also, a large and extensive assortment of Vices, Files and Rasps. Stove-Rod Iron, Mah. Veneers, &c. Mill and Cross Cut Saws, Hand Saws, Chisels, Planes, &c., &c.
All goods sold at the lowest Market Prices.
AGENTS FOR MENEELY'S SUPERIOR CHURCH BELLS.

In 1878 Henry Anthony withdrew and disposed of his stock to his brother Immanuel Meister and to his nephews, Rudolph Frederick's sons Luther Reily and William Anthony, who operated the business under the name Kelker Brothers. Immanuel Meister together with his sons George Beatty (1852–1896) and Frederick (1858–1929) opened his own hardware business under the name Kelker & Sons.

DISSOLUTION OF PARTNERSHIP.

THE PARTNERSHIP HERETOFORE existing between Immanuel M. Kelker and Henry A. Kelker, under the firm of Kelker & Brother, in the General Hardware business, has been this day dissolved by mutual consent.

All persons having claims against the late firm will present them, and those indebted please call and settle with either of the undersigned, without delay.

INMANUEL M. KELKER,
HENRY A. KELKER,
No. 17, East corner Market Square.

HARRISBURG, May 1, 1878.

The undersigned having this day retired from the hardware business takes this occasion, publicly, to thank the citizens of Harrisburg and the surrounding counties for their long continued and very liberal patronage.

HENRY A. KELKER.

HARRISBURG, May 1, 1878.

KELKER & SONS.

Immanuel M. Kelker, of the late firm of Kelker & Brother, having associated with himself his sons, George B. and Frederick, will continue the hardware business at the old stand under the name of Kelker & Sons.

Thankful for the patronage heretofore bestowed on the late firm, they respectfully solicit a continuance of the same.

HARRISBURG, May 1, 1878.   123

Harrisburg Telegraph, May 1, 1878, page 4

NEW HARDWARE STORE.

LUTHER R. KELKER.   WILLIAM A. KELKER.

KELKER BROTHERS,

DEALERS IN

Hardware, Iron, Steel, Saddlery and Coach Hardware, Gum and Leather Belting, Mechanics' Tools, Paints, Oils, Glass, Varnishes, &c.
6½ MARKET SQUARE (Northwest side), four doors above Market street. P. O. Box 114.

WE offer a well-selected stock of Goods at reasonable prices. Every effort will be made to oblige our customers. We respectfully solicit a share of public patronage.

KELKER BROTHERS.

HARRISBURG, May 13, 1878.

TO THE PUBLIC.

LUTHER R. KELKER, of the above named firm, was in the employ of the late firm of KELKER & BROTHER for the past eleven years, and has gained a practical knowledge of the business. He has united with his brother, WILLIAM A. KELKER, in establishing the present house. The new firm has my best wishes for their success, and I cheerfully recommend them to the patronage of the public. HENRY A. KELKER,
Of the late firm of Kelker & Brother.

HARRISBURG, May 13, 1878.   1.3.5-193

Harrisburg Telegraph, May 1, 1878, page 4

Kelker Brothers, (1878–1892) and Kelker & Sons: (1878–?). Luther Reily and William Anthony continued operations of Kelker Brothers until 1883 when William Anthony retired. Luther Reily ran the business alone under the name Luther R. Kelker until 1892, when at age 48 he became ill and was forced to retire (see Chapter 5). During his forced retirement he found himself following his lifelong interest in the history of early Pennsylvania and he spent the rest of his career studying and publishing historical records of Dauphin County. Kelker and Sons was the last of the Kelker hardware businesses. (from Luther R. Kelker's vol. 3, *History of Dauphin County*)

A Massive Explosion at the Kelker Blower Factory in 1916. Although this story has nothing to do with my family, I include it because "Kelker" is not a common name and as a cautionary tale that things have to be carefully researched.

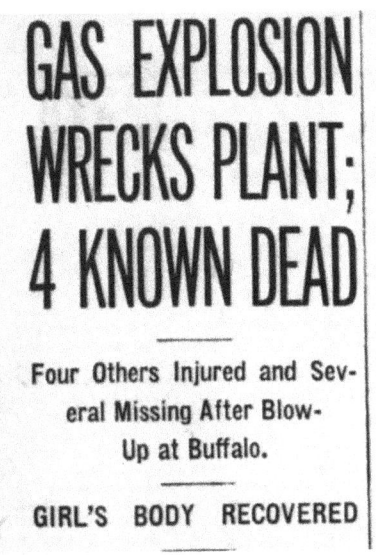

> # GAS EXPLOSION WRECKS PLANT; 4 KNOWN DEAD
>
> Four Others Injured and Several Missing After Blow-Up at Buffalo.
>
> GIRL'S BODY RECOVERED

A massive explosion in January of 1916 in the Kelker Blower Factory in Buffalo, NY made headlines nationwide. The force of the blast not only leveled the factory but shattered almost all the glass windows within a block of the factory and caused great panic at a nearby grammar school. Helen Kelker, the wife of owner Charles Kelker, had both legs severed and died within a few hours. Three more died and three others received injuries that were not life threatening although one of them, a James Kramer, had his ear torn off. (Pittsburgh Daily Post, Jan 25, 1916, p.7)

I include this story as a caution to family history researchers. Kelker is a very uncommon name and someone reading about the explosion might assume that factory owner Charles Kelker was a descendant of Heinrich and Regula Braetscher Kölliker. But he is not. He was born in Germany about 1864) and immigrated to the United States in 1892 (U.S. census of 1910). It is unlikely that he is in any way related to the Swiss Köllikers, otherwise his name would very likely be Kölliker, not the Americanized Kelker. My lesson from this story, "don't assume!"

Afterword

So, there we have it, stories from almost three centuries of the Kelker family in America.

Most of us grow up hearing stories about ancestors, and we form images of who they were and the times they lived in. But as with most hand-me-down tales they are often incomplete, vague, inaccurate and exclude any bad behavior. I have here tried to seek out and relate something of the lives of some Kelker family members and recount the good, the bad and the interesting.

But what has been most satisfying in the preparation of this book is that the lives of nearly forgotten ancestors have been brought to light. This is the result of the historians, independent historians and others who have been so helpful in providing the history, historical context and a sharper focus of those nearly forgotten people. Their cooperation, collegiality and friendship have been vital. They enriched my knowledge, inspired my interest and spurred my motivation.

Because the ancestors included in this book were written about in newspapers, I was able to find numerous articles and stories about many aspects of their lives that added immeasurably to the content of the book. The Historical Society of Dauphin County in Harrisburg holds a vast collection of Kelker archives that covers the four generations of the family who were active and prominent in that community. I recognize that others searching out their family histories may not have that advantage.

But the question that intrigues me and that I can't quite answer is why I ever wanted to write a book. I spent my professional years as a scientist, and my writing was limited to scientific publications and grant proposals. But the science experience has carryover benefit to writing history, e.g., objectivity, exhaustive research, a strict observance to established fact and clear and concise presentation. I guess that, like most of us, my curiosity was piqued by stories heard from family members. And I believe that we all have an inborn curiosity about where we come from.

Also, I had an Uncle Rudolph Frederick Kelker and I had heard about Kelker Street in Harrisburg, and I had a genealogical history of the Kelker family (the Kelker Family Record) that was completed in 1883, all there to stimulate my interest. As the research progressed and more stories were found the task became more and more intriguing. Not much more to say except that it's been a joyous adventure.

Sic transit gloria mundi.

Index

Author's Note

I t seems to be a rather common phenomenon that as we grow older our curiosity about where we come from grows, and some of us are curious enough about our family histories that we search through archives, old newspapers and available records. My venture into history began after my professional career as a microbiologist, geneticist and biotechnology executive ended.

Most of us pass through life from birth, youth, schooling, professional career and then to retirement, and my life has followed that course. I was born in Chillicothe, Ohio where my father, Aaron Kelker, taught science at the local high school, and my mother, Martha Taylor Kelker, was a music school graduate who spent her time taking care of me. We moved to Hiram, Ohio, a tiny village in northeastern Ohio in 1943 when my father accepted a teaching position at Hiram College where he and my mother, and later my brother and I, graduated. I attended the local public school from first through twelfth grades and graduated in 1957 in a class of twenty students, the largest in the school's history. The village of Hiram had about six hundred residents, so our class size reflected the population of the town and township. The enriching presence of the college opened my youthful mind, and those of many others, to a greater appreciation of life's offerings.

After high school came the big question of what college to attend. Ohio is blessed with a rich offering of excellent small liberal arts colleges like Hiram. But I settled on Hiram, probably because it was in my comfort zone and because my father, who had moved on to the administrative staff, was so fully committed to his work and the college. Four years and then graduation and the accompanying shock of leaving home and college life to face the real world. I settled on a graduate program in biology at Purdue University where I received a Master's degree in 1964 and where I met my future wife, Hanna Chroboczek. I left Purdue to enter a Ph.D. program in the Department of Microbiology at Michigan State University. In 1965 Hanna and I got married in her home country of Poland, and we returned to MSU where she pursued her Ph.D. in plant biochemistry. We ended up spending six years of graduate and postdoctoral studies on the East Lansing campus.

Then another decision, educational pursuits are over, now go find a job. I joined the Department of Microbiology at New York University School of Medicine where I ended up spending ten years. I studied bacterial genetics that was a hot topic in the 1970s but has been rendered obsolete by the rapid and ever evolving progress in molecular biology and genetics.

Hanna also joined the NYU School of Medicine where she spent most of her career studying the immunology of the AIDS virus. In 1980 I joined Enzo Biochem, Inc., a New York biotechnology company and spent the rest of my career there.

Hanna and I are proud of our family that includes our son Adam (born 1974) and our daughter Kristina (born 1978). Adam and his wife Michelle Fierro live and work in Chandler, Arizona where they enjoy life with their three children. Kristina and her husband Daniel Gerschel live in New York City where they work and take care of their two children.

So, there it is, a scientist turned historian who now immensely enjoys digging into times past. It's been a great journey of discovery with warm friendships, rewarding associations and a newly found appreciation for the many fine people I have come to know and admire in Harrisburg and its surroundings. It's been a great experience.

Life's been good. Live, learn and appreciate.